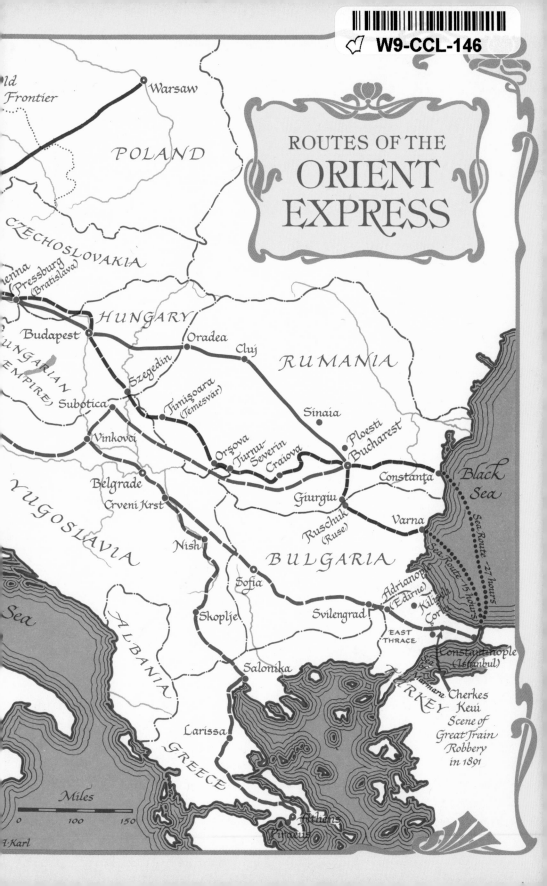

ROUTES OF THE ORIENT EXPRESS

Old Frontier

POLAND

Warsaw

CZECHOSLOVAKIA

Vienna (Pressburg (Bratislava))

HUNGARY

Budapest

(HUNGARIAN EMPIRE)

Subotica

Szegedin

Oradea

Cluj

RUMANIA

Timişoara (Temesvár)

Vinkovci

Orsova

Turnu-Severin

Craiova

Sinaia

Ploesti

Bucharest

Belgrade

Crveni Krst

Giurgiu

Constanţa

Black Sea

YUGOSLAVIA

Nish

Ruschuk (Ruse)

Varna

Sea Route 27 hours

BULGARIA

Sea Route 15 hours

Sofia

Adrianople (Edirne)

Kilindj Çor

Skoplje

Svilengrad

EAST THRACE

ALBANIA

Salonika

Constantinople (Istanbul)

TURKEY

Cherkes Keui Scene of Great Train Robbery in 1891

Larissa

GREECE

Sea

Miles

0   100   150

Athens Piraeus

i-Karl

ORIENT EXPRESS

The Life and Times
of the World's
Most Famous Train

E·H·COOKRIDGE

Random House
New York

Library of Congress Cataloging in Publication Data
Cookridge, E H
Orient Express, the life and times of the world's most famous train.
Includes index.
1. Railroads—Europe—Express-trains—History.
*2. Compagnie internationale des wagons-lits et
des grands express européens—History. I. Title.*
HE3008.C66   385'.22'094   78-57119
ISBN 0-394-41176-5

To Gail, Bob, Sean, Duff, and Jessie,
who love travels but missed
the Orient Express

Acknowledgments

FOR ALMOST A CENTURY THE STORY OF THE ORIENT EXPRESS WAS INEX-
tricably woven into the tempestuous history of Europe. The most
famous train ever to operate, the Express spanned a continent and
became not only the wonder of railroad engineers but the setting for
novels, films, television features, and sensational news stories. Kings
and crooks, millionaires and refugees, big-game hunters and smugglers,
prima donnas and courtesans traveled on it; tycoons and financiers
clinched their deals across its sumptuous dining tables; diplomats, spies,
and revolutionaries on board the train moved secretively to their moments of history. This unique caravansary on wheels was a microcosm
of the world's intrigues, human passions, and unbridled ambitions.

In this book I have attempted to record for a more mundane
generation—for whom a trip means the bustle of crowded airports, jet
lag, or the frustration of motoring—the glamour and drama that were
rarely absent from the slower but infinitely more exhilarating mode of
travel represented by the Orient Express, the queen of the Railroad
Age. My own fascination with the Express began with my journeys in
the heyday of the train between the two world wars when, as a young
newspaper reporter, I first visited the ramshackle Balkan kingdoms, and
it continued after 1945 when I reported on the new regimes within the
Communist orbit.

For my more recent research into the history of the Orient Express
I am greatly indebted to the archivists and former executives and
employees of the Compagnie Internationale des Wagons-Lits; the staff
of the Bibliothèque Nationale in Paris; the Bibliothèque Albert I and
the Musée de la Dynastie in Brussels; national archives, libraries, and
transport museums in Vienna, Belgrade, Bucharest, and Istanbul; the
French SNCF; the Austrian, Romanian and Turkish State Railways
administrations; the Railroad and Locomotive Historical Society of
Boston; and, above all, to M. Roger Commault.

Grateful acknowledgments are due the authors and publishers of books and newspaper and magazine articles from which I gleaned some additional information or quoted a few passages; they are mentioned in the Bibliography, on p. 275. I should like to single out here the excellent standard work by George Behrend, M.A., F.R.G.S., on *Grand European Expresses* (Allen & Unwin, London, 1962); the writings of the railroad historians C. Hamilton Ellis (Britain), Julien Pecheux and Jean des Cars (France), and Fritz Stoeckl (Austria), who provided much inspiration; the articles by Pierre Rénon, former public relations officer of the Compagnie, M. Harand, formerly chief engineer of the Chemins de Fer de l'Est, and John Price, the editor of Cook's International Timetable. I wish to thank the following publishers for permission to quote from the books by Edmond About (Hachette), Opper de Blowitz (Plon and Arnold), Sir Robert Bruce Lockhart (Putnam), Paul Morand (Gallimard), R.E. Crompton (Constable) and R.A. Vogeler (W.H. Allen), and to use some fictional descriptions of Orient Express journeys from the novels by Agatha Christie (Collins), Maurice Dekobra (Paul Elek), Den Doolard (Barker), Lawrence Durrell (Faber), Graham Greene (Heinemann and Bodley Head), Ian Fleming (Cape, Glidrose Productions and the Macmillan Company, New York), Cecil Roberts and Eric Ambler (Hodder & Stoughton) and E.L. White (Collins).

The book would never have been completed without the unstinted help and research work of my friend F. George Kay, the author of *Steam Locomotives,* whose technical knowledge of railroads far exceeds my own. I am grateful to Jacqueline Granger-Taylor for meticulously preparing the typescript. Last but certainly not least, I wish to express my thanks to my friend and editor at Random House, Robert D. Loomis, for his unwavering kindness and most valuable advice.

E.H.C.

Contents

One · *The Birth of an Idea* · *3*

Two · *The Man from Ohio* · *19*

Three · *Maiden Voyage of the Land Liner* · *29*

Four · *To the Bosporus* · *49*

Five · *The Great Robbery* · *70*

Six · *Full Speed Ahead* · *86*

Seven · *The Man in Compartment No. 7* · *104*

Eight · *The Royal Train* · *124*

Nine · *The Famous and the Notorious* · *151*

Ten · *Travels of an Oil Tycoon* · *186*

Eleven · *The Train Lost in the Snow* · *207*

Twelve · *The Train in Fiction and on the Screen* · *228*

Thirteen · *Through the War and the Iron Curtain* · *247*

Fourteen · *Journey's End* · *264*

Bibliography · *275*

Index · *281*

ORIENT
EXPRESS

Chapter One

THE BIRTH OF
AN IDEA

THE INVENTION OF THE STEAM ENGINE AND ITS ADAPTATION TO A mechanical device that could move from place to place brought about social and economic changes in the history of mankind comparable to the advent of the wheel at the dawn of the Stone Age. The Industrial Revolution was rapidly developing a complex system of mass production in new factories and mills; new sources of raw materials were being discovered; and the speedy transportation of commodities and manufactured goods became imperative.

Although in the eighteenth century the roads, as well as the breed of horses, had been greatly improved throughout the civilized areas of the world so that heavy, lumbering carriages could be dragged over long distances, it remained impossible to take heavy goods—such as coal and iron—along the roads except in good weather. Even then the average speed of a carriage was rarely more than three miles an hour. River and canal traffic was as important a means of transportation as roads but quite inadequate to satisfy the ever-growing needs of industry and commerce. Mail coaches carried travelers, but even the shortest journey was an uncomfortable and often hazardous adventure.

When on September 27, 1825, the world's first railroad worked by a steam locomotive was opened in the industrial northeast of England between the towns of Stockton and Darlington—a distance of eleven miles—it heralded the beginning of an era of phenomenal social and technological progress. In a mere quarter of a century the communication system of the entire civilized world, and with it the development of human enterprise, was revolutionized. In that period the initial eleven miles of track in Britain had grown to six thousand. In Europe, France opened its first railroad in 1832, Belgium and Bavaria in 1835, Austria and Prussia in 1838, Italy and Holland in 1839; Denmark and Spain followed in 1848.

In the United States in 1830, in advance of any country on the continent of Europe, Peter Cooper sent his steam locomotive, the famous *Tom Thumb*, on a successful first run over thirteen miles between Elliscott's Mill and Baltimore—which was the modest beginning of the Baltimore & Ohio Railroad. By the end of the same year work was going ahead fast on the 135-mile track in South Carolina, between Charleston and Hamburg, at a time when in England only a 40-mile line had been established between Manchester and Liverpool. Within ten years trains were running on 2,818 miles of American tracks. The frenzied energy put into the race during the "heroic" phase of the Railroad Age was matched only by the eagerness of investors and speculators to finance construction. Great fortunes were founded, and as many lost, on uneconomic projects. The general aim was to get a railroad running at the maximum possible rate of progress and at the minimum cost. Freight was the main source of revenue, and in most cases the transportation of passengers was merely an ancillary means of making some extra profit. Passenger cars were at first not much more than stagecoaches chained together behind a locomotive, or open freight wagons fitted with a few wooden seats and a roof. The travelers were subjected to billows of smoke and sparks that covered them with soot and burned holes in their clothing. When the slack in the chains was taken up suddenly, the passengers were sent sprawling out of their seats.

But as the railroads were extended and linked together journeys of several hundred miles became commonplace. It was now essential to provide some degree of comfort, and protection from the weather.

The open passenger car on American railroads was characteristic of a nation devoted to the democratic way of life, in contrast to the typical carriages in Britain and continental Europe, with boxed-in small compartments—some upholstered and others with hard wooden seats—to separate the social classes. For some years there was nothing comparable in Europe to the American trains, in which the passengers could walk about, sleep on reclining seats, enjoy washing facilities, and even cook a snack.

The railroads had come of age. The pioneers of England and Europe slowly and grudgingly were beginning to accept that the pupil now had something to teach the master. Those European railroad managers and engineers who were not prejudiced about the New World opportunism, or were not hidebound by tradition, began to study the innovations developed in the United States. And one young man, a Belgian, the citizen of a country justly proud of its early railroad system, was one of the few who admired the dynamic enterprise in the United States—where Pullman had devised the first sleeping car—and he decided not only to emulate the Americans but to score off them.

GEORGES NAGELMACKERS LOVED RAILROADS. BORN IN 1845 AT LIÈGE IN Belgium, he grew up in that new country which boasted that it had the best-designed and most efficiently managed network of railroads in Europe, except for Britain. This small state, densely populated and busy with new industries, had gained its independence from the Netherlands in 1831. Under the driving force of its first monarch, King Leopold I, duke of Saxe-Coburg-Saalfeld and uncle of Queen Victoria, Belgium had linked every important center with a railroad by the time young Georges could go with his father to watch yet another new locomotive rumble out of Liège for Ostend.

His father was heavily involved in railroad finance. He owned a banking firm which had been financing trade and industry since the Middle Ages. Georges's mother came from one of the wealthiest and most distinguished families of the country, the Frère-Orbans. The Nagelmackers' social prestige and wealth ensured personal friendship with the King, and through him with his relatives in virtually every ruling dynasty in Europe.

Georges grew up to become a strikingly handsome man, dark-eyed, tall, with the black bushy beard regarded as a symbol of probity and conservatism in business. But in reality he felt little enthusiasm for the sedate routine of banking. His character was that of an entrepreneur, a merchant adventurer. Almost inevitably, thanks to those childhood memories of watching those primitive trains steaming off to distant places, his thoughts turned to visions of the fortunes being made during that era of railroad mania. And those thoughts were grandiose: to organize a train that would span a continent, running on a continuous ribbon of metal for more than 1,500 miles. He was then twenty years old.

To cross Europe from west to east in the mid-nineteenth century was an expedition considered only by gypsies and generals—the former could take years to do so; the latter planned it as theoretical logistical campaigns of war fraught with disaster, as Napoleon had discovered. Not since the breakup of the Roman Empire, when military roads, one language, and one currency had made it feasible for the fortunate few, had the entire span between the Atlantic coast and the gateway to Asia enjoyed a safe highway of communication. Those who had to travel from one end of Europe to the other undertook most of the journey by sea.

But as young Georges was quick to point out to his father when discussing his idea, every European country, great or small, had been frantically constructing railroads for prestige, profit, industrial expansion, and future military use. The reasons were more often than not economically unjustified, except for the promoters who could sell stock in any company if its name included the magical word "railway." Yet the overall picture was of a mass of local tracks which, with a little engineering work and a lot of political and financial persuasion, could be linked to span the Old World from East to West.

Cautiously Nagelmackers Senior told his son that international cooperation between the many railroad companies in countries so diverse and often hostile was improbable if not impossible, and that financial investment would be unwise and risky. In the West, France and the emerging German Empire glowered at each other with bellicose suspicion, pretending to pursue a policy of peaceful coexistence while preparing for war. In Central Europe, the monarch of the vast Austro-Hungarian Empire regarded any form of easy communication, even within his dominions, as a potential danger to his autocratic rule. The Balkan countries, under the domination of one or another of their powerful neighbors, were largely unknown and unvisited lands, where internecine warfare was a way of life.

To this prudent objection young Georges had a forceful reply: their principal client, debtor, and fellow railroad buff, Leopold II, had just succeeded his father as the new king of the Belgians. The thirty-year-old monarch had, like young Georges, inherited a genuine enthusiasm for railroads from his father. But more important from the Nagelmackers' point of view, was the fact that he badly needed money and had the contacts to influence financiers to invest in a business proposition designed to net lucrative profits in a dozen or more countries.

Louis Philippe Marie Victor Leopold was a typical scion of the Saxe-Coburg family, whose eugenically incestuous marriages of convenience and illegitimate liaisons had over five centuries produced generations of rulers, aristocrats, landed families, and petty princelings and dukes the length and breadth of Europe. For good measure Leopold II had Queen Victoria as an aunt, King Louis Philippe of France as his maternal grandfather, and the Archduke Joseph of Austria as his father-in-law.

Through all these relationships the peripatetic monarch—he was out of his kingdom almost as often as he was in it—was a frequent guest at every palace and château in Europe, as his royal, aristocratic, or wealthy hosts knew to their cost. But with the ties of blood and the trappings of power, so avidly coveted by the Saxe-Coburg-Gothas, he could usually rely on favorable ears to listen to his business propositions.

"With the King's name formally linked with the business," Georges suggested to his father, "not only will we get the required finance, but the necessary engineering work and running facilities will be approved by the stockholders anxious to see the enterprise succeed."

"His Majesty won't invest a franc himself," said his father thoughtfully. "However, there is something in what you say. If he is amenable, no doubt we can arrange some paper investment on his behalf. His cooperation would compensate for the overdraft we've been very patient about for so long. I think some more definite ideas would be worth drawing up: finance, methods, routes, and so on. See what you can do."

But the grandiose and imaginative plans for what was ultimately to be the Orient Express suffered a long delay for an improbable reason. Georges fell in love with a woman some ten years his senior. Accustomed from birth to get what he wanted on account of his family's wealth and reputation, he was dumfounded when she laughed aloud at his formal proposal of marriage, explaining with frankness unusual for unmarried ladies of uncertain age in those days that she did not love him.

The rejection hit Georges hard. He abandoned all interest in his banking job and in his railroad project. His father, worried that his son was making himself ill, suggested that he take a long vacation. Georges did—choosing a destination as far as he could conveniently go: America.

The visit to New York was a revelation to him. Like most continental Europeans of his social class, Nagelmackers regarded the United States as a land of opportunity for those to whom opportunity was a forbidden word in the countries of their birth; as a nation that had torn itself to pieces in a civil war; a world where such civilized progress as there was depended on European invention and industrial production. Instead, he found a country of burgeoning cities, booming industries, and a spirit of enterprise and ingenuity which was rapidly healing the scars of war. Nothing impressed him more than the railroads. As a fervid student of steam traction, he knew that the early American railroad companies had been dependent on British know-how, as indeed had Europe, importing locomotives, rails, and even engineers to get started on hastily constructed routes, or to replace road and canal transport over short distances between seaport and town. He had no conception of the miles of new lines which had been opened year by year, even during the upheaval of war. Long journeys which involved days of travel, admittedly with a change or two from one company's lines to another and maybe a stagecoach link here and there, were now commonplace.

Fascinated by schedules that listed scores of towns which to him were just names in geography primers and newspaper articles, Georges traveled hither and thither, enjoying the new experience of big passenger cars built as saloons, without compartments, and decked out with mirrors, carved woodwork, and ingenious methods of turning the upholstered seats into sleeping bunks for night travel. The Americans were building specially designed vehicles—not, as in Britain and Europe, adapting the traditional stagecoach to run on rails.

A long, heavy car was, as Nagelmackers knew, essential for the luxury transcontinental train he had dreamed about; here, in the New World, he saw the proof of its viability. And the secret was in having not merely powerful locomotives to haul them but the proper wheel design. American engineers had been forced to equip their rolling stock with bogies because the majority of tracks had been poorly laid. There were innumerable bends and the routes often undulated like switchbacks. By supporting locomotives and cars on a framework consisting of two or three pairs of wheels, not only was the vibration reduced, but violent curves could be negotiated without the fear of derailment. The idea of the bogie meant in effect that the car ran on two entirely separate trucks, thus spreading the weight evenly over a considerable length of track.

The stimulus to forget his emotional troubles and to transform his dream of a transcontinental European express into reality came almost every day. He read in the newspapers of the fantastic scheme to bind the young nation together with a band of steel from coast to coast, as gangs of workers began transforming Abraham Lincoln's vision of the Pacific Railroad into fact with the first lengths of rail from Omaha laid in July 1865. Progress was reported in daily bulletins, sometimes announcing completion of one and a half miles in each direction in a single day toward the target of a link between the Union Pacific and the Central Pacific in the desolate terrain north of the Great Salt Lake. That historic occasion was still four years away, but the confident certainty that it would be achieved was yet a further example to Nagelmackers of what could be done with enterprise and imagination.

He also learned of yet another American idea which might be useful to him. George Westinghouse was conducting experiments with various types of brakes. The practice in both Europe and America was to have brakemen at the front and rear of trains, only two cars being fitted with brakes, in addition to those of the locomotive itself. When the engineer wanted the brakes to be applied by manual operation by the brakemen he used a whistle code. Not only was this system almost useless in an emergency, but braking power on a long and heavy train was inadequate to bring it to a stop in anything under several hundred yards. Westinghouse planned to use power brakes operated solely by the engineer and working on every vehicle of the train. He finally decided on using compressed air to operate the brakes, and his invention, by the time Nagelmackers was in the United States, was avidly discussed by engine builders. The railroad companies were not particularly enthusiastic, for equipping every locomotive and item of rolling stock with the new brakes would have been very costly. Many of the directors were not unduly worried by the thought of a minor accident, which in any event they regarded as unlikely, considering the comparatively low speeds of their heavy trains and the absence of converging tracks and crossovers.

It took Westinghouse three years to obtain recognition. In the spring of 1869 he managed to get approval to equip an experimental train, and in September it made its first run from Union Station in Pittsburgh. Just as it began to gather speed at the end of Grants Hill tunnel a car drawn by two horses began to lumber slowly across the level crossing immediately ahead. The frightened horses reared and became entangled in the harness; no train with the standard braking system could possibly have pulled up in time. But this one did, thanks to the Westinghouse air brakes, within a foot of the horse wagon. It made a splendid news story. Orders poured in for the Westinghouse system.

NAGELMACKERS WAS NO ENGINEER, BUT HE HAD AN ENTHUSIASTIC INterest in the mechanical ingenuity of experts. The benefits of bogies and braking systems were just details to be described to technicians back in Belgium. What really interested him were the stories about the man who, by clever publicity and salesmanship reminiscent of a fairground barker, was regarded as the sleeping-car king of America—George Mortimer Pullman.

Born in Brocton, New York, in a family of ten children, Pullman was selling farm implements at the age of fourteen. A couple of years later he traveled around the eastern states selling wooden cabinets and closets made by a brother. A born public-relations man and never too reticent about embellishing a good story with romantic color, he later in life claimed that the idea of building luxury saloon cars for railroad travel came to him in the winter of 1853, when he was twenty-two. He was taking his heavy samples of cabinetwork to Westfield from Buffalo, a distance of fifty-eight miles, a journey lasting four hours. Heating was nonexistent. A few candles provided flickering light. The seats were wooden. Wind howled through the ill-fitting windows.

In Westfield his cabinet selling was quickly forgotten. Pullman recalled that by the end of the day he had roughed out a plan for a parlor-cum-sleeping car. He had a good knowledge of carpentry, though his original design, merely a general outline of something as decorative and solid-looking as the cabinets he sold, took little account of the technicalities of railroad-rolling-stock construction.

This incident, if the story vouched for by the publicity-conscious Pullman in later years had any basis of truth, had little practical result. Soon afterwards Pullman's father fell ill, and when he died George found that the business had been left to him.

He moved to Chicago, which he was told was the fastest-growing city, with rich pickings for contractors able to move buildings to make way for new urban development. There he promised to move a small hotel a few yards back without disturbing the furniture or guests by jacking it up and placing rollers underneath. This feat was completely successful and one which he saw got the maximum publicity in all the important newspapers, obtained through lavish hospitality for a crowd of reporters he had invited to watch the proceedings.

But the number of buildings in Chicago which needed moving was decidedly limited, and he was soon in financial trouble. He returned to New York and revived his father's more modest carpentry business. There he met an ex-senator of New York State, Benjamin Field, who, with his brother, Norman, had set up a business to run sleeping cars on the Alton, Galena and Chicago railroad. The Fields offered Pullman the job of fitting out two ramshackle wagons they had bought for conversion into sleeping cars. The enterprise was not a success, passengers objecting to paying the fifty cents' supplement for a sleeping berth on what were for the most part fairly short journeys. On the outbreak of the Civil War in 1861 both cars were taken over by the Union army and contributed to the success of moving men and matériel rapidly over long distances. The cars, each built for twenty passengers, carried an average of fifty troops—and more during the historic occasion in 1863, when thirty trains operated day and night to carry twenty-five thousand men over a distance of 1,200 miles from the Potomac to the upper reaches of the Tennessee River.

During the war Pullman ran a general store in Gregory Gulch, Colorado, a site of a gold rush quite unaffected by the hostilities. He had to organize his supplies from Denver, but even with the cost of packhorses and wagons his profits brought him more money than he had ever previously earned, and before the end of the war he was able to return to Chicago with sufficient capital—reputedly $20,000—to gamble the entire sum on building the first real Pullman car. The work took him a year, with much of the wood and iron work carried out by himself. He was down to almost his last dollar when the job was finished.

He named his car *Pioneer*. Its décor became the theme that prevailed in every luxury train coach for nearly a century. The interior was paneled in inlaid walnut with framed mirrors between the windows. The seats were covered with embroidered cloth. Polished brass was lavishly used on lamps, toilet fixtures, and doors. Deep-pile carpeting covered the floor. It was by far the heaviest passenger vehicle ever built and was regarded by Pullman's prospective customer, the Chicago & Alton Railroad, as too heavy for the track and too wide and tall to negotiate the tunnels and bridges. *Pioneer* remained in the siding outside Pullman's workshop, unused and unusable. Its creator had to concede, when he tried to hire out his car to railroad after railroad, that the car was too heavy and too big.

Then, on April 15, 1865, he read in his morning newspaper that President Lincoln had been shot; the fact that the bullet had entered the brain meant there was little hope. A horror-struck nation awaited the inevitable news. When it came, there were also reports of the funeral arrangements. The dead President's body was to be taken from

Washington to his hometown of Springfield, Illinois. Ever the opportunist, Pullman saw the chance both to pay his respects and to get his car on the rails. He learned that a banker he knew, Colonel James H. Bowen, had been ordered to make arrangements for the funeral journey. Pullman approached him and said his *Pioneer* car was at his disposal. Then he went to see Mrs. Lincoln and, after a few minutes' conversation, had his offer accepted with gratitude.

The railroad could not risk public opprobrium by refusing to provide transit facilities for the President's body. Gangs of workmen labored on widening tunnels, strengthening bridges and adapting depots so that *Pioneer* could travel along the route. The long journey of the funeral train, moving hardly beyond walking pace, was seen by tens of thousands. Long descriptions of the train and drawings of the funeral car, with the name *Pioneer* prominently displayed, were featured in every newspaper in the United States and in many journals all over the world, which had reported in great detail Lincoln's assassination and obsequies.

After the funeral, *Pioneer* was returned to Chicago, stopping at every depot so it could be inspected by local dignitaries and journalists. This was the first installment in a publicity campaign that was to continue throughout Pullman's spectacular career. A second one came almost immediately. Five days before Abraham Lincoln was assassinated, Lieutenant General Ulysses S. Grant had received the capitulation of General Robert E. Lee and his Confederate army at the Appomattox Courthouse. When Grant announced that he would be returning to his hometown of Galena, Illinois, Pullman managed to get *Pioneer* to Detroit, where Grant was starting his hero's journey. The future President gladly accepted Pullman's offer to travel in his luxurious car. Once again tracks were altered and rebuilt to permit the transit of the Grant train through hundreds of miles in Michigan, Indiana, and Illinois. The result of all this publicity was contract after contract for Pullman cars.

Georges Nagelmackers was among the thousands who inspected *Pioneer* and, as a distinguished foreign visitor, was invited to enjoy a free trip. Accustomed to the heavy décor and lavish use of high-quality woods, brass, and gold leaf in European mansions and châteaux, he was not unduly impressed with the interior beyond marveling that such a weight was feasible for a train of several such cars that he envisaged for his Orient Express—this was the name he had privately given the train he was determined one day to create. He was even more interested in the structural side, and saw that the two heavy bogies, each of four wheels, supporting the train with massive springs, had a real innovation —shock absorbers made from thick rubber.

It is not recorded that Pullman and the young Belgian banker got on particularly well. Long meetings with a young man on a vacation in the United States—with no definite program, vagaries about the necessary capital, and not a single agreement with any European railroad company—were, in Pullman's view, of dubious profit. However, always ready to boast of his accomplishments, he gave Nagelmackers the run of his workshops and proudly displayed contracts that gave him a monopoly for running his cars over thousands of miles of railroads, passing from one company's tracks to another's, without hindrance.

That through-running facility was the feature of the Pullman enterprise which deeply impressed Nagelmackers. He carefully read and memorized the legal jargon of the contracts, knowing that the knowledge would be invaluable once he tackled the problem of persuading highly independent and suspicious railroad enterprises in Europe to give him what amounted to overriding control of a special train: stipulating when and where it ran, at what speed, and what fare could be charged. The bait he had decided to use was that he would supply the cars at no cost whatever to the railroads. They would not merely enjoy the prestige of the finest train in the Old World servicing their routes but take all the basic passenger fares as well. The only revenue accruing to Nagelmackers would be the supplementary charge for each passenger and whatever could be gained by providing meals, drinks, and extra luxuries.

Nagelmackers spent just over a year in America. Back in Liège, he recounted to his father all the details of the Pullman cars. The old man was impressed by his son's enthusiasm. Possibly his banker's caution was weakened by the affection of an indulgent and wealthy father. Two men with a single thought, they reminded each other of their earlier intention to get Leopold II directly involved.

Off to the royal palace in Brussels went father and son for an audience with the King. His Majesty, conscious of his unpaid installments on overdue loans, was undoubtedly relieved to discover that the conversation concerned making money, not repaying it, and he was amenable. Finance aside, Leopold was genuinely interested in Georges's description of American railroads and eager to further the prestige of Belgium as a leading railroad country in Europe. Not only did he agree to his name heading the list of subscribers—with an informal and private arrangement for his contribution to come from the bank—but he signed a letter of introduction and recommendation for Georges, headed "To whom it may concern." Thereby the King provided the new company of Nagelmackers et Cie. with literature for stock-sales promotion warranted to tempt every social climber in Belgium and those of Leopold's innumerable relatives and acquaintances in the rest of Europe who had not learned from experience that financial partnerships with the King of the Belgians rarely benefited anyone but himself.

The company proposed, as an initial enterprise, to organize a luxury train to run from Paris to Berlin. Apparently, neither Leopold nor the Nagelmackers realized that war between France and Germany was probable, even imminent. Whatever warnings they received, the readiness of the railroad organizations involved to cooperate on the project seemed to contradict the Jeremiahs who forecast war. One reason for this helpful attitude was that both France and Prussia, with their war plans already drawn up, were both anxious to secure an alliance treaty with Belgium. The country's neutrality was regarded by both sides as a hindrance to a rapid advance into enemy territory. Consequently a proposition clearly supported by the King of the Belgians offered the chance of commercial cooperation which might well be exploited as a preliminary to a political and military treaty.

Georges Nagelmackers, with the necessary credit to finance the construction of his luxury cars, ordered five of them from a Viennese wagon-construction firm. He selected it in the hope of gaining a favorable reaction from the Austrian Emperor when the time came for running his Express through the imperial territories. Each car had three compartments, with four armchairs in each, the backs of the chairs built in such a way that they could be lowered at night and covered with a mattress and bedding. By the beginning of July 1870 the cars were ready and hauled to Liège, where King Leopold inspected them. Final touches were made to the interior, the running schedule worked out, and the train's first trip advertised. Then, on July 19, France declared war on Prussia.

For a man less determined than Georges Nagelmackers this would have been the end of the enterprise, at least while hostilities continued. But he refused to abandon his idea. By assiduous study he had acquired unrivaled knowledge of the network of European railroads—they totaled some eighty thousand miles by then—and he worked out a route from Ostend in neutral Belgium to Brindisi on the heel of Italy.

In those days warfare did not result in complete destruction of the civil fabric of nations and the rights of a neutral country were usually meticulously respected. Thus there was no unsurmountable difficulty about running a train owned by a Belgian company through France, whether the territory was held by the invader or still defended. In any event, both nations in conflict were anxious not to arouse the anger of Britain by molesting a small nation ruled by a close relative of Queen Victoria.

And Britain was soon to prove the best customer for the new train. Scores of government officials, diplomats, and army personnel, as well as quantities of urgent mail, had to be carried quickly and safely between the mother country and India, "the pearl in the Imperial Crown of the British Empire," and to Egypt and Africa. If an express train existed running from a Channel port on the coast of France to southern Italy, up to ten days' traveling time could be saved as compared with the stormy and uncomfortable sea route through the Bay of Biscay and the western Mediterranean. The principal British maritime carrier, the Peninsular and Orient Line, readily agreed to use Brindisi as the western terminal for their liners. The service was an immediate success, with the once-weekly schedule doubled to a three-day one as soon as five more cars had been built.

But the triumph was short-lived. Despite the pressures of war, France had continued with one of the major engineering projects of the time, tunneling through the Alps under Mont Cenis. On September 17, 1871, nine months after the end of the war, the tunnel was opened for rail traffic. Nagelmackers, using the only feasible rail route through the Alps available at the time of his train's debut, had been forced to arrange contracts with railroads in Switzerland and Austria, the route going far to the east in order to use the railroad through the Brenner Pass. The French railroads, largely controlled by the government, rejected Nagelmackers' application for running rights through the Mont Cenis tunnel and started their own service, cutting the time from the English Channel ports to Brindisi by some eighteen hours. The contracts Nagelmackers had with Britain for conveyance of mail and government officials included a clause for termination of the arrangements without notice. The British government used it. The Belgian train continued to run for a time, usually with only a few passengers. Losses mounted, and the service was quietly terminated.

Nagelmackers remained as determined as ever. Without any assets beyond ten cars no one wanted to travel in, lapsed contracts with a few railroad companies, and debts exceeding the capital originally available, he made a new start by reregistering his enterprise under the name to become world-famous: La Compagnie Internationale des Wagons-Lits.

For some months the only evidence that this splendid-sounding enterprise was actually in business was one or two of its sleeping cars tacked on to French expresses. The journeys were not long enough to justify anyone but the most luxury-loving and wealthy traveler in paying the surcharge. The returns indicated that the average number of passengers per individual journey was 0.5. It was clearly a matter of days rather than weeks before the new enterprise would have to end. Georges and his father would have to face angry subscribers, including Leopold II, who was fearful that his numerous royal and ducal relatives as well as financier friends would think he had again tempted them into one of his semifraudulent enterprises.

In fact, this depressing stage in Nagelmackers' career, when he was almost resigned to his father's advice to cut his losses and settle for a mundane career as a director of the family bank, marked the brink of permanent and spectacular success.

The first hint of it came in a cordial letter inviting him to travel to London to "discuss matters of mutual commercial interest." The invitation was signed by Colonel William d'Alton Mann, an American with a reputation for unconventional business methods sufficient to make any banker shudder with alarm, but with a personality of considerable charm and self-confidence.

Colonel Mann had decided that Europe's train services were due for his attention as a source of yet another fortune to gain, to spend, or possibly to fail to attain at all. He had heard of this young Belgian banker with an enthusiasm for railroads and, more important, with all the right contacts with the influential families of Europe. This was the partner, Mann thought, who would help him to emulate—and probably beat—George Pullman as a railroad Croesus.

Chapter Two

THE MAN FROM OHIO

THE RECEPTION OF THE YOUNG BELGIAN BANKER BY THE EBULLIENT Colonel William d'Alton Mann was designed to be impressive. The American had taken a luxury suite in the Langham Hotel, at the top of London's fashionable Regent Street, where he entertained Americans who had been on the Confederate side and had exiled themselves, along with their safeguarded fortunes, to England. The colonel's other newly acquired friends presented a motley assortment of both notorious and aristocratic Englishmen and foreign entrepreneurs seeking their luck in the upsurge of industrial and financial activities of Victorian Britain and Empire—the only factor common to them.

At the time the colonel set up his business in London, he was in his mid-thirties, but despite his youth he had behind him a checkered and dubious business career. The son of a farmer in Perkins, Ohio, he had learned a smattering of engineering as a student at the technical college at Oberlin, but left for Grafton, West Virginia, halfway through the course when he inherited a tavern there—incidentally neglecting to tell his newly married wife where he was going.

His charm and joviality made the tavern a success. The profits were good, far better than they would have been if its owner had bothered about paying his bills from the brewery and other suppliers. When their demands for payment became pressing, he decamped and later turned up in Detroit, where, the Civil War having broken out, he joined the U.S. cavalry, mainly to move out of the sight of his creditors. He was sent to the Washington area, somehow managed to obtain the command of the 7th Michigan Cavalry Regiment, and became at the age of thirty the youngest colonel in the Union army. After a number of fairly successful skirmishes he was placed under the command of General George A. Custer. At Rommel's Farm Colonel Mann's unit was badly mauled and he decided to end his further participation in the war. He left the command of his regiment to a junior officer and resigned. But his military experience had not been unprofitable. He had taken the initiative of patenting various ideas of his own and of others to improve horse trappings and cavalrymen's equipment, selling the designs to the War Department as a patriotic if remunerative enterprise.

With his newly acquired capital Mann went into oil exploration. Since that August day in 1859 when Edwin Drake struck oil in Pennsylvania at a depth of sixty-nine feet, "liquid black gold" had become the new El Dorado sought by American investors, matched only by the great drive of making a fortune in railroad development. He bought a few hundred acres of farmland within sight of the new Pennsylvania oil rigs. This barren land was the sole asset of the company he then registered as the United Service Petroleum Co., whose name he conveniently abbreviated to the U.S. Petroleum Co. on stock certificates, thus creating the impression that it was either owned or sponsored by the government. With a colorful prospectus and a jar of refined oil bought in a hardware store as a sample of the product from his nonexistent drilling, he set himself up in Washington, D.C. In advertisements in many newspapers and to investors who came to see him in his office he promised that his oil would be gushing out by the barrel within sixty days. He sold most of the stock to paid-off army officers—professional investors were much less gullible. He netted $59,000 before he was arrested for fraud. He eluded punishment on the technicalities put forward by clever defense lawyers, and hardly any of the unhappy investors thought it worthwhile to sue him in the civil courts after he declared himself bankrupt.

Mann next turned up as a tax collector in Mobile, Alabama, a post he obtained through the help of a dishonest politician, to whom he promised a share in the receipts. He produced orders to sequester the property of those who fought with or supported the Confederates. Influential people got off lightly; those who could cause no trouble lost everything. The federal treasury received $4.7 million as the result of Mann's efforts. Later investigations proved that he had pocketed over $5 million for himself and had paid a handsome commission to his politician friend.

Before the investigations began—they dragged on for some years —Colonel Mann established himself as the uncrowned king of Mobile, buying up the two local newspapers and reissuing them as his own *Register*, which soon gained a wide circulation. He stood as a Democratic candidate for the Forty-first Congress, but by then law enforcement officers from Washington were on his trail. An indictment to charge Mann with embezzlement of government money was prepared. Mann won his Mobile seat in Congress with a handsome majority, but his election was followed by investigations of his manipulation of the polls. A recount of the ballots reversed the election result. Yet the citizens of Mobile still regarded him, now branded as a villain, as their hero and benefactor, and he remained in the city, a wealthy and popular personality.

Mann had registered another company for the exploration of oil in Alabama and succeeded in selling worthless stock, but in the end, knowing it was impossible to announce oil strikes, he turned his attention to railroads. Another company was formed to build a line between New Orleans, Mobile, and Chattanooga—an enormously long route mainly across swamp and shifting sand. (Rather surprisingly, the railroad was eventually built by others, the construction taking twice as long as forecast and swallowing up many times the cost announced in Mann's stock-promotion literature.) Before contractors and investors made life too uncomfortable, Mann took off for New York, boasting there about the impressive engineering feat and prosperous new railroad he had launched, and so joined the highly venerated and exclusive coterie of American visionaries—the railroad tycoons.

Typical of his undoubted courage in rejoicing in any proposition that offered a challenge—a virtue marred by his unprincipled methods of besting an adversary—Mann decided to do battle with the wonder man of the era, George Mortimer Pullman. In his works at Detroit, Pullman was building his saloons and sleeping cars as fast as a thousand craftsmen could turn them out. Demand was obviously outstripping supply. So Mann went into direct competition with Pullman. His slogan was "Unexcelled luxury." Calling them boudoir cars, Mann got his designers to divide the cars into private rooms, each car accommodating only sixteen passengers, who enjoyed the comfort of deeply upholstered armchairs and, at night, real beds. The Mann car cost more than the Pullman saloon to build. Its prospective revenue, because of the fewer passengers it could carry, was far less. In any event, Pullman was determined to smash his rival by undercutting whatever price Mann charged for his cars and reducing the supplementary fare charge.

Mann had to admit defeat on direct confrontation with Pullman, but still managed to make a good profit by building private railroad cars for the business magnates—a status symbol eagerly taken up by anyone wealthy enough to be able to travel around without any contact with the ordinary fellow passengers.

Without doubt, Mann's greatest coup was to build a special car for Lillie Langtry. The daughter of a reverend dean in the Channel Islands, "Jersey Lily"—the name was a nickname given to her because of her immaculate white skin—had become a national celebrity as a vaudeville star in England when she was only eighteen. She could not move from her home in London's fashionable Eaton Place without a police escort to keep off the gaping crowds. Millais, Watts, Pointer, Burne-Jones, Lavery, and Whistler painted her portrait. From a music-hall performer she developed into a talented actress. Among her many lovers were two sons of Queen Victoria—Prince Leopold, Duke of Albany, and Edward, Prince of Wales. She had a platonic friendship with Oscar Wilde, who wrote *Lady Windermere's Fan* for her and also *The New Helen*, dedicating it to "Helen, formerly of Troy, now of London."

When she went to the United States, she had a rapturous reception in New York and rode in state down Fifth Avenue. For her appearance at the Park Theatre, tickets were auctioned to the highest bidder. They each fetched $2,000. Two hours before the performance the theater was burned down. A group of infatuated businessmen decided to provide the Jersey Lily with a railroad coach for her tour through the States. Colonel Mann got the contract. He built a car which he claimed was a replica of the barge in which Cleopatra (one of Lillie's most famous roles) had met Marc Antony at Tarsus. It was painted in blue and decorated with lilies of white and gold. The car's bathroom and lavatory fixtures were of solid silver. The bedroom was padded in silk and the walls of the saloon were covered in brocade specially woven in Lyons, France. There were two rooms for friends invited to accompany her, a maid's room, a kitchen, and a pantry. The car ran for thousands of miles and was seen by tens of thousands of people, giving publicity to its glamorous passenger and the man who had built it. Mann's bill for the job was $100,000, a vast sum in those days.

Whether the profits from this enterprise were sufficient to finance Mann's assault on the European railroad market or whether he had other sources of income is uncertain. It was alleged by his many jealous critics that he was not above inveigling wealthy men to finance him by blackmailing them, adopting the then well-known and lucrative method of starting a scandal sheet, drafting articles exposing the illicit sexual and business activities of well-known American personalities in industry, commerce, and government, and then offering to abandon publication for a substantial payment.

However that may be, he had sufficient cash and credit to go to the expense of shipping two of his boudoir cars to England and having them hauled from the Liverpool dockside to a London railway siding, where they could be inspected by prospective customers. He then began issuing invitations to journalists and British railways directors, to lavish receptions at his Langham Hotel suite. Possibly through the colorful stories the journalists published about this successful businessman from the New World, and as a result of introductions supplied by Lillie Langtry, with whom he had become very friendly, scores of the socially prominent came to his parties. They were potentially useful contacts and sources of finance, but could give him no direct business. The European railroad experts were unenthusiastic despite the champagne dinners Mann threw in their honor.

The exception was young Georges Nagelmackers. He swallowed hook, line, and sinker everything Mann told him about his grandiose plans. The agreement the two men signed was one of a partnership. In reality, Mann bulldozed Nagelmackers into acquiescing to his every proposal. The upshot of their many meetings was the formation of the Mann Boudoir Sleeping Car Company, registered in London, and the purchase of an empty factory in Oldham, Lancashire, to build the cars. Nagelmackers' Compagnie Internationale became a subsidiary of the Mann company, and Nagelmackers was persuaded to step down from the position of senior manager. Another Mann company was set up in Paris.

Without any definite contracts, Mann sent the first two boudoir cars to France, where they were used for demonstration runs. He then played a master stroke. He learned from the "Court Circular" in the London *Times*—Mann was a devoted student of the column in order to acquaint himself with the names of influential notables—that the Prince of Wales was to represent Britain at the wedding of his brother, Prince Alfred, Duke of Edinburgh, to Marie Alexandrovna, the only daughter of Alexander II, czar of Russia, in St. Petersburg on January 2, 1874. He knew also that Lillie Langtry had told the Prince of Wales about the wonderful rail car Mann had designed for her. With the brashness of an American he ignored all protocol and sent a letter direct to the Prince, offering him the free use of one of his boudoir cars to travel from the English Channel port through France and Germany to the Russian capital.

To Mann's satisfaction and the consternation of palace officials who had been busily making formal arrangements for several separate royal trains, and for suitable ceremonies at each European city where a change of train was necessary, the Prince accepted Mann's invitation. It was a publicity scoop comparable to that of Pullman with his car for President Lincoln's railroad cortege. It paid off just as satisfactorily— so much so, indeed, that an angry Pullman hurriedly launched a separate company to build and run Pullman cars in Europe.

With Pullman's resources and readily available cars, Mann and Nagelmackers were faced with severe obstacles to get any of their cars into operation. Mann thereupon attacked the Pullman cars—on moral grounds, which was amusing to those close enough to know him well. Mann said that, with their open interior, they were hotbeds of immorality at night. Those bent on illicit romance could indulge themselves with impunity; ladies of virtue were open to indecent assault while they lay asleep in their bunks. It was even known, he hinted, that prostitutes worked on some of the Pullman night expresses, offering comfort and companionship to men traveling without their wives. Whatever safeguards decent people took to protect themselves from the temptations of sex, there was always the embarrassment of undressing and dressing while hardly concealed by a flimsy curtain from a carful of strangers of both sexes.

Mann's Mrs. Grundy campaign found an immediate echo from railroad operators and the public in that age of strait-laced Victorian morality. If people did travel on one of the few Pullman cars running in Europe, they now kept quiet about it. But no one seemed to have studied the interior layout of Mann's boudoir cars with sufficient attention to realize that his private cubicles for two persons were infinitely more improper than a completely open car, and in later years were indeed used by many gentlemen as convenient places for discreet peccadilloes.

Steady, routine work did not appeal to Mann. His aim had always been for a quick killing and then to move on to other ventures. While Nagelmackers traveled around Europe arranging contracts to supply boudoir cars—he quickly sold more than fifty in France, Germany, Austria-Hungary and to Balkan kings—Mann enjoyed himself in London on the money that was rolling in. His last practical effort in the European market was to build a magnificent car for the personal use of Leopold II and his famous mistress, the dancer Cléo de Merode, who was constantly complaining about the discomfort of the trips across Europe. Leopold's boudoir car was, of course, paid for by the Nagelmackers bank.

Eventually Georges Nagelmackers could not stomach Mann's business methods any longer and offered to buy him out. After much haggling, Mann sold out his interests to Nagelmackers and a cartel of financiers for $5 million, and then returned to New York. The original company was reinstituted under its old name, Compagnie Internationale des Wagons-Lits, with the obliging King of the Belgians again allowing his name to head the list of chief subscribers. The company had a capital of four million Belgian francs. In the inaugural year, 1876, Georges Nagelmackers traveled week after week negotiating new contracts. The discomfort of most of the trains he used, and the frequent changing and long waits at interchange stations, accentuated his conviction that an international train, composed entirely of luxury sleeping cars, would be a success. He inspected the royal train of Ludwig II of Bavaria ("Crazy Ludwig") and was impressed with the degree of luxury that money could buy. The train was painted in royal blue on the outside, with heavily gilded decorations above the windows. Inside, the saloon had the appearance of an eighteenth-century drawing room. The washbasin was inlaid with gold and the water closet cushioned in swansdown to minimize discomfort should the train sway badly while the king was *in situ.*

But such a degree of luxuriousness was not, in the opinion of the railroad directors Nagelmackers met, for those of nonregal blood, even if they were very rich. All he managed to get were several short-term contracts to attach one of his company's cars—with the Mann name emblazoned on the side now deleted—on expresses running between Paris and Vienna, Paris and Menton, Paris and Cologne, Vienna and Munich, and Ostend and Berlin.

The new standard car was equipped with tables, each with four chairs, the backs of the seats being lowered to form a lower sleeping berth, with an upper one let down from the ceiling. A boiler at one end provided heating and water for washing. There were two water closets in separate compartments. A bigger car, mounted on six wheels, had a large saloon and two separate sleeping compartments. The first so-called restaurant car appeared in 1877 on the Berlin-Bebra line; Bebra was then a junction station for Frankfurt and Kassel. It merely provided tables, with cutlery and glassware. Food was sold in luncheon baskets or passengers could bring their own meals.

In confirmation of Nagelmackers' forecast, and to the barely concealed amazement of the railroad companies, these special cars were well patronized. All over Europe the new rich were spreading their wings. They were far better and more numerous clients of the excess-charge services than the often impecunious aristocrats, who considered that a seat in the luxury car was their birthright rather than a privilege for which they had to pay.

But Nagelmackers was still far from achieving his vision of running a complete luxury train across Europe. The route, which he checked by personally touring the whole length of the Continent from the English Channel ports to the borders of the Black Sea, was now techni-cally feasible, the pressure of the demands of freight and passengers having resulted in numerous independent lines building additional tracks and linking them together. Commercially he met with a wall of resistance. Railroad companies were happy enough to enjoy the addi-tional revenue brought by the existence of the Wagons-Lits, but they insisted that they had to be hauled by their trains, on their chosen routes, and at their scheduled times. There could be no question of an independent company without a mile of track to its name running an international express on the established tracks.

Persistence, plus some encouragement by Leopold II to his numer-ous royal relatives to exert pressure where a company was privately owned, and to calculate their own profits where they could benefit from state railroads, slowly broke down objections. Some idea of the difficult negotiations Nagelmackers had to conduct, usually single-handed, can be gained from a glance at some of the agreements which he completed by May 1883.

They were made between the Wagons-Lits Compagnie and the Eastern Railway Company of France, the Imperial Railways of Alsace-Lorraine, the Kingdom of Württemburg State Railways, the Grand Duchy of Baden State Railways, the Royal Bavarian Lines of Commu-nication, the Imperial and Royal Austrian State Railways, the Royal Rumanian Railways, and the Austrian Lloyd Shipping Company (for the last section by sea to Constantinople).

The route selected by Nagelmackers ran from Paris through Mu-nich, Salzburg, Vienna, Budapest, and Bucharest to Giurgiu, forty miles southwest of Bucharest and on the left bank of the Danube, which formed the border between Rumania and Bulgaria. Ferries plied regularly across the wide river to Ruschuk (now Ruse), and Nagelmackers had a somewhat shaky agreement for a special Bulgarian train to take those of his passengers booked for Constantinople as far as Varna on the Black Sea coast.

The timetable for the Orient Express entailed complicated calculations, as there was no synchronization in time from one country to another, and in some—particularly in the Austro-Hungarian Empire—even from one city to another. Eastbound, the scheduled time from Paris to Constantinople was 81 hours 40 minutes; westbound, 77 hours 49 minutes.

Although the proposed name was not yet used in official announcements of the new direct service, it was being dubbed the Orient Express in the newspapers, and Nagelmackers decided to make its formal "inaugural" run in October under this name.

Chapter Three

MAIDEN VOYAGE
OF THE LAND LINER

L/ONG BEFORE DARKNESS FELL ON THAT EVENING OF OCTOBER 4, 1883, Parisians began to stream along the Boulevard de Magenta and Boulevard de Strasbourg toward the Gare de Strasbourg (later renamed the Gare de l'Est). The official inaugural journey of the Orient Express, well advertised beforehand and highlighted in newspaper headlines, had caught the public's imagination. The people of Paris, always ready to take to the streets for any kind of celebration, had been excited by the stories in the press describing the luxury of the new train, the exotic foods and costly wines that were being delivered to the station, and the list of the distinguished personages who had been invited to join what was variously recorded as a "land liner" and a "grand hotel on wheels," only comparable to the standards of comfort and luxury of an ocean-going passenger ship or a first-class hostelry. Even more colorful was a headline proclaiming that the new express was "The Magic Carpet to the Orient."

In fact, this early exercise in public relations, proclaiming that this was the first run of the Orient Express, was not entirely truthful. There were several trial runs of the new Wagons-Lits cars, the first a year earlier, on October 10, 1882, but the Paris express had terminated its route at Vienna, where passengers had to change to a *Schnellzug* of the Austrian State Railways, continuing to Orsova, the Rumanian town on the frontier triangle between Rumania, Serbia, and Bulgaria. Only when—after many months of negotiations with several governments and eight railroad managements, and after discreet distribution of generous payoffs to various officials—Nagelmackers had signed the agreement at Constantinople in February 1883 was the route to Bulgaria secured. Even so, for six years thereafter, passengers had to disembark at Nish in Serbia and cross the mountain in bone-shaking diligences to the Turkish railhead at Tatar Pazardzhik, in Eastern Rumelia, which until 1885 had remained a Turkish province.

For the inaugural journey Nagelmackers did not dare to inflict on his guests such an exasperating route. He decided to take the Orient Express as far as Giurgiu in Rumania, then make them cross the Danube by a ferry to Ruschuk, and hence by a special train he had borrowed from the Austrian State Railways to the Bulgarian port of Varna, from where they were to continue the trip aboard an Austrian packet boat across the Black Sea to the Turkish capital. But this improvised route had been kept secret from them, and when embarking in Paris they were under the impression that they would travel all the way to Constantinople by the luxurious new express.

At the Gare de l'Est the earliest sightseers on that historic October evening were admitted in small groups to the station's quais, where they could marvel at the new electric lights which illuminated it. They could look, albeit at a distance, at the Orient Express, a ghostly train lit up from its interior by gas lamps. Shrewdly, Nagelmackers had arranged for several of the aging Mann boudoir cars, unwashed and with peeling green paint, to be lined up on the adjacent track. They contrasted dramatically with the sparkling exterior of the Orient Express.

First to arrive, all in top hats and tail coats, were the hosts of the distinguished guests. They were led by Georges Nagelmackers himself and included Napoleon Schroeder, his French representative; the Belgian banker Delloye-Matthieu, who had become president of the Compagnie des Wagons-Lits; another of its financial backers, Etienne Lechat; and several of the company's directors.

The Belgians, invited so as to stress that this was a Belgian enterprise as well as an international occasion, were the first to arrive. There was the Minister of Public Works, the manager of the Belgian State Railways, several members of the Wagons-Lits board, and journalists from Brussels. The French party of nineteen guests included the son of the Minister of Posts and Communications—the Minister himself had at the last moment sent his apologies for his absence, caused by a sudden political crisis of the Grévy cabinet—and the Secretary of State for Finance. With them were six directors of the French railroad companies. The Ottoman Empire was represented by its Paris chargé d'affaires, Mishak Effendi.

The many journalists invited to report on the journey included two of the best-known writers of the time: Edmond About and Henri Opper de Blowitz. About was not only a versatile contributor to Paris journals but a best-selling author. He was born in 1826 in Alsace, where he lived and wrote until the Franco-Prussian War of 1870, and then went into exile to Paris, eventually settling down at Pontoise. He had turned out a stream of books in the social-realist style of the English novelists such as Trollope and Thackeray, and of the early novels of Henry James. As a young writer he had extolled Voltaire and had written anticlerical essays in which he condemned the political influence of the Catholic Church. But he soon conformed to his readers' more fashionable tastes, writing stories that did not question the social conventions of his time. An inveterate traveler, he had visited Egypt and the Near East, and in many of his books he injected Oriental glamour by taking his characters to the more exotic parts of the world. He also could be regarded as one of the earliest science-fiction writers, like his contemporary Jules Verne, having produced a fantastic tale entitled *The Man with the Broken Nose,* still popular with French readers. In the pursuit of his profitable writing career he avidly cultivated friendships with the wealthy. A valuable friendship, which flourished as a result of his partygoing, was Delloye-Matthieu, the president of Nagelmackers' company, who invited About to join the inaugural journey of the Orient Express as his personal guest. The book which Edmond About subsequently produced, *De Pontoise à Stam-*

boul, * was largely a paean of unstinted praise for the new international express, certain to attract many important passengers, but it remains the most vivid and probably fairly accurate account of this first official journey of the Orient Express.

Henri Opper de Blowitz was an even more important guest of the Wagons-Lits company. A native of Bohemia, with a somewhat mysterious past which he was loath to reveal, he had become in midlife the Paris correspondent of the London *Times* and gained international fame as "the Prince of Journalists" by procuring for his newspaper the text of the Treaty of Berlin of 1878, including all its secret clauses, before it was signed. Pompous and verbose as his reports were, they always got worldwide circulation; James Gordon Bennett paid large sums of money for publishing Opper's *Times* reports in the *New York Herald.* Anything Opper wrote about the Orient Express could be guaranteed to be read by hundreds of thousands.

Another passenger was a youngster of only seventeen, Léon Daudet, the son of the famous French author Alphonse and nephew of Ernest, the historian, neither of whom was able to accept Nagelmackers' invitation. Daudet was to become notorious as one of the accusers of Dreyfus, as the founder of the royalist and militant anti-Semitic *Action Française,* and a collaborator of the Nazis during the Second World War.

While the guests were being received, while ebullient speeches were made and many bottles of champagne emptied in toasts in honor of the great venture, the locomotive which was to haul the train on the first leg of the long trip was being coupled.

In this era of supersonic speed the rate of travel a century ago is often regarded as little better than that of the horse, which, since time immemorial, had been the fastest means of getting from one place to another. Not so; railroad trains in the latter half of the nineteenth century matched—and sometimes exceeded—the speeds of today's expresses. Already on the drawing board by the time locomotives were being selected for the debut run of the Orient Express was New York Central's famous engine No. 999, which on May 10, 1893, was to reach 112.5 mph near Batavia, New York.

*Librairie Hachette, Paris, 1884. It was not published in English.

For his heavy Orient Express Nagelmackers knew that powerful and reliable locomotives were readily available. There were two types in general use on Europe's railroads, both originally of British design and either built in Britain or under British supervision at European works. The first, the Crampton, built by T.R. Crampton, the chief designer of England's famed Great Western Railway, was well known to the Belgians. Two of them were bought for the Liège and Namur Railway. Its 1–1–1 axle arrangement put most of the thirty-ton weight of the locomotive on the front wheels, thus helping adhesion. The driving wheels of seven-foot diameter gave the locomotive a speed potential of 75 mph. The performance of the Cramptons on the Belgian line impressed railroad managements all over the Continent, and more than three hundred of them were in operation by 1864, and still running thirty years later. In France they hauled the crack expresses and the phrase *prendre le Crampton* (to take the Crampton) became a colloquialism for taking an express train.

The other, and eventually more popular, engine in France was the Buddicom, a 1–2–0 locomotive originally built from 1845 to 1858 at the famous railroad engine works at Crewe, England. It was comparatively small, light, and economical to run. The French versions were built at a locomotive foundry set up by W.B. Buddicom and another Englishman, William Allcard, in Rouen. The Buddicom, as any locomotive with its wheel arrangement was known in France until diesels replaced steam, had driving wheels five feet in diameter and weighed twenty tons. Its outstanding feature was the inclined outside cylinders, which reduced friction on the bearings and virtually obviated the fractures of crank axles which often occurred with inside cylinders. It was one of these engines, a modernized version of the original and built in 1878, which was selected for the maiden journey of the Orient Express. It was in the class known as 500 and was equipped with the pumping apparatus for the Westinghouse compressed air braking system.

Immediately behind the locomotive tender, stacked high with soft-coal briquettes, came a six-wheel covered truck, known as a fourgon. It carried mail, the only source of revenue on that inaugural run. Then followed "three houses on wheels," as About, in one of his less happy similes, described them. The first two were sleeping cars mounted on bogies. Each had accommodation for twenty passengers. Above the windows in raised bronze letters were the words *Compagnie Internationale des Wagons-Lits et des Grands Express Européens,* the second part of the title displayed for the first time. Behind the sleeping cars came the restaurant car, also mounted on bogies. Through its wide windows the crowd could already see the snow-white napery on the tables, the gleaming glassware and the silver cutlery.

At the rear was a four-wheel fourgon loaded with the passengers' baggage, alongside the containers of food and crates of wine, champagne, port, brandy and liqueurs. There was not sufficient room in the storeroom adjacent to the restaurant car's kitchen for the huge quantity of provisions Nagelmackers had insisted on being in readiness for the gastronomic delights with which his guests were to be regaled. The fourgon was equipped—apparently for the first time—with refrigeration supplied by huge blocks of ice. About later recorded that he was able to enjoy "the freshest butter of Isigny even when the train was roaring across the Hungarian *Puszta,* a thousand kilometers distant from France."

To the annoyance of the engineers who had to damp down the locomotive's fire and release surplus steam, and to the chagrin of the *chef de train,* a fine figure of a man with a white Vandyke beard and waxed mustache who wore an immaculate gold-braid uniform, the guests continued to talk and empty their champagne glasses despite the pleas of the stationmaster when the scheduled time of departure—6 P.M.—came and went. When at last everyone had been escorted aboard to the respectful but urgent calls of *En voiture, messieurs, s'il vous plaît,* with the deferential aid of the conductors standing at the doors of the cars, the train rather jerkily began to steam off to the cheers from the crowd of spectators. Local trains had been held on branch lines to give the Orient Express a clear run, and it made up the lost twenty minutes long before it reached Strasbourg. Even allowing for reduced times for the locomotive to take water and more coal at Châlons-sur-Marne and Nancy, the train must have exceeded 55 mph on the straight sections.

Meantime About was making copious notes. He had been allocated compartment No. 7 (a number later to become famous as the accommodation permanently reserved for the Orient Express's most regular VIP, the armaments king Sir Basil Zaharoff). His companion in the two-berth compartment was the Turkish diplomat Mishak Effendi, whom About records as an agreeable roommate, courteous while awake and not in the habit of snoring when asleep. It seems he felt great satisfaction that he was quartered with a diplomat while his rival, Opper de Blowitz, shared compartment No. 3 with merely another journalist—a Dutchman named Jantzen, as obese as the *Times* correspondent.

About had something of a reputation to maintain as a man of taste, thoroughly familiar with the arts and readily capable of discriminating between the restraint of real luxury and the vulgarity of ostentation. His eulogistic description of the train's interior can be taken as an accurate reflection of the reactions of all the passengers, accustomed as they were to authentic elegance in this high noon of French artistry and culture. In his account he extolled the teak and mahogany paneling with inlaid marquetry of the compartment walls and car doors, the deep armchairs covered in soft Spanish leather embossed in gold patterning, the spring-loaded roller blinds that could be lowered to exclude drafts and ensure complete privacy, augmented by the flowered-damask drapes held back when not in use by silk cords and tassels of gold thread. When the seats were converted to beds for the night, they were covered with silk sheets, the finest wool blankets, and counterpanes filled with the lightest of eiderdown. He pressed the bell, which instantly brought an attendant, and tested the speaking tube, which provided direct communication with the car *conducteur* at his seat at the end of the car. Then he walked along the gently swaying car to the toilet cabinet, which had Italian marble fixtures and decorated porcelain basins. He was intrigued by the servant standing outside the door; his duty, About discovered, was to clean the cabinet after each use by a passenger. He was greatly impressed by the fresh towels, tablets of soap, and vials of toilet water beside the washbowl— a service, he mentioned, that was not provided even in the most expensive hotels he had so frequently patronized in all parts of Europe. Already in his sleeping compartment About had been pleasantly reminded of the comforts of his own home at Pontoise when he discovered on the small mahogany cupboard beneath the washbasin a brass plate with the engraved inscription which read: *Sous le lavabo se trouve un vase.* The *vase* proved to be a rather small but conveniently placed chamber pot, adorned on both the inside and outside with prettily painted garlands of colorful flowers.

This preliminary survey of the train took About more than an hour because of numerous conversations with his fellow passengers in the deeply carpeted corridors. As the train began to run through the Champagne country the *contrôleur* visited each compartment to announce that dinner was about to be served. The autumn night was a cold one, and About noted how excellent was the train's heating system when he passed to the car's vestibule and met the gust of wind while he cautiously stepped from the end of his swaying wagon-lit to the door of the dining car. Later, replete with food and alcohol, he was to claim that a few moments on this breezy lookout place was a refreshing change.

Entering the dining car—or, in the words of the Compagnie's prospectus, the *wagon-salon-restaurant*—About first looked into a double compartment that was designed as a drawing room for ladies. There were no women aboard, but two were to join the train at Vienna. This *petit salon pour les dames* was furnished in exquisite taste, with Louis XV chairs and taborets, a miniature chaise longue, all covered with petit-point embroidery, a couple of dainty tables, the walls padded with tapestries adorned with scenes imitating Watteau's *fêtes galantes* and with hanging silk drapes covering the windows. It was indeed a miniature boudoir, as if transferred from the lady's wing of a French château. At the other end of the restaurant car—as About was later to discover —was the gentlemen's smoking room, furnished with heavy leather fauteuils and footstools and a bookcase containing reading matter, which included travel guides and maps of the countries the train passed, and French, English, German, and Austrian newspapers and journals, thus almost creating the atmosphere of a London club. Opper de Blowitz characteristically described it as the *salon de société.*

The self-appointed publicist of the Orient Express insisted that the sight of the dining salons "took his breath away." The décor certainly bore witness to the ostentatious taste of the Victorian age. The wall paneling was of finest woods—mahogany and teak, inlaid with rosewood—with carved scrolls, cornices, and scallops at friezes and borders, adorned with gilded metal flowers and reaching the arched ceilings embellished by rather garish paintings. Students of the Paris Art Academy had excelled themselves in copying the stereotypical figures of Greek mythology, but About's usually so discriminating taste must have let him down when he claimed that those writhing gods and goddesses and rubicund cherubs "reminded one of the great Masters of the Renaissance and were executed with such artistry that they had little to justify their standing as inferior to a Veronese, Correggio, or Raphael." About's critical qualities must indeed have been dulled when he jotted the notes for the subsequent description of the dining salons in his book. Perhaps he did this when reclining in one of the deep fauteuils, which unlike those in the Pullman cars (and subsequently also installed in the Compagnie's restaurant cars) were not fixed to the floor but could be freely moved. This enabled the more obese trenchermen to adjust the distance from the tables according to their girth. With a glass of Napoleon brandy in front of him and an outsize Havana Corona between his fingers, he could inspect the décor at leisure, relaxing after a meal. And he certainly did not overlook even the smallest detail. The racks into which the diners could deposit some small articles, such as a book, a pair of binoculars, a cigar case, or a tobacco pouch, ran the length of the car on both sides, and their gilded brackets were handwrought and adorned with intricate ornaments. Between the windows were small gold frames with original aquarelles and etchings by some of the most celebrated artists of the nineteenth century, such as Delacroix, Decamps, Meryon, Schwind, and Seymour. The tables were arranged on the off-side for four sitters and across the gangway more intimately for only two, with couples on honeymoon or on a more discreetly romantic peregrination in mind.

The dining salons were lit by huge gas chandeliers which, though producing a pleasant luster of the cut-glass pendicles, gave only a subfusc illumination. The soft light was not devised with any intention of producing a particularly *gemütlich* ambience but was dictated by necessity. The flames of the candelabras had to be kept low to minimize the risk of fire. At that time gas mantles had not been invented, so that each outlet produced a naked flame and was a fire hazard.

The car was pleasantly warm on this chilly October night. The central heating system based on hot water from the low-pressure boiler was something of a novelty, first tried out on Belgium's Grand Central Railway only the year before. Hitherto, if there was any heating at all on European trains, it was in the form of foot warmers filled with acetate of soda which gave off heat while passing from a liquid to crystalline state. The hot-water system did not in fact greatly raise the temperature in a vehicle subject to really cold winds on the roof and underside. But the new cars built for the Orient Express had not only heavy paneling at the sides but excellent insulation of the ceilings and floors, the latter being covered with close-fitted deep-pile carpets; windows were draftproof. In any case, it was as well for About and his fellow passengers that they were that evening—and on every following day—lavishly fueled internally.

At precisely 8 P.M. the *conducteurs* gently knocked at the compartment doors and announced that dinner would be served fifteen minutes later. The tables were laid with snow-white damask cloth, the napkins artistically folded to form butterfly patterns, and About noted with agreeable surprise that lined up at each place were four glasses "of finest Baccarat crystal from Louis XVI's famous Lunéville factory." The cutlery was of solid silver, the plates of finest porcelain, gold-rimmed and adorned with the crest of the Compagnie. The waiters—most of them carefully selected from among many applicants with experience of service in Parisian and Swiss luxury hotels—wore powdered wigs, tail coats, breeches, and silk stockings. The wigs were abandoned soon afterwards when a passenger complained that some of the powder had dropped into his soup.

The gargantuan meal, described on huge menu sheets in gold lettering, consisted of ten courses—the usual size of a formal banquet in that era of gross overeating. It started with soup, followed by hors d'oeuvres which included lobster, oysters, and caviar. Then came fish, a gigot of game, capon—all garnished with fresh vegetables and salads —and, finally, elaborately decorated cakes, sorbets, a selection of more than a dozen cheeses, and baskets of fresh fruit. The ride was so smooth, About recalled, that "not a drop of the champagne and wines was spilled, and the passengers reclined in their fauteuils as if they were in a building firmly rooted to the ground." More mundane, Opper de

Blowitz remarked in his book* that on the first morning of the journey he was able to shave "without my hands trembling in the least"—a tribute not merely to the well-sprung train and robust French track but also to his recuperative ability, in view of the amount of wine and spirits lavished on the guests the night before.

About, a gastronomic connoisseur of rank, rightly expressed his admiration, not only at the triumph of producing such an array of delicious dishes in the tiny kitchen, but at the freshness of the salads and fruit. He asked for, and was readily given, permission to inspect the kitchen and express his gratitude to the chef and his assistants. The *chef de cuisine* was a huge Burgundian with a coal-black beard, and they discussed gastronomy like the two experts they were. The chef was in command of three subchefs and three general handymen—they doubled as baggage and kitchen boys—and two cleaners, who looked not only after the pots, crockery, and cutlery but had to peel potatoes and wash the vegetables. Conscientiously About inspected every nook of the chef's realm and reported that "so tiny was the kitchen, most space taken up by the gas-fired stove, that it seemed as if the cooks could hardly move without spilling the boiling contents of their huge copper pots and pans over each other." In fact, they occasionally did; scalds were regarded as both the inevitable dangers of the job and as battle honors of service well performed.

The dinner lasted nearly three hours. From time to time Nagelmackers and his directors got up and stopped at some of the tables to exchange a few words with guests they had had no opportunity to welcome at the Gare de l'Est. In turn, several passengers walked up to others to introduce themselves. There were two or three German journalists in the party, but they were able to make few friends. About remarked that he could "neither praise them nor complain about them because none of us exchanged as much as two words with them during the journey, even though we eat the same bread . . ." The memories of Sedan and the siege of Paris were still too fresh; the Germans, sensing this, kept to themselves.

After lingering over their brandy till nearly midnight, the guests

* *Une Course à Constantinople* (Paris: Plon, 1884). Not published in English.

finally took themselves to bed. Cautiously About had brought along a vial with *dragées pharmaceutiques* prescribed by his doctor—anti-travel-sickness pills or sleeping tablets. But he suffered neither from nausea nor sleeplessness; indeed, he slept soundly during that night and every following one during the whole trip.

The train pulled into Strasbourg station, three hundred miles from Paris, shortly before dawn, running slowly on the last stretch in order to arrive just in time for the official reception. The station was brilliantly illuminated. It was one of the few in the Reich that could boast electric lighting, the generator having been installed by the American Edison Company. Its European president, Mr. Porges, was waiting with his engineers to show the train's guests around the plant, but only four of them emerged from the Orient Express. About, Opper de Blowitz, and the rest of them remained in their curtained sleeping compartments, unaware even of the change of locomotives and the resumption of the journey for its run, via Karlsruhe, Ulm, and Munich, to Vienna. The French passengers were determined not to view the scenery of the passing countryside, or to get involved in the courtesies of meeting German station officials and local bigwigs. About rather sarcastically recorded that when the train was running through the vineyard districts of Württemberg, he left his compartment for the toilet to relieve himself. He wrote: "In Bavaria, beyond Ulm, where the train stopped to take on water and fuel, we reached for the first time the beautiful blue Danube, which one must rather describe as the dirty Danube. On this stretch we also experienced some fault in the construction of our restaurant car and our carriages were penetrated by an unpleasant smell . . . though I do not wish to dwell on this mishap."

The mishap he referred to happened before the train reached Munich. The dining car was brand-new and not adequately tested. The additional weight of the stocks of food and the wine "cellar" located next to the kitchen, plus the long stretches at high speed, produced severe friction on the axle bearings. When the train passed Mering, some miles beyond Augsburg, black smoke began to penetrate the crevices in the floor of the kitchen and the corridor of the restaurant car. At least one axle box had run red-hot and the stench of its boiling grease, used for lubricating the bogies, and the biting smoke offended the nostrils of the passengers. The train was stopped, and Nagelmackers himself led the locomotive engineer, the fireman, and three of the train's guards down the track to inspect the damage. The Bavarian locomotive engineer, who had taken over at Stuttgart, wanted the restaurant car uncoupled then and there, which would have meant shunting the Orient Express onto another track and causing a long delay. Nagelmackers could not bear the thought of it and persuaded the engineer to take the train slowly as far as Munich, some thirty miles distant. There the restaurant car was uncoupled. The resourceful Nagelmackers, prepared for almost any eventuality along the entire route, had arranged beforehand to have another restaurant car (as well as a sleeping car) standing in reserve in Munich. Nagelmackers had taken a risk because the hot axle could have set the car afire and the flames might have spread. But the run was completed without fire breaking out, and the passengers remained unaware of the danger.

About was amused by the variations in time shown by the clocks at the stations at which they stopped. "In my native Alsace," he commented, "the Germans had introduced a time two hours ahead of Paris time. But Munich had again a different time from Stuttgart, and yet another change took place in Austria. Mercifully our clocks in the train had no intention of being involved in these horological complexities. I was told that, wisely, the keys of the clocks of the Orient Express were left at home in France, so that Paris time never changed for us."

And so the train crossed the Austro-Bavarian frontier at Simbach and into the lands of the Austro-Hungarian Empire, with its capital of Vienna 270 miles distant from Munich. The express had taken about thirty hours since it steamed out of the Gare de l'Est in Paris.

The reception of the Orient Express in Vienna was organized as a semistate occasion. Emperor Franz Josef, then forty-four years of age, cold, stubborn, and reactionary as he remained for the whole of his unhappy reign, was, however, now as enthusiastic about the potentialities of railroads as his unimaginative character allowed. This was for reasons of prestige and military advantage, which he hoped would outweigh the dangerous facilities speedy communication would give to the peoples of his vast and restless empire. To all intents and purposes, the Austrian railroads were the personal property of the Hapsburgs. The earliest steam-operated railroad in the country—from Florisdorf, on the northeastern outskirts of Vienna to Wagram, scene of Austria's defeat by Napoleon in July 1809—was named the Kaiser Ferdinand Nordbahn, and was in effect the Emperor's mechanical toy. Most of the railroads built subsequently were named after members of the imperial family, and their "owners" took needless trips on them, usually still in their horse-drawn coaches hauled onto tracks and lashed to the sides, with flunkeys attempting to stand motionless before and behind the coach.

The reception arranged for the train and its passengers was a nicely balanced mixture of formal ostentation and spontaneous celebration. With the rigid regard by the imperial court for etiquette, no person of royal blood could lower himself or herself to greet the visitors of plebeian origin. The compromise was to send a committee headed by the Court Chamberlain, Ritter von Hollan; the imperial and royal Vice-Minister of Roads and Communications, Karl von Scala (accompanied by his wife and sister-in-law); the director of the Austrian State Eastern Railways; and several state officials and railroad functionaries who managed to obtain permission to attend and thus satisfy their curiosity about the new international express.

While the Austrian dignitaries inspected the train and the rather weary passengers politely listened to eulogies about the Austrian railroad system, the band of the Imperial Guards played the national anthems of all the nations through whose territories the train had passed or was due to pass, continuing with *The Blue Danube* and other tunes by Johann Strauss. Out of rather grudging courtesy to the French guests, a potpourri was also rendered from the *Tales of Hoffman*, the opera by Jacques Offenbach, first presented after the composer's death three years earlier.

By now the hour was very late, but the ceremony was not over. The passengers were escorted to the station restaurant, where a champagne supper was served. For reasons of national prestige Imperial Tokay was also pressed on the guests, with the result that only a few of the hard-drinking journalists were in any condition to accept the next invitation on the agenda. This was to embark in state carriages awaiting them outside the station in order to visit the International Exhibition of Electric Lighting. This was being held to display the latest developments in illumination by the American Edison Company and the German firm of Siemens. Not only had the exhibition been kept open long after its normal closing hour but the municipality of Vienna had rushed ahead with the replacement of street gas lighting with electricity along the Ringstrasse, bathing the Hofburg (the imperial palace), the Opera House, and the recently completed House of Parliament in an early version of floodlighting. This tour, designed to demonstrate both the allegedly progressive policy of the empire and also its historic prestige, was something of an anticlimax: the majority of those it had been intended to impress were fast asleep in their train compartments. Both About and Opper de Blowitz failed in their journalistic duties and missed this nocturnal view of the Austrian capital. Perhaps wisely they concentrated on subject matter of greater human interest—for example, the fact that two Austrian ladies were joining the train.

Even in the 1880s, for a woman to travel by night on a train was regarded by most Europeans as unconventional if not actually dangerous. Colonel Mann's alarmist revelations of the goings-on in American sleeping cars had been read, marked, and taken to heart by those who treasured their reputation. Indeed, perfectly serious advice was offered in Viennese periodicals to those ladies forced by circumstance to travel by train in the company of strangers, whether by day or night. Day travel involved regular phases of pitch-black darkness when a train went through a tunnel; obviously, at night the menace of assault was omnipresent, aggravated rather than prevented by the twilight dimness of the illumination. A widely approved method of self-protection was for women to equip themselves with hatpins or long needles, which they clenched between their teeth when darkness demanded defense.

The two ladies who joined the Orient Express needed to have no qualms. Mme. von Scala, traveling in the company of her husband, the Vice-Minister of Roads and Communications, was—according to About—most beautiful. "She is somewhat of the type of a great English lady, but more animated and with Viennese features that make her even more alluring," he wrote. Her sister, Mlle. Leonie Pohl, was

afforded what seems like a double-edged compliment—probably unin-
tentionally—in About's assertion that she was "exactly the opposite of
a classical beauty." However, he conceded that she had "such a pretty
wit, with a wonderful figure and a profusion of blonde hair, that I could
not but glance again and again at her. The two ladies will certainly
make extremely agreeable traveling companions."

The run to Budapest, a distance of more than 150 miles, was
covered at a low speed and the train stopped for water and fuel at the
ancient capital of Hungary, Pozsony (now Bratislava). About was awake
and able to watch dawn break over the low-lying and fertile lands
watered by the Danube, where the peasants were gathering the last of
the harvest of corn, sunflower seed, and wheat—a bucolic scene which
inspired some of About's more flowery prose. But determined not to
mar his account with any hint of even slight discomfort, he omitted
to mention that the restaurant car was by now somewhat congested.
In conformity to the agreement Nagelmackers had signed with the
Austrian railroads, the rear fourgon had been uncoupled at Vienna. Its
load of baggage and reserves of food and wines had to be crammed into
the remainder of the train.

After breakfast—for once a simple meal served to the more som-
nolent passengers in their sleeping compartments—Nagelmackers,
freshly barbered and in his usual formal dress of morning coat and top
hat, toured the train to announce that in a few minutes they would be
drawing into the station at Budapest. "The Orient Express has now
traveled 1,500 kilometers since we left Paris," he proudly informed his
guests. In fact, the Railroad Magician, as he had been named by the
passengers, was understating the distance. The track distance between
Paris and Budapest at that time was 1,048 miles, according to the
careful data compiled from the records of British surveyors and engineers when the train was planned. This was the equivalent of 1,671
kilometers.

Even the most sophisticated and jaded of the travelers caught the
sense of excitement as the train moved at barely above walking pace
toward the gap between the two hills that dominated Buda, the town
on the west bank of the Danube. This was the first glimpse for the
majority of the passengers of a place tinged with the atmosphere of the

East. The town had been attacked and captured time after time by waves of Eastern invaders—Tatars, Mongols, Turks. In the slanting light of a late autumn morning the rocky mass of the Gellert hill rose sheer from the river, crowned by a military citadel built in 1851 to extend the old Turkish fortress. Beyond it was the Varhegy hill dominated by the neobaroque palace built by Maria Theresa a century before. The Austrian passengers were at pains to point out that construction had already begun to transform it into a huge Hapsburg residence with nearly nine hundred rooms.

The train eased gently onto the bridge across the Danube, groups of railroad officials and workmen supervising the transit on the shaky track. Nagelmackers noted the creaking and groaning of the structure and privately felt relief that the train weight had been reduced to eighty tons. Over the Danube was the bustling community of Pest, standing on low-level land and therefore capable of expansion. Since the new city of Budapest had been formally inaugurated by imperial decree a dozen years earlier by bringing Buda, Pest and the old Roman city of Obuda under unified control, industrial and residential growth of Pest had been rapid. Belying the view of the foreign journalists on the train that the Austro-Hungarian Empire was an anachronism treasuring the outmoded glories of the past, Pest had been planned in a modern style not unlike Napoleon's center of Paris. The plan was roughly concentric with three semicircular boulevards (the koruts), the foremost forming the city boundary. Straight roads radiated like the spokes of a wheel from the center to connect the koruts. Just after crossing the bridge, the train gave the passengers the opportunity to observe the site that had been cleared for the new Parliament building which, the Court Chamberlain explained, would be in the Gothic style and was so vast and splendid that it was estimated it would take ten years to complete (in fact it took twenty and the building was not finished until 1904).

The leisurely pace of the train enabled the formal reception at Pest station to be held in midmorning. A military band, this time in colorful Honved uniforms and feathered shakos, played the train in with traditional Hungarian czardas music. After local dignitaries had been invited to inspect the train and enjoy a glass or two of French champagne, the Hungarians returned the hospitality with a lavish buffet set up on the platform. For those able to face yet more rich food there were steaming tureens of goulash, seasoned with throat-constricting hot paprika. Less robust appetites were catered to with exquisite *nuss-beugeln,* crescent-shaped pastries containing crushed walnuts. And there were endless glasses of Tokay wine as well as the famous, notoriously powerful apricot brandy. Whether, after the train resumed its journey, the passengers sat down and were able to tackle luncheon is not recorded.

The empire's final gesture to the Orient Express had been secretly arranged in cooperation with Nagelmackers during the stop in Vienna. It came when the train reached Szegedin, an ancient city standing at the confluence of the Tisza and Maros rivers, which had been the sources of both prosperity and disaster for the town. Since the ninth century it had been a center of river trade dealing in fish, cereals, paprika, and fruit—and, most important, in salt from Transylvania. But four years before, in 1879, the most catastrophic of the many inundations caused by the two rivers devastated the town. When the Orient Express came to a halt in the primitive station, ruined houses could still be seen beside the river. This somewhat depressing scene was quickly forgotten when a band of Tziganes—Hungarian gypsies—in their traditional costume came dancing along the street toward the station. They were playing fiddles, flutes, and tambourines as they progressed, with two gypsies carrying big drums and struggling to keep up with the others. Their leader, a swarthy giant of a man with a huge black mustache, greeted Nagelmackers with a torrent of Romany words which a local railroad official condensed into German as: "He is explaining that he is Onody Kahniar, the king of the gypsies." With courtesy appropriate to his royal guest, Nagelmackers invited him to enter the train and bring his troupe with him.

Meantime the waiters had moved some of the tables and fauteuils at one end of the restaurant car to make a space for the musicians and their audience. Blending with the discordant blast of the locomotive whistle, the lively music burst out as the train began moving once more. The next scheduled stop was at Temesvar (now Timişoara in Rumania), some 70 miles distant. For the entire duration of the journey, which took over two hours, the gypsies played and sang without a break, encouraged by the applause of the enchanted audience. Mishak Effendi, the Turkish diplomat, persuaded Fräulein Pohl to dance with him. Some of the journalists, unable to partner Frau von Scala, grabbed one another and danced around the confined space as best they could. Opper de Blowitz seemed deeply impressed when, after some whispering between the Burgundian chef and the gypsy king, the musicians launched into what was a just recognizable rendering of the "Marseillaise." In a burst of patriotic zeal the *chef de cuisine*, pushing back his tall white hat, began to sing. "His hand on his heart, his eyes aflame, his face in ecstasy," Opper de Blowitz reported, "and with a voice strident from the heat of the kitchen fire, he rendered the great anthem in tones that were sonorous and profound—the song of the Marseillaise!" With enthusiasm for the country he regarded as his adopted motherland along with England, the Prince of Journalists joined in the singing, waving his wide-brimmed hat in the air.

The performance ended as the train came to a halt at Temesvar. A collection was quickly organized, the gypsy king graciously accepting this practical testimony to the skill of his eleven musicians. Opper de Blowitz, forgetting for a moment his "entirely Belgian origin" and his adopted Anglo-French background, involved the gypsy king in a most animated conversation, which he apparently conducted in a rapid mélange of German, Hungarian, and Rumanian. He later told his fellow passengers that the band was not the haphazard group of wandering gypsies it appeared to be, but a professional band of musicians due to perform at a Temesvar music hall that same afternoon and evening. The chance to travel by train from Szegedin quickly, comfortably, and earn some money while doing so, had been too good to miss, and they had shown their satisfaction in the only way they could. Asked by Opper de Blowitz whether he and his band were not exhausted after the nonstop concert, Onody proudly retorted: "We Tziganes play as easily as you breathe; we get tired only when we do not play."

The Temesvar stop was only as long as was necessary to take on fresh food and change locomotives while the dining-car staff hurried ahead with preparation of the delayed luncheon. When it was served in the cleaned and restored car, the passengers got their first glimpse of the Transylvanian Alps while the train labored on the gradient, which became steadily steeper. A brief halt at the border, and the train was in Rumania, the fifth country of the itinerary.

Chapter Four

TO THE BOSPORUS

For most of the passengers and the train personnel, except for the Austrian locomotive engineers and guards, the border crossing represented an expedition into unknown—and rather alarming—territory. Gone was the all-embracing dominance of the Austro-Hungarian Empire, through whose territories they had been traveling for more than twenty hours. The passengers amused themselves by reading the difficult Hungarian station names, alongside which were the German names also. The two last Hungarian places were Herkulesbad, a renowned spa, where wealthy visitors bathed in the iron-saturated waters —allegedly a cure for rheumatism—and the appropriately named frontier station Porta Orientalis. Beyond was Orsova and the Danube's Iron Gate. The train had entered Rumania and the Balkans.

For two thousand years the area bordered by the Transylvanian Alps, the Carpathians, the river Danube, and the Black Sea remained a Latin enclave, despite invasions in passing centuries by Goths, Tatars, Huns, Magyars, Turks, and Slavs. Its original inhabitants, the Dacians and Gets, who had wandered north from Thrace, had established a kingdom in 200 B.C. which was to become a dangerous neighbor to the Roman provinces. Eventually conquered by the Romans, they remained comparatively peaceful and obedient to Rome, and Roman troops and merchants enjoyed a good life in the fertile country. Many Dacians married off their daughters and sons to them, and by the time the Roman Empire broke up, much of the Latin language and customs had been absorbed by them. The Turks, having conquered the Balkans and subjugated the Slavs, afforded the Rumanians a sort of autonomy, exercised by tribal voivodes. In modern times, after the Crimean War between England, France, and Russia, the Great Powers had tried to give the country a taste of Western-style democracy, and in 1859 Alexander Cuza was elected Prince of Moldavia and Wallachia. But the voivodes and boyars—the rich landowners—preferred their ancient ‘feudal rights to any notion of freedom for the peasants, and forced him to abdicate.

In the perpetual wrangle over the "Eastern Question," the Great Powers clinched a compromise by producing a princeling from Germany, that bottomless well of candidates for any European throne, great or small: Prince Charles of Hohenzollern-Sigmaringen became Rumania's ruler. In the Russo-Turkish war of 1878 he had attempted to keep the country neutral, but after it was invaded by Russian troops, he decided to ally himself with the Czar and secure his protection. When the Orient Express crossed her borders, Rumania was still suffering from the economic ravages of the war, having been compelled by the Treaty of Berlin to cede her fertile province of Bessarabia to Russia as a price for full independence and the elevation to a kingdom. All this historical reminiscence was retailed by Opper de Blowitz to any of the Orient Express passengers prepared to listen.

Until the train began running through Europe's southeastern terrain Opper de Blowitz had been somewhat eclipsed as a literary personality by Edmond About, a writer whose forte was descriptive prose liberally mixed with social gossip. The absence of really influential statesmen on the train and Opper de Blowitz's failure to find anyone at the Vienna welcome ceremony prepared to give him yet another journalistic scoop resulted in the rotund little man being deprived of the limelight in which he was accustomed to bask.

But now, with the Orient Express laboring onto the foothills of the Transylvanian Alps, he was coming into his own. With his usual political acumen he knew that Rumania, being wooed by Austria, Germany, Russia, and France, was about to play a more important role in European politics. He had carefully studied the historical background of the country, and he had a genuine and personal interest in Balkan affairs. The fact that he had never previously traveled in Rumania did not prevent him from implying that the desolate country passing before the train windows revived "memories" of his childhood and youth.

When interviewing European statesmen, he invariably let it be known that he was the descendant of the Seigneur Opper von Blovsky, a legendary Bohemian count, as remote in time as was geographically the family castle towering over the village of Blovsky (or Blowitz), not far from Pilsen. When some of his French adversaries—particularly during the Dreyfus affair in 1896 when anti-Semitism was rife among the reactionary accusers of the Jewish general staff officer—insinuated that Opper de Blowitz (who had taken Dreyfus's side) was himself a Jew, he indignantly retorted that he had been baptized at birth into the Catholic faith of his ancestors. In his memoirs* he produced a good story, telling, not without humor, of his birth at the castle of Blovsky: "a child with a big head and a feeble body, who was declared by the doctors summoned to the mother's bedside as having a weak heart so that it would not live." Hence the Catholic priest, Father Vasck, was hurriedly brought from the village church to the castle. "The Parish register may be taken in evidence that I was born a Catholic," he wrote, "baptized twenty and four hours after my birth, given the names of Henri Georges Stephane Adolphe, and that I did not have time to become a Jew, which I regret for the sake of the People of Israel . . ." The truth, however, was that he was the son of a Jewish merchant, Marcus Opper, who had kept a small general store within sight of the castle of Blovsky, the property of the counts of Kolovrat. One of them, in the fashion of the time, became the bright boy's benefactor and paid for his initial education at a school in Pilsen which otherwise would have remained closed to the Jewish storekeeper's son. He left his native village in Bohemia at the age of fifteen

* *My Memoirs*, Edward Arnold, London, 1903, p. 3.

to seek his fortune in the West. In his memoirs he gave a more romantic reason for his departure: he had been kidnapped by gypsies. Whatever the truth, he traveled widely—to Russia, Germany, Switzerland, Italy, and France—and, having a remarkable linguistic flair, acquired a good knowledge of several languages, in addition to his native German and Czech.

In 1849 Opper, at the age of twenty-four, was eking out a livelihood as a teacher of German in a boys' school at Tours. He had undoubtedly a great flair for languages, and for several more years he found employment as a teacher in various lycées in French provincial towns, such as Limoges, Poitiers, and eventually in Marseilles. His opportunity came in 1858 in Marseilles, when at the age of thirty-three, still an impoverished tutor, he met and married a wealthy lady. In his memoirs he described her as Mlle. Anne-Amélie Armand, the daughter of a naval officer and, on her mother's side, related to the Bourbons. In fact, her father had been a purser, and she was forty-five—twelve years older than her diminutive and already very corpulent bridegroom, over whom she towered by more than a foot. She was the widow of an Englishman, a Mr. Bethford, who had conveniently died soon after their marriage, leaving his widow a tidy fortune, which Opper accepted as adequate compensation for his bride's ripe age and intimidating size. The marriage, apparently a happy one, lasted for more than thirty years, and Opper, who survived her by many years, seemed to have had genuine affection for her, describing her as "a lady for whom love was an affair of the heart, even of compassion," thus explaining why his marriage had remained childless.

The former Mme. Bethford had, through her first husband, excellent connections. During the elections of 1869, when Napoleon III approved a new parliamentary system, Opper ingratiated himself with the man who had formed the Third Party, Adolphe Thiers (he became the President of the Republic in 1871) and was a parliamentary candidate in Marseilles. His opponent was Viscomte Ferdinand de Lesseps, a national hero as the designer of the Suez Canal. When there were riots in Marseilles after the fall of the monarchy, Opper wrote some excellent reports, which he offered to Laurence Oliphant, the flamboyant Paris correspondent of the London *Times*, a former diplomat and world traveler. Eventually Oliphant invited Opper to come to Paris and become his free-lance assistant. Opper soon impressed him, not only as a fount of intriguing information about the political scene, but also as an accomplished linguist. His one-time Marseilles political boss, President Thiers, undoubtedly confided to him some political secrets, and Opper used this information cleverly and with restraint. He also took good care that his stories were dispatched to London under his own by-line so that *The Times'* famous editor John Delane would know about this new and enterprising member of Oliphant's staff. In 1873, on Oliphant's retirement, Opper—who now hyphenated his name with that of "de Blowitz" became the great newspaper's chief Paris correspondent.

As was not usual, he had been approached earlier by the British secret service to work as an intelligence agent. He was sending reports direct to Brigadier General Sir Henry Brackenbury, head of the British military intelligence. Having produced some amazing exploits for both *The Times* and his secret contacts at the British War Office, the rise of his prestige was meteoric. He frequently visited London, was introduced to Disraeli, Lord Salisbury, and Gladstone and managed to gain their trust. He implied later to his friends that the information he provided for Disraeli about his *bête noire,* Ferdinand de Lesseps, and the financial situation of the Suez Canal Company had decisive bearing on Disraeli's coup in November 1875 in buying a controlling interest in the canal from the khedive of Egypt. The Rothschilds were closely involved in this deal, and Opper de Blowitz had earlier established a personal contact with the head of the French banking house of that great financial dynasty, as he did later with its English branch. His exploits at the Berlin Congress of 1878, at which he was accepted as the doyen of the two hundred journalists from all over the world, culminated in his obtaining the secret parts of the treaty—probably with Disraeli's assistance—and publishing them in *The Times,* a feat which caused a furor throughout the diplomatic world. With such a reputation, it was not surprising that Opper de Blowitz was convinced that every mile of the journey, as the Orient Express entered the Balkan countries, took him nearer yet to other great journalistic scoops. He had secretly arranged with Rumanian diplomats and the Turkish ambassador in Paris to obtain interviews with King Charles and Sultan Abdul Hamid.

Before nightfall the passengers were able to view the Iron Gates, the narrow defile between the southern end of the Carpathian Mountains and the Miroch range of the Balkan Mountains. So called because of the massive boulders partly emerging from the rushing Danube at this point, the Gates provided spectacular scenery and not a little fear among the more nervous passengers as they noted how close the track was to the water, built on foundations which in places were merely piles of rock taken from cuttings blasted through projecting cliffsides. The train ran even more cautiously than before, yet it still occasionally lurched and jerked where storms had eroded the subsoil and hasty repairs had still not settled firmly. When darkness fell, dinner was served. This time neither About nor Opper de Blowitz could praise the manner in which their soup and their glasses of wine and champagne remained unspilled. Progress was slow and bumpy, with the engineer bringing the train to a complete stop when, peering into the darkness, he suspected that the track had moved or a small avalanche of debris from steep slopes carried the risk of derailment. The schedule had allowed for this cautious movement, and the stretch of about 180 miles from the Iron Gates to Bucharest took some seven hours, the train arriving without mishap in the capital at 5 A.M., with daylight still nearly two hours away.

As a result, the reception at this untimely hour was modest by comparison with previous stops of the train—merely the director general of the Rumanian State Railways, Olanescu, and his managerial staff were present. But a regal reception had been arranged for a more appropriate hour and in more splendid circumstances—in the royal palace at Sinaia, some 85 miles away.

The train was shunted to a junction outside the station and then steamed northwards, at first through well-tilled farmland and then into the mountains. During the four-hour trip there was a brief stop to change locomotives at Ploesti (sixty years later the target for the historic daylight attack by 177 USAAF Liberators on August 12, 1943, involving a flight of 2,460 miles). The passengers were intrigued by the sight of wooden derricks scattered around the outskirts of the town.

The knowledgeable Opper de Blowitz was able to explain that they were the rigs of the wells sunk to obtain the rock oil which the Americans called petroleum.

Beyond Ploesti lay forests and streams swollen by rain as far as the small community of Sinaia, built around an ancient monastery. Above the area towered mountain peaks, capped with snow. For centuries this beautiful spot on the lower slopes of the Transylvanian Alps had been favored by the powerful and wealthy tribal chiefs as a secure bastion, and later because of its invigorating climate during the heat of summer. When the train pulled into the tiny station, the passengers had their first glimpse of two impressive buildings—one the small but attractive palace of Pelishor, the ancient summer residence of Rumanian princely boyars, and close to it the much more grandiose Castel Peles, completed only a few months earlier. It was the pride and joy of King Charles I. The country's economy had been badly strained to finance the building of this summer palace and to decorate and furnish its hundred and fifty rooms with the best that German and French emporia and artisans could supply.

On the advice of his cousin, the King of the Belgians, Charles planned the reception of the Orient Express travelers as a political maneuver, hoping that the journalists—and especially Opper de Blowitz—would transmit edifying reports on the prestige and progress of Rumania and the benevolent rule of her monarch. But King Charles was not the sort of man to unbend and engender friendliness. Though only forty-four, he had the manner of a much older man. He was austere and taciturn. His only real enthusiasm was for forestry and horticulture and the one sure way to arouse his interest was to talk about trees. He personally supervised new plantations and shared the work of digging and planting with the peasant laborers, much to the disgust of his court officials.

His morose character had not been improved by the unhappiness of his marriage. In 1869 he had married Elizabeth of Wied, member of a family that had furnished minor princelings in a Rhineland principality dating back to the twelfth century. She had been approved as a potential mother of a future ruler of Rumania who would strengthen German influence. She duly gave birth to a child who was weakly and died at the age of three. Moreover, the birth had involved surgical work no better than butchery, permanently injuring the mother. The royal doctors had to inform the king and queen that any further conception was highly improbable and, in any event, would create a highly dangerous situation for both mother and child. The royal couple had perforce to cease living as man and wife, and the marriage, never compatible, degenerated into mutual dislike. Charles was planting his trees and Elizabeth finding solace in romantic literature. To the general consternation of the court, she announced that so far as her professional activities were concerned, she was to be known as Carmen Sylva. She wrote her poems and romances in German, but used as themes ancient Rumanian folklore. The queen attended fewer and fewer official functions, and the shaky façade of her marriage and royal duties was maintained only with difficulty. But she was told by her husband that the Orient Express reception was a state occasion she must attend. She obeyed readily when she heard that two notable authors were in the party—especially Edmond About, whose romances were more to her taste than the political reports of the correspondent of *The Times*.

Characteristically, Charles did not invite the Orient Express party to stay at his palace, although he had plenty of room to put up the weary passengers. They were taken by Olanescu to the newly built Grand Hotel Nouls at Sinaia, where lunch was served on the large veranda. A few court officials acted as hosts and a Tzigane orchestra entertained the foreign visitors with a program of Hungarian czardas, Johann Strauss tunes, and Rumanian folk songs. Nagelmackers appeared to be restive; he had been promised that his party would be received by the King and Queen, but the officials remained noncommittal and were visibly embarrassed. Obviously, something had gone wrong, and Opper de Blowitz did not disguise his disappointment, loudly complaining that he had been promised an interview with the King.

Suddenly an officer of the palace guard arrived and announced that their Majesties desired to welcome the members of the Orient Express party at the Palace of Peles. There was a whispered conversation between the royal messenger and the Compagnie's directors. Nagelmackers then informed his guests that the king had waived etiquette and would receive the party in their traveling clothes, as there was no time to return to the train and unpack more formal attire. Opper de Blowitz seemed very pleased to have his revenge for the belated invitation: according to About, the famous journalist wore a crumpled hiking jacket, a pair of very wide knickerbockers, rough woolen stockings in the Tyrolean fashion, and a hat "as those favored by Calabrian bandits." The party was told to set off without delay. Looking to the palace, towering hundreds of feet above the hotel, About inquired whether fiacres would be provided to convey the party across the uninviting mountain road. But he was informed that the idea was to give them a pleasant walk so that they could enjoy the vista of the valley of the Prahova River below.

So the guests, instead of enjoying a pleasant rest after the excellent meal, began climbing the steep road to the castle. It soon became a muddy path, and when a sudden downpour caught the party midway, they all got drenched. About, a portly gentleman of fifty-seven, not used to such strenuous exercise, recalled with gratitude that two of his younger compatriots—Georges Boyer of *Le Figaro* and Jules Trefeu of *Le Gaulois*—supported him on long stretches of the climb, while Opper de Blowitz scornfully recorded that "the royal road was more suitable for mountain goats than for human beings." At last, footsore and soaked to the bones, they reached the old monastery, but there was still half a mile to march on; fortunately, the rain stopped and the road had somewhat improved.

After a short rest at the monastery, which dated from the early seventeenth century, About could observe the castle, still several hundred feet above: "Five minutes' walk from the monastery brought us to an opening from which we saw the silhouette of the castle high above our heads, an edifice as elegant as it was bizarre, such as none of us had ever seen but in our dreams or in a book of fairy stories. It is a building at which conception, knowledge of archaeology, and fantasy appear to have been jumbled up in a riot of timber, stone, marble, glass, and shining metal. . . . Every gust of wind brought to us strains of martial music. At last we arrived at the palace, where a handsome officer—I saw no other but handsome officers in Rumania—awaited us and conducted us to the great portal . . ."

Opper de Blowitz was more critical when describing the party's arrival. "A small crowd of people had collected at the gates of the royal park, soldiers and officers were marching up and down, and Orthodox priests, holding up their black cassocks to avoid the mud, their dark beards dripping with rain and their tall hats, the *kamelavkions*, limp and sodden. They were leaving the palace, where some ceremony had just ended. When we arrived, our clothes soaked and our boots covered with mud, the flunkies and soldiers looked at us with bewilderment and suspicion. At last an officer, informed by Monsieur Nagelmackers and his officials of the royal command, arranged our admission. We entered the hall, deposited our umbrellas and wet cloaks and then marched on, our forty pairs of boots, weighted down by the mud from the terrible road, sounded like thunder when we mounted the marble stairs."

The palace was indeed an architectural nightmare. Its construction began ten years earlier, in 1873. Its original design was by Wilhelm Doderer of Vienna, but the King had found it not magnificent enough and called in a fellow German, Johann Schultz, who had designed several palaces for German princelings. But even he could not satisfy the King, and many additions were eventually designed by a Czech architect, Karl Liman. Started on the ground floor in Italian Renaissance style, it was continued above with half-timbered façades of golden plasterwork, with dormer windows, a cross between a huge Swiss chalet and a medieval German castle, surmounted by an array of turrets, ornamented lintels, balustrades, terraces, and absurd-looking little balconies. As a present-day travel editor remarked, "Seen through the parkland trees, Peles Castle was pure Walt Disney."*

Bedraggled as they were, the guests of the Orient Express were led between two long rows of bizarre stone statues and past ornamental fountains into the courtyard and to the entrance hall with its grand staircase of Italian marble and hence to the Hall of Honor, paneled from floor to ceiling in carved and inlaid walnut with wainscoting of alabaster reliefs and a ceiling of dark mahogany. In one corner was a corkscrew staircase leading to one of the towers, in another a huge pulpit, both with carvings in Byzantine style. The floor was covered

*T. Appleton, *Rumania*, London, 1963.

with carpets from Mosul, Bokhara, and Fergana, and the rooms were full of heavy German furniture, Oriental divans, French chaises longues, Chippendale chairs, taborets and odd pieces of every period and style, which later prompted About to record that he had never before seen such an overwhelming display of bad taste.

In the center of the Hall of Honor stood the King and Queen. He, a slight, bearded figure in the parade uniform of a general, his chest bedecked with glittering orders and medals, on his head a tall plumed hat with heavy gold tassels, a truly Ruritanian monarch; she, much taller, her full-bosomed Valkyrie figure wrapped in a flowing Rumanian national costume. Although still only forty years of age, Carmen Sylva had lost the slender beauty of her youth and had run to fat. The royal couple and their courtiers in tails and uniforms presented a farcical contrast to the members of the Orient Express party, in their crumpled and wet travel clothes and muddy boots; they were given no time for a good brush.

The King looked sullen, and he might have been forgiven for not enjoying the invasion of his privacy by that motley crowd. He insisted on a tour of the castle even before refreshments were served. The King led the party to the Armoury, proudly pointing out his collection of eighteenth-century flags and some good Oriental weapons, many encrusted with precious jewels. Then the guests were taken to the Music Room, the Column Room, and the French Drawing Room and shown the private theater, seating an audience of about sixty. To About's and Opper's amazement, the walls of all these rooms were full of paintings by Titian, Raphael, Veronese, Rembrandt, and other old masters. About identified several which he knew were in the Louvre and the Uffizi in Florence, and he quickly recognized that each and every one of the pictures was a crudely executed copy, apparently painted by not too talented art students. Indeed, in the whole palace there was not a single original of real value and the King's "art collection" was but a forger's dream.

The Queen waylaid About as soon as the formal ceremony of welcome was over, describing how she worked on her literary effusions and quoting long excerpts from her poems in German. The Frenchman, who always preferred to talk about his own books, was saved from utter boredom by the presence of Elizabeth's ladies-in-waiting, whom he described as "these ravishing Parisiennes of the Danube." Opper de Blowitz soon monopolized the conversation, however, with personal reminiscences about the famous personages he had met, and the King, obviously eager to pump "the grand interviewer of popes, kings and statesmen" for some more discreet information, asked Opper to follow him into his study, where they could talk in private. The King's study was an awesome place, with an enormous desk and a huge carved chair standing on a rostrum. Visitors had to settle themselves into chairs placed below in front of the desk, thus being dwarfed by the undersized monarch. One can imagine that Opper disliked this arrangement. The King bitterly complained about the Treaty of Berlin, which gave the rich and fertile province of Bessarabia to Russia; he was pessimistic that peace could be maintained in the Balkans, and when Opper remarked that the King had succeeded in building up the Rumanian army, Charles replied that "if and when things blow up again in this corner of the world, we shall have to be reckoned with." Opper politely agreed, even though he might have had doubts about it.

Eventually the King and Opper rejoined the party to listen with hardly disguised boredom to arias sung by the famous Rumanian prima donna Carlotta Leria. The Queen had chosen to accompany her on the piano, "a rather unfortunate decision," About later recorded. After the concert tea and cakes were served, and then the King suddenly beckoned his chamberlain to call an end to the reception. Nagelmackers had tried to involve the royal couple into a conversation about the Orient Express, pointing out the economic importance of the train's inauguration for Rumania, but the King showed little interest except to murmur that he was pleased.

Then the party was led out, but after collecting the guests' cloaks, an official apparently lost his way in the maze of corridors of the new palace and took the group to the servants' staircase, which led into a dark backyard. Sentries guarding the door took the bedraggled party for workmen, who were still putting the finishing touches to the construction of the palace, and sternly ordered them to stand in a group and await the arrival of an officer who would give them permission to leave only after they were searched. "We stood immediately under an overflowing gutter and were drenched once more," About noted. "It was raining still, raining as it only does in Brittany . . ."

The party had to march down the muddy road, by now in almost total darkness, accompanied by a few torchbearers. At last they reached Sinaia station and boarded the train, which took them back to Bucharest. They reached the capital after ten o'clock at night, seventeen hours after their first arrival on the Orient Express. A fleet of fiacres took the party for dinner at one of Bucharest's best restaurants. Opper's humor had improved somewhat. (He later noted that "the cabmen, half-barbarian, half-Turk, with a smack of the Muzhik, skillfully drive the small, lean horses, which gallop like the wind on the primitive paving of the city's suburbs . . ." and, apparently looking out the window of the carriage, added: "Right and left of the station are squalid houses, mud hovels, worm-eaten little shops, while in the gutters between the spaced-out flagstones are beds of slimy, smelly mire. But as soon as one leaves the suburbs behind, the visitor's sight is impressed by the ambitious capital. New, fine houses, of smart and modern construction, dwarf by their splendor the old low buildings, which have not yet emerged from the fetters of the past and poverty . . . Everywhere is the striking contrast of a city and a country, growing and beautifying themselves and marching onward toward a better destiny. . . .) It was long after midnight and after many toasts that the party again embarked on the Orient Express.

When the passengers woke up, probably most of them late in the morning, the train was slowly steaming on toward Bulgaria and leaving the snow-covered Transylvanian Alps a long way behind. Seven hours after leaving the Rumanian capital, the Orient Express stopped at Giurgiu, the frontier port on the Danube. It was a miserable place, almost completely destroyed by the Russians in 1829, and recaptured with heavy cost in lives by the Turks in 1854. The inhabitants had only half-heartedly troubled to restore their city to the ancient standards set by its founders, the Genoese merchants of the Middle Ages.

The passengers now had to leave the comfort of the train for a small steamship to be ferried across the wide river to the Bulgarian border post at Ruschuk. Their reception at the station, close to the steamer quay, was correct and formal but hardly cordial. Bulgaria was under Russian political and military control. Her ruler, Prince Alexander, had been told by his chief minister, the Russian General Shepelev—the Ministers of War and of the Interior were also Russian officers—that it would be safer for him to remain in his palace in Sofia. The Russian regarded the new direct railroad communication with Western Europe by the Orient Express with undisguised suspicion and hostility.

The ruler of Bulgaria, Prince Alexander of Battenberg, was—like the monarch of neighboring Rumania—a German princeling, who had been put on the throne as the result of a political intrigue between Queen Victoria and the Czar, despite the German Emperor's protests. The Prince's father was a son of the Grand Duke of Hesse-Darmstadt; he had morganatically married an impoverished Polish countess, Julia Teresa Hauke, and had renounced all his ducal privileges, taking the title of a Prince of Battenberg. This marriage produced the high-flying clan which, in 1917, assumed the name of Mountbatten. Prince Alexander's sister, Marie of Hesse, had married the heir to the Russian throne; his uncle Grand Duke Louis was the husband of Queen Victoria's second daughter, Alice; his younger brother, Prince Franz Josef, a godson of the Austrian Emperor, married a princess of Montenegro. The clan had done extremely well through all these matrimonial links, and even better in the next generation. Queen Victoria's granddaughter Ena of Battenberg became the wife of Alfonso XIII of Spain; another, Louis of Battenberg, married King Gustav VI of Sweden; and Princess Alice of Battenberg became the wife of Prince Andrew of Greece and the mother of Prince Philip, the Duke of Edinburgh and consort of Queen Elizabeth II. The brother of the two queens (and Philip's uncle) is Admiral Earl Mountbatten of Burma, the Allied supreme commander in Southeast Asia during the Second World War.

At the time in question Alexander of Bulgaria was, for all practical purposes, a prisoner of his Russian "advisers." Three years later he was ousted when his cousin, Alexander III, the new Czar, withdrew his support and agreed with the German Emperor to replace him with Ferdinand of Coburg-Gotha.*

Thus, when the train arrived at Ruschuk, there were only a few

*See p. 81.

Russian officers on the platform. Opper described the continuation of the journey to the Black Sea port of Varna thus: "The train ran through a countryside of most barren and melancholy monotony. The fields appeared untilled; we saw only stunted underbush and sandy soil. Here and there was a little hamlet with a few miserable cottages, hovels built of mud and timber, many riddled with bullet holes—reminders of some past skirmishes of war and bandit attacks. In a cemetery a hungry goat and some mangy cattle were browsing; perhaps only decaying human bodies could provide manure for this infecund soil."

Before the Orient Express reached Sheytandjik, a miserable town which meant Little Devil in Turkish, the passengers were told by the car attendants that they were passing through bandit country. A few days before—as Opper de Blowitz recounted—"a gang of robbers had attacked the station at Votova, bound, gagged, and nearly strangled the stationmaster and his few railroad workers, in order to force him to surrender such money as he had in the cashbox, poured petroleum on the wooden building, and would have burned all the men alive with the station had not by a lucky chance a truck with some workmen arrived in time; the bandits fled, carrying with them the stationmaster's thirteen-year-old daughter." Opper and a few of the passengers followed the example of the attendants and took out their pistols to be ready for an expected ambush by brigands, but the journey continued without incident.

Lunch was served at the Sheytandjik station. Nagelmackers thought this would be a special attraction for his guests and enable them to enjoy the Oriental ambience. But About, as well as most of his fellow passengers, grumbled that one needed the strength of a very large devil to chew the flesh of the partridges served as the main course. However, the Turkish-style meal included Turkish fruits and desserts —peaches and chopped almonds flavored with rose syrup; kabak tasthi (pumpkin cooked in syrup and served with pounded walnuts); and pastries filled with raisins, pine nuts, and pistachios, followed by cups of thick, strong Turkish coffee. To mollify his guests, Nagelmackers had told one of the train attendants to bring along as many bottles of wine and brandy as he could carry, so the passengers could be fortified against the cold.

Edmond About described, in a similar vein as Opper, the ruined villages he saw from the train, pillaged and burned to the ground during the war between Russia and Turkey four years earlier. Only the occasional glimpse of a mosque, standing intact among a cluster of hovels, indicated some sign of normal life, impressing the observers gazing out of the slowly moving train that this was Moslem country, a finger of the East still stretching into Christian Europe, and that the seemingly cowed and miserable peasants in the fields, who studiedly avoided looking at the train, were the same people, the Pomaks, who had massacred thousands of their fellow countrymen because they were Christians only seven years before in the Bulgarian atrocities that horrified all Europe.

At long last the train pulled into Varna (the Odessus of ancient Greece, the Tiberiopolis of Rome, and between 1949 and 1955 named Stalin), on the edge of the Black Sea. The Turks had held the port against periodic assaults for more than six centuries, until in 1878 it had been ceded to Bulgaria. Built on a sandy isthmus, the town was still Turkish in character and the Bulgarian presence merely superficial. Apart from beggars and railroad officials, no one seemed to take much notice of this historic occasion as the passengers from Paris were marshaled by Nagelmackers and his staff to the jetty, where a steamship was moored in readiness to take the party to Constantinople. She was the *Espero*, owned by the Austrian Lloyd-Triestino Shipping Company. The vessel had left Trieste three weeks earlier and showed signs of the battering it had endured in stormy conditions encountered in the Mediterranean and the Black Sea. The local shipping manager had exploited the opportunity of the sailing for Constantinople by selling tickets to Turkish families who had been existing in appalling conditions in Varna after expulsion from inland villages as part of the policy to "Bulgarize" the mainly Turkish-populated eastern region. Edmond About gave a description of the stench of bodies and bundles of bedding, of the wailing children, mothers in rags breast-feeding their babies, and sallow black-mustached men, who glared at the wealthy Westerners with undisguised hatred. He was relieved that ropes and a hastily erected timber barrier isolated the refugees on the deck. "We kept mostly to our cabins," he recorded. "They were stuffy and we

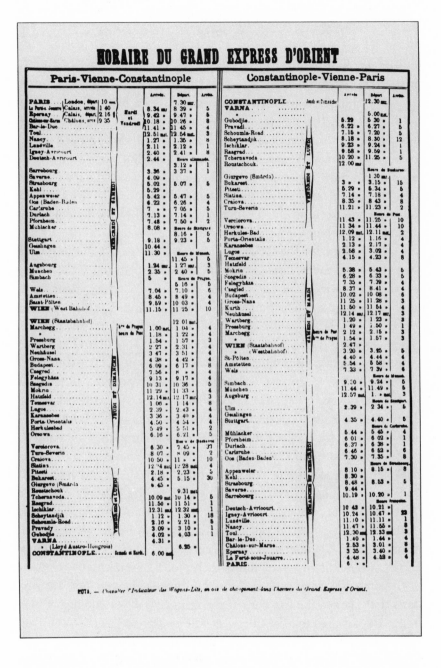

One of the earliest timetables of the Orient Express, showing the sea-route connection from Varna to Constantinople before the completion of the railroad track in Bulgaria.

missed much of the majestic views of the Black Sea, but we felt safer under cover than on deck."

The ship, heavily laden and, because of its flat keel, subject to rolling in even the slightest of seas, left Varna as dusk was falling. Although Nagelmackers had ensured that a good dinner, cooked by one of the Viennese chefs employed by the shipping line, should be served, no one had much of an appetite. The night was cold, the sea choppy, and the aging engines set up a tremendous vibration while dense billowing smoke from the low-grade coal burned in the firebox penetrated every cabin.

The distance to the Golden Horn in the center of Constantinople was about 170 miles, discounting the vessel's drift through the strong northeasterly wind. The passage took more than fourteen hours, making the average speed about twelve knots. The misery of the open sea ended when the *Espero* entered the Bosporus just as dawn broke. About recalled a knock on his cabin door: one of the Compagnie directors, Regray, informing him, "I have good news. It is sunrise, a beautiful morning, and we have entered the Bosporus."

This was an experience none of the passengers wished to miss. Even the two Viennese ladies did not trouble to complete their toilette before leaving their cabins to join the men watching the panorama on each side of the 19-mile strait separating Europe from Asia, with rolling hills sloping steeply to the blue water, forming tiny bays and inlets. The first sight they had were of the two castles at the entrance from the Black Sea—the Rumeli Hisari, on the European side, built by the Sultan Fatih Mehmet in 1452, and the Anadolu Hisari, on the Asian bank, built by Mehmet's grandfather in 1395. Ahead were the gleaming domes of the mosques and churches of Constantinople.

Slowly the vessel moved along the sinuous channel, first past the forts that marked the two ends of the massive walls extending for nine miles around the city, then between the two great palaces—the Dolmabache, on the western bank, and the Beylerbeyli, on the eastern side. The vessel threaded its way among the fishing boats, ferries, and merchant ships till it swung right to enter the long neck of water of the Golden Horn. While the *Espero* was maneuvered to the quayside, the passengers gaped at the fantastic scene that spread before them. Close at hand were the domed roofs of the Kapali Carsi, the covered bazaar, a city in itself, with streets and alleys bordered by hundreds of shops and workshops. A little farther off towered the cupola of one of the greatest churches in the world—the Basilica of St. Sophia, first built in A.D. 347 by the Emperor Constantine, destroyed by fire, rebuilt, again destroyed during war, and rebuilt by the Emperor Justinian. The more devout among the passengers expressed sorrow that this magnificent building was now dedicated to Islam. But there could be nothing but wonder and admiration for the six graceful minarets and the immense dome of the Blue Mosque.

The Orient Express party was greeted by the Belgian ambassador and a crowd of Turkish officials, headed by the Sultan's chamberlain, Sheker Pasha. Horse-drawn carriages were waiting to take the visitors to the Grand Hotel of Pera (now the Pera Palas), then a newly built hotel under French management. Considering the strained relations between the Ottoman Empire and the Western powers, the hospitality accorded the visitors was generous. All the sights of the city—the Roman hippodrome, the column of Constantine, and the exteriors of the Topkapi and other palaces—were the subjects of organized tours. A ferry took them across the Bosporus to Uskudar (Scutari), past Leander's tower, where, according to legend, Hero was imprisoned. In the grounds of the Beylerbeyli palace, the residence of the French Empress Eugénie when she visited Constantinople, the group was entertained by belly dancers. The high spot of the sightseeing was a long drive through the Dolma Valley to the Yildez Kiosk, where Sultan Abdul Hamid was due to review a parade of his Cherkees Cavalry and the Imperial Guards. Always fearful of assassination, the Sultan rarely appeared in public, and the visitors were permitted to view the military ceremony only from a distance.

Opper de Blowitz had separated himself from the party soon after their arrival. He was a close friend of the Turkish ambassador in Paris and had arranged with him not only a series of visits to the highest officials in Constantinople, including the Grand Vizier, Said Pasha, and the governor of the city, General Ahmed Pasha, but also a secret audience with the Sultan, who carried the ancient titles "Emperor of Powerful Emperors; the Sole Arbiter of the World's Destiny; Refuge of Sovereigns; Distributor of Crowns to the Kings of the World; Ruler of Europe, Asia and Africa; High King of the Two Seas; and Shadow of Allah upon the Earth"—alas, titles that were as empty as his declining power over the Ottoman Empire—while contemptuously referred to by foreign statesmen and political columnists as "the Sick Man of Europe."

Judging from the many pages that Opper de Blowitz filled in his *Memoirs* about his interview with the Sultan—the first ever granted to a journalist—it must have been less a conversation than a monologue by the loquacious correspondent of *The Times.* Opper described Abdul Hamid II as a sullen, taciturn, sickly-looking man, obviously living in constant fear for his life, threatened either by a rebel's bullet or dagger or by the poison administered by his own courtiers. The Sultan hardly ever left his palace of Yildiz Kiosk, rarely sleeping two nights in the same room, and though guarded round the clock by devoted and trusted servants, always keeping a loaded pistol under his pillow. It is, of course, a historical fact that he was a ruthless and cruel man, who had disposed, by murder, of several members of his family and of scores of his ministers, generals, and officials, including the Grand Vizier Midhat Pasha, who had helped him to depose his brother Sultan Murad V. The massacre of Armenians, which Abdul Hamid ordered, brought a universal reaction of horror: he was called the Great Assassin by Gladstone, and Abdul the Damned by the world's press.

Yet the celebrated and versatile Prince of Journalists was obviously unafraid of the imperious Ottoman ruler. According to his report of the interview, which lasted three-quarters of an hour, he had proffered advice to the Sultan on how he should shape his future policy, gave him a survey of European politics, explained the British government's attitude to Turkish interests in Egypt and the Middle East, and hinted that he could be helpful in arranging with the Rothschilds and other financiers in London and Paris badly needed loans to Turkey. The Sultan must have been impressed because on leaving the audience room, Opper was handed the Order of Medjidieh Third Class. He took the decoration, but regarded it as an insult. In view of the valuable advice and information he had provided, he considered that the order should have been of a higher grade.

Nagelmackers and his party again embarked on the *Espero* on the afternoon of October 13. Arriving at Varna before dawn the next morning, they were back in the comfort of the Orient Express cars late that afternoon. For the now seasoned travelers, the return journey was uneventful, with receptions in the main cities en route reduced to brief welcomes, except for a longish stop in Vienna when Herr von Scala and his two intrepid ladies made their farewell, much to About's regret. The exchange of promises to visit their new friends in their own countries and return to be entertained in Vienna increased the delay in the train's schedule by two hours. Thanks to splendid work by the locomotive engineers and the Austrian, German, and French railroad managements, the lost time was made up and the Orient Express halted in the Gare de l'Est in Paris precisely on schedule, at 6 P.M.

The celebrations were not quite complete. Nagelmackers wanted to express his thanks to his guests for accepting his hospitality. That meant one last dinner together. Edmond About recorded in his book: "The eleven wonderful days of a unique and historic journey were over."

Chapter Five

THE GREAT ROBBERY

Shortly before midday on may 31, 1891, a telegram arrived at the offices of the Compagnie with a terse report of an incident that had been a dreaded eventuality ever since the train was routed through Bulgaria. The Orient Express, westward bound for Paris, had been derailed, the passengers robbed, and an unstated number of hostages taken.

The scene of the holdup was near the Turkish village of Cherkes Keui, in East Thrace, some 60 miles west of Constantinople. No further details were given in this first telegram, but it was all too obvious that this was an operation by Greek bandits, who would demand ransom.

The next development was a message handed to the Turkish governor in Adrianople telling him to send a rescue party to the scene of the holdup. The rough-looking horseman who delivered it galloped away before the guard on the gates could detain him. Almost simultaneously the railroad telegraph at the Karagaj station of Adrianople began to receive detailed information. A Turkish official on the train had struggled through the darkness along the track for five miles to the station of Cherkes Keui to give the alarm. His message was that the track had been torn up and the locomotive and some of the cars derailed. Injuries to the train crew and passengers were not believed to be serious, but several of them had been abducted by the bandits, estimated to number about twenty. Their captives' fate was unknown. A great deal of baggage and money had been stolen. Help was urgently required. The governor, Weissel Pasha, a German colonel in the Sultan's service, mindful of the reaction in Constantinople if he failed to take precautions at what might be the overture to yet another rebellion, alerted all military and police posts in the area. Next he compiled a report on what he had done and wired it to the Ottoman capital. Only then did he order railroad officials to assemble a train and send it to the holdup scene. It did not leave until close to midnight, moving very slowly in case there had been further sabotage on the line, and arrived three hours later. The frightened and shivering passengers were crammed into the two cars of the rescue train, which steamed back to Adrianople. As soon as it arrived and the passengers had been taken care of, the train set out again with a repair crew. At dawn, the men began repairing the torn-up track and pushing the wrecked locomotive and cars out of the way.

The full story of the attack was given by the survivors. The engineer, a Swiss named Freundinger, who had been bruised as he jumped, along with the fireman, when the locomotive toppled down the embankment, said that he had seen that the track was damaged but was unable to stop the train in time. The tender, a baggage van and two cars—one for third-class local traffic and one second-class—had been dragged down the embankment by the locomotive. The coupling between the second-class car and the first of the three Wagons-Lits cars snapped under the strain and they remained upright on the track.

At first there was complete chaos. From the derailed cars the passengers, many bruised and cut by shattered glass, struggled to free themselves, creeping out from windows and through the open roof of one of the cars. The Wagons-Lits passengers, who had been on the point of retiring after dinner, crowded at the windows and doors, at first unaware of what had occurred but soon alarmed by the sight of the wrecked local cars and the hissing steam from the overturned locomotive. Amid the babel of screams in several languages, alongside their undamaged luxury cars they saw armed men with rifles, pistols, and daggers. Some of them were rounding up the men and women who had escaped from the derailed cars; others began to clamber aboard the sleeping cars and the restaurant car. They ordered all fifteen employees of the Compagnie—conductors, chefs, and waiters—to get off the train and to lie on the ground. There, at pistol point, they were bound hand and foot.

Inside the Wagons-Lits cars passengers were moaning that they had been hurt when baggage had toppled off the racks, and several of the eight ladies had hysterics. Bandits burst into the compartments, smashing doors that were locked, and ordered everybody to come out and stand in the corridors; the passengers were given no time to dress and many believed that everybody would be killed. Then the leader of the gang arrived in the first corridor. He was a giant of a man, about forty years of age, with a flowing black beard. He shouted in a mish-mash of French, German, and Greek, trying to calm the excited men and women: *Non tuer! Calmez vous!* (No killing, calm yourself). Then with a broad grin he announced, "Anasthatos, leader of rebels," jabbing a finger toward his chest, and then assured the passengers in broken French that no one would be harmed if there was no resistance. His almost polite behavior contrasted with the menace of the huge old-fashioned pistol he waved in the faces of the frightened passengers, and with the long dagger thrust through a dirty red sash around his big waist. Going along the corridors, followed by several of his rambunc-tious companions, he ordered the men and women back to their com-partments. He took no direct part in opening and rifling their hand baggage, content to watch his men going from compartment to com-partment and taking their time removing moneybags, wallets, rings, brooches, watches, and any other valuables they could find. When one man resisted, he was hit by a brigand's point-blank pistol bullet, which just nicked his upper arm. Anasthatos heard the shot, and he ran along the corridor, pushing aside some of the bandits standing guard. On entering the compartment and seeing what had happened, he knocked his henchman to the ground with his huge fist. Then he motioned to the slightly injured passenger to remove his coat and skillfully bandaged his arm with a handkerchief and a scarf, all the time murmuring apologies. The gang leader was obviously anxious to avoid bloodshed and to persuade the passengers that he was not a common ruffian but the leader of rebels.

The search for valuables was conducted without further violence, three or four bandits having the job of collecting all the loot taken by their comrades and packing them into bags. The booty was impressive. Some of the passengers were carrying large sums in gold coins, and all had articles of jewelry. A later estimate put the total value of the robbery at about $160,000, at least a million dollars in present-day value. Anasthatos, reacting to the tears of the women and the pleading by some of the men, chivalrously handed back wedding rings and trinkets they had described as being of sentimental value. For this gesture he demanded some reward, however, and confiscated all cigars and tobacco pouches.

Only about twenty minutes had passed since the train was derailed. Now the bandits gestured for everyone to line up on the track alongside the wagons-lits where there was a little light. Anasthatos walked slowly along the row and selected his hostages. They included the bruised engineer, Freundinger; the chef of the British embassy in Pera, who was going on vacation in Bulgaria, one Georgius Kviat; five German businessmen—Moritz Israel (a Berlin banker), Oskar Greger, Albert Marquet, Oskar Koelsch, and Franz Roet. They had been negotiating mineral and land concessions from the Ottoman government in connection with the Baghdad Railroad. It later developed that the gang leader had attended the German Evangelical mission's school in Adrianople for a year or two and knew German quite well. He probably decided that taking the prominent Berlin businessmen as hostages was the most promising means of extorting a substantial ransom.

After ordering the rest of the passengers to get back in the undamaged cars, he told them that they should wait for help, which he would arrange to be sent from Adrianople. Then he gestured to his men to shoulder the loot, which also included most of the stores of food and drink in the restaurant car and the mailbags from the fourgon. Loaded with the heavy bags, the men and their hostages started moving northward into the forest. Within minutes they had all disappeared into the dark woodland. As soon as they could no longer be seen and heard, some of the less daunted passengers unbound the Compagnie employees, who, in the tradition of their service, immediately set about tidying the mess in the compartments, consoling the distraught men and women, and making coffee, which they laced with brandy from a few bottles the bandits had missed.

Apart from the belated appearance of the rescue train, the next incident was the arrival of the exhausted Georgius Kviat at the Cherkes Keui railroad depot shortly after dawn. He said he had been released after the bandits had marched some five miles on the mountainside. He was shown a track running in a southeasterly direction, which he was told would get him to Cherkes Keui. He was presumably selected as the bandits' messenger because he spoke both Bulgarian and Greek as well as English. He told the stationmaster and the local gendarmes, who were waiting for the relief train, that Anasthatos had ordered him to convey the message that the ransom for the German hostages was £8,000, payable in gold sovereigns. Kviat had no instructions as to the method of payment, nor could he help much in regard to the location of the hideaway. The bandits and their prisoners had moved off as soon as he got his instructions about getting to Cherkes Keui. It was clear that there was no chance of finding the bandits and their captives in the vicinity even if Kviat could lead the gendarmes back, and that the whole attack and escape route had been carefully prepared in advance.

That the bandits had put maximum distance between the derailed train and their position by the time daylight came was proved later that morning, when the Berlin banker Moritz Israel arrived on horseback in Kiliseli, a small Turkish town on the river Tunja; a large proportion of the town's inhabitants were Greek, and the bandits could count on their compatriots' assistance. Kiliseli lay some sixty miles from the scene of the attack, and this meant that the Anasthatos gang had penetrated fast and far into wild and rugged countryside, clearly having a good knowledge of the shepherds' trails, which enabled them to make good time. Israel was accompanied by one of the bandits, who made it clear to the gendarmes that if he was detained the hostages would be shot. The banker told the gendarmes that he and his escort had left the bandits' hideout two hours, he thought, before his arrival at Kiliseli, the horses being ridden hard and probably covering at least fifteen miles. He was not sure about the time because his watch had been taken away.

The banker had brought two letters for the Turkish authorities. One was in German; he had written it himself under Anasthatos' dictation, the second was in Greek and the gang leader had scrawled it himself. Both were similar in content:

We, the undersigned, are prisoners. Our captors demand a ransom of 200,000 French francs or £8,000 sterling, in gold, to be deposited at Kirk Kilisse. In default of compliance with this demand we shall be shot. We beg you therefore instantly to send the money. Only Herr Israel or Herr Marquet can bring it. At the first appearance of soldiers or police we shall be put to death.

Below the message, on both letters, were the signatures of all the captives. His mission accomplished, the bandit then rode off, leaving Israel with the gendarmes. During the day the courier of the German travel agency Stangen, which had organized the German businessmen's trip, arrived from Adrianople and interviewed Israel. The courier, Walter Gerlach, had been on the train and, being regarded as a Compagnie employee, had been one of those tied up by the bandits. He was a man of action and took Israel on the first available train to Constantinople, where they saw the German ambassador, Von Radowitz. The ambassador promptly demanded an interview with the Grand Vizier and asked that Sultan Abdul Hamid should be informed that German citizens had been taken prisoner in Turkish territory. The Turkish officials talked about action being taken to discuss the means for providing the ransom money, but nothing concrete resulted.

The incident was rapidly developing into an international crisis. Kaiser William II, who had strenuously tried to develop an alliance with Turkey and had visited the Sultan in 1889, was incensed at this assault on his subjects. The mailed fist came out of the velvet glove, and he threatened to send German troops to Adrianople to deal with the bandits. This was tantamount to declaring war. Whether the Kaiser was bluffing or not, the Sultan took the threat seriously; he authorized the German ambassador to obtain the necessary gold coins from the Ottoman Bank, with a pledge that Turkey would refund the loan. Thereupon, all problems were quickly resolved, and Israel was given an escort of twenty-eight Turkish gendarmes, with four mounted Greek scouts each carrying a bag of two thousand English sovereigns. The Swiss engineer Freundinger, as a neutral, joined the party, which arrived in Kiliseli on June 4, five days after the bandits had taken their hostages.

Four men, with proof that they were authorized by Anasthatos to negotiate the payment of the ransom, had been given a promise of safe conduct by the military commander at Kiliseli, and were staying at a caravansary outside the town. As soon as they saw the police escort they refused to cooperate. Acceding to pleas by Israel and diplomats of Austria and Germany, who had also arrived on the scene, the Turkish commander withdrew his troops. Then, after hours of argument on both sides, the four bandits agreed to accept the courageous Swiss engineer in place of Israel as the representative of the authorities. Along with the four Greeks carrying the gold, the emissaries set off for the hideout, whose location was still not revealed. It was a village named Edis Baba. Anasthatos had prudently shifted from his original hideout when the lack of overtures from anyone in Adrianople hinted at the possibility of a planned military search. (If that had in fact been launched, the Turkish troops would have meandered for days, and possibly weeks, in the remote hideout area without success.)

The meeting took place on June 9, four days after leaving Kiliseli. The length of time taken for a journey that was not particularly long or difficult suggests that the escorting bandits mistrusted the authorities and made frequent checks that they were not being followed, adopting different routes for a few hours just to put any concealed scouting party off the scent. In fact the Turks had managed to keep on the party's trail, but, fortunately, in view of the bloodbath that would have occurred if they had attempted to interfere, they remained in the background until the hostages' release was completed. Then they came forward to escort the freed prisoners back to Kiliseli.

The released hostages proved to be in good health, though dirty, hungry, and badly in need of fresh clothing. All were clutching five gold sovereigns (taken from the ransom money), the personal gift of Anasthatos. After an overnight rest in a hotel at Adrianople and a morning spent purchasing new clothes and footwear with money brought by

Israel from Constantinople, the heroes took the Orient Express to Belgrade. A crowd of reporters, including a London *Times* correspondent, awaited them.

Possibly to build up a story which was becoming somewhat anticlimactic in the complete absence of facts as to who the bandits were, where they came from, or what had been done with the fortune they had obtained, many newspapers, including the restrained London *Times*, claimed that Anasthatos must have had accomplices among the Turkish railroad employees or the Compagnie staff on the train. How else could they have known that there were wealthy Germans, Austrians and French passengers traveling on it? The answer, of course, was that there were always rich and influential people on the Orient Express. A more interesting theory advanced in the popular London papers was that the bandits had indeed prior knowledge of the identity of one passenger who had reserved a sleeping compartment—Sir Stephen Ralli, a British millionaire banker who had been undertaking business deals in Constantinople and was the real target for capture. But Ralli had canceled his return to England at the last moment. None of the allegations was ever confirmed or denied because Anasthatos and his gang were never found, and not a cent of the ransom or any of the valuables ever recovered.

The reaction of the Ottoman government to the outrage was to dismiss the governor of Adrianople, Weissel Pasha, and replace him with a Turk, Marshal Hamdi Pasha, who had a good reputation as commander-in-chief of II Corps of the Turkish Army, based in Thrace. The Adrianople police chief, Blunt Pasha, an English officer in the Sultan's service, put forward a scheme to organize a rural police force to guard all trains passing through Eastern Thrace, with armed guards aboard all express trains. The Adrianople garrison was reinforced with six thousand additional troops, who were to be deployed all along the railroad between the frontier, Adrianople, and the stretch regarded as most vulnerable—from Cherkes Keui to Uzunkopru. These plans were rushed through because of a rumor in the Ali Bazaar at Adrianople that Anasthatos was planning a second ambush of the Orient Express for the night of June 20. It was presumably a false story circulated by political malcontents to harass the hated Turks.

In fact the bandits did strike again. On August 10 they swooped on the headquarters of the Ormandji Vineyard Company, near Eregli, a small town overlooking the Sea of Marmara and 30 miles south of the site of the attack on the Orient Express. The two French managers, Eugène de Raymond and François Ruffier, were kidnapped and held for two weeks. They were freed after a ransom in gold Napoleons equivalent to a total of $20,000 was paid. From the Frenchmen's description of the bandits' leader he was clearly Anasthatos.

Once again the Ottoman government lost face in not being able to protect citizens of foreign nations within its territories. The French ambassador in Constantinople lodged a strong protest and conveyed his government's warning that French marines would be brought in to protect French citizens and property. The press branded Turkey as a country "in a state of political as well as social anarchy."

Infuriated by all the criticism, and at least as angered by the expense of remitting the large sums to cover two ransom coups, the Sultan issued a personal ordinance on September 28, 1891, requiring the immediate suppression of brigandage in Eastern Thrace. His command took the form he had found so effective during other crises of state: it was either the officials' heads or those of the people they were supposed to suppress. All *muttessarifs* and *kaimakams* (provincial and local semimilitary functionaries) were to be held personally responsible for any and every act of brigandage committed in their districts. Some officials, too aware that brigandage was a way of life for many of the inhabitants enduring Turkish rule, took to their heels and went to live in self-imposed exile. Others, pursuing the familiar and disastrous policies that had fomented revolts and minor wars for generations, issued orders to intimidate the population. Peasants were forbidden to carry weapons (meaning that farm implements and knives could be regarded as an excuse for their arrest) and anyone with a hunting gun had to report to the local police office. Condign punishment was threatened on all those who knew of the existence or whereabouts of brigands and failed to inform the authorities. As there was hardly a family without some relative liable to be dubbed a bandit under the expansive concept of the Turks, or a village from which a neighbor had not taken to the mountains to live as best he might, this was again an all-embracing intimidation of the people. That rewards offered for the capture of a brigand dead or alive produced no result whatever is an indication of the loyalty of the people to the alleged criminals and their loathing of their rulers.

Inevitably, the Compagnie suffered some criticism for failing to ensure adequate protection for passengers on the Orient Express. There were allegations that criminal assaults on the train had occurred on other occasions but news of them had been suppressed. A well-known Austrian banker and member of the Vienna parliament, Eugene von Rappoport, told reporters that in February 1886, when he was traveling on the Orient Express to Constantinople, a group of bandits boarded the train at Uzunkopru, threatened the train conductors with shotguns, robbed a number of passengers, and alighted when the train made its usual stop at Pichlon, simply walking off without anyone attempting to stop them. Why he postponed telling this story for five years and did so only when the Cherkes Keui attack became big news is not clear. In any event the Compagnie categorically denied that there was any truth in it.

More justifiable perhaps was the criticism about the Compagnie's policy in routing their train through Bulgaria and European Turkey when fully aware that the entire area was politically unstable and unrest involving military skirmishes a virtually permanent situation. To understand Nagelmackers' reasons one needs to appreciate the situation after the first few months of the train's operation.

At the outset the Compagnie had wanted the northern route in Eastern Europe, running through Bucharest to the Rumanian border, because it involved a minimum of operation in Bulgarian territory— a matter of only sixty-five miles from the border to the port of Varna, on the Black Sea. Rumania was well equipped with railroads, as compared with other Balkan countries, because of the degree of independence from Turkish suzerainty guaranteed by the major powers, and their financial support. By taking a more southerly route from Belgrade and across Bulgaria, a direct rail link with the Turkish-run railroad was possible, with only a short break to be covered by road transport. It was far shorter than the northerly route and, of course, obviated the uncomfortable eighteen-hour Black Sea passage. The objections included slow and difficult running through the Balkan Mountains in contrast to the comparatively easy route along the Danube basin, the dubious reliability of Bulgarian tracks and locomotives, and, above all, the political instability of Turkish controlled areas, always threatened by outbreaks of insurrections or outright banditry.

But by 1885 the Compagnie was sufficiently satisfied with the plans and promises of the Bulgarian government to run a train for the first time from Budapest via Belgrade to Nish, in Serbia, as a test for the eventual rerouting of the Orient Express. From Nish a team of engineers and traffic experts headed by Nagelmackers inspected the route planned for an extension of the railroad along the banks of the river Nishava through Bela Palanka, and then through the foothills of the mountains to Pirot and the border with Bulgaria. Almost 120 miles were without a reliable rail track from the border to Tatar Pazardzhik and Plovdiv. Thereafter the railroad was complete as far as Constantinople. The journey of survey and exploration through an area where the terrain was as savage as the people who sparsely inhabited it was enough to intimidate any with less optimistic determination than Nagelmackers. He and his team traveled in the height of summer, but the condition of the roads and the number of cascading streams running down the mountainsides were sufficient to hint what travel would be like in wintertime. However, there was definite evidence of some new sections of a railroad being under construction, and Bulgarian officials, eager to prove that theirs was not a backward country, displayed plans to prove that sooner than their visitors could believe a splendid line would stretch from the western border to the existing railhead of Plovdiv.

Already the Orient Express had attracted passengers of a type that surprised the Compagnie. The original conception had been that it would cater to officials, businessmen, and the wealthy nobility who were the only committed long-distance travelers of the time. In the event, a large proportion of the clientele proved to be tourists ready to spend large sums simply to visit places of scenic and historical interest and to see countries previously almost unreachable.

The southerly route through Bulgaria was both spectacularly scenic and fascinating historically. Though geographically part of

Europe by custom and ethnic origin, the country had much of the glamour and mystery of the East. The towns that would appear on the revised Orient Express timetable, unknown except to students of history and Balkan politics, were redolent of Europe's past. Nish was one of the oldest towns in Eastern Europe outside Greece. The birthplace and summer residence of Constantine the Great, it had been destroyed by the Huns in the fifth century and promptly rebuilt by the Emperor Justinian.

Pirot, the next community on the route, was the ancient town of Turres and famous for carpet making, an industry introduced by the Turks. In the 1880s, because of war and the retirement of the Turkish garrison, the place fell into ruins, through which ran a maze of alleys. But it did boast a hotel, Le Roi de Serbia, charging one Belgian franc for a meal and one franc for a room—the latter, whatever its location in the building, always being described as the regal bedchamber in memory of the night some unnamed monarch had slept in it.

After the long trek through the mountains Nagelmackers and his party rested at Sofia. He was anxious to meet Prince Ferdinand—just elected the country's ruler after the deposition of Prince Alexander of Battenberg—to secure a contract for the running rights for the Orient Express. As the Prince, an astute and cunning monarch, was a scion of the house of Saxe-Coburg and Bourbon-Orléans, Nagelmackers had taken the precaution of bringing an extravagant letter of introduction from the King of the Belgians. But Ferdinand, accustomed to looking for underlying motives from the politicians and militarists who tried to advise him purely to further their own interests, made excuse after excuse about his regrettable inability to grant an audience. Nettled, Nagelmackers decided to go ahead with his survey, leaving his principal assistant, Count de Richemont, to hang around until an invitation came from the palace. When it arrived and he presented himself in his rather creased and stained formal clothes, he was told by the court chamberlain that protocol demanded that every person addressing the Prince had to be in uniform. The resourceful Belgian managed to persuade the police captain on duty at the palace to lend him his parade uniform. When he duly entered the audience chamber and gave what he hoped was a smart salute, the Prince roared with laughter, exclaiming "What a ridiculous country this is!" But the incident put his Highness in a good mood, and De Richemont walked out with the agreement required.

Nagelmackers had meantime reached Tatar Pazardzhik, some 70 miles from Sofia, which was one of the outposts of the Mongol invasion of Europe. It had a nondescript appearance but was significant in that it marked the end of the difficult mountain region; ahead was reasonably easy terrain all the way to Constantinople, with the Ottoman Railway already in operation.

The line passed through Plovdiv, then the second largest city of Bulgaria. It had been founded by Philip of Macedonia, named by him Philippolis, and was subsequently captured by the Romans, who made it the capital of their province of Thrace. But most of the classical buildings had disappeared in the earthquake in 1818 which devastated the entire city. The 125 miles from Plovdiv to the Turkish town of Adrianople took six and a half hours by train, and from there to Constantinople a further seven and a half hours. Named after its founder, the Emperor Hadrian, in the fourteenth century, Adrianople became one of the summer residences of the sultans and had a wholly Oriental appearance, with two large and beautiful mosques built in the sixteenth century. When Nagelmackers visited it for the first time, many of the buildings had remained in ruins as a result of the Russian bombardment and subsequent occupation during the war in 1878. The stay of the Compagnie's chief there was brief. He wanted to move ahead and satisfy his long-treasured ambition: to approach the city of Constantinople by land. And there it was, at last, as the train of the Ottoman Railway Company jolted slowly along the edge of the Sea of Marmara. The direct rail route from Paris to Constantinople, with some minor and, he hoped, only temporary breaks, could become a reality. But there was still the missing link—that formidable stretch where the railroad track in Bulgaria had still to be completed. The official brochures issued to attract travelers did not entirely conceal the possible dangers, but assured prospective clients that the "numerous and highly experienced staff of the Compagnie is well trained and able to cope with any untoward event."

Nish, then the second city of Serbia, was the last outpost of safety inside the comfortable cars of the Orient Express. The train arrived there in the early evening, and in summertime there was a chance for the passengers to see the sights before their memorable journey the following morning.

The Compagnie had bought a string of diligences to transport the passengers by road right through Sofia to Tatar Pazardzhik, a road distance of 175 miles, of which the first 44 miles as far as Pirot were through savage and depopulated country. Diligences had been chosen because they were of light weight compared with traditional coaches, and with the body hung on leather straps, they gave a fairly comfortable ride. In Western Europe and the United States diligences were often called flying coaches because of the speed they attained, averaging 10 to 12 mph with frequent changes of horses. But in Bulgaria, with the road little better than a rutted track and the innumerable fierce gradients, anything more than 5 mph was out of the question. The wagons used to carry the passengers' baggage moved even more slowly, and hours often elapsed at each overnight stop before the passengers could obtain their nightgowns or a change of clothes.

The schedule allowed two days for the journey and indicates how carefully the Compagnie had organized frequent changes of horses in any benighted village that could boast a stable, as well as suggesting the many exhausting hours the passengers had to spend in the tiny vehicles. The time might even be longer; the Compagnie advised passengers that if the diligences were delayed by bad weather they should remain overnight in the vehicles rather than patronize some inn which was not on the authorized list of resting places, both for reasons of safety and hygiene.

One passenger has left a personal account of his experience: "The diligences were comfortable, and had excellent springing and upholstery, which was appreciated particularly during the ascent of Mount Platcha. Each diligence was drawn by two horses and usually there were no more than four travellers in each vehicle. The interior was small with tiny windows, the latter for reasons of safety from brigands' bullets."

From their diligences the passengers were able to see gangs of peasants working on the construction of a railroad running parallel to the road and the river Nishava, working eastward from Nish. The

Compagnie, whose wish was doubtless echoed by the diligence travelers who contemplated making a similar journey in the future, stated in their brochure:

We anxiously await the day when the Orient Express will be able to continue the full distance beyond Belgrade. Meanwhile we have recently provided a new wagon-lit with ten berths to establish a temporary service beyond Nish to Bela Palanka. This car will run thus far next October; this will reduce from three days to two the journey that now has to be made over the whole distance to rejoin the railroad at Tatar Pazardzhik. The car will certainly make the journey more comfortable and pleasant; further, it will enable passengers to sleep in their own berths at Nish and thus spare them the trouble and expense of seeking hotel rooms. An excellent meal will be available at the station buffet at Nish, and the next morning the train will take the passengers in two hours or so to Bela Palanka.

As this rail link was only 28 miles long, the schedule of "two hours or so" gives some indication of the difficult gradients and formidable curves of the track, as well as the lack of power of the locomotives. There was, indeed, a constant worry about breakdown or derailment. Beyond Belgrade the Compagnie was permitted to use a train weighing a hundred tons, but if there were thunderstorms, heavy rain, fog, or snow, or the thermometer dropped to 6 degrees Fahrenheit below freezing, the weight was limited to eighty tons. This meant leaving one sleeping car at Belgrade, the passengers being given makeshift beds in the restaurant car if all other berths were occupied.

When this section of the railroad was in operation, there still remained the primitive road as far as Tsaribrod, now Dimitrovgrad,* the last Yugoslav town before the Bulgarian frontier, a distance of 45 miles. Conditions as far as Pirot were comparatively good—the road and river were fringed by vast sloping stretches of scrub and grass, with flocks of sheep kept for the wool used in producing carpets, Pirot's main industry. The town lies in the shadow of 5,800-foot-high Mount Trem, a hint of the formidable mountain area that lay ahead. The road wound

*Named after Georgi Dimitrov, the Bulgarian Comintern leader who in 1933 was accused by the Nazis of having set fire to the Reichstag in Berlin. He became Bulgarian prime minister in 1946 and died in 1949.

through defiles and traversed innumerable mountain streams, usually with no bridges and only a bed of loose stones to form a ford, invariably impassable in times of heavy rains or melting snow. The Compagnie's publicity staff did their best to make this section sound like an attractive experience: "The road towards Slivnitza plunges into a succession of majestic gorges, at first perhaps a little forbidding but always notable for their dramatic quality."

The sense of drama was not solely that imposed by nature. Peering through the windows of the diligences, the passengers noted with an understandable sense of foreboding the military strongpoints perched on the crags, the occasional groups of ruined hovels, burned down and demolished in the interminable skirmishes between Turkish, Serbian, Bulgarian, and Macedonian bands of raiders. The area was so infested with bandits that the Compagnie arranged for mounted police or troops to escort the diligences through the more notorious places of attack.

Despite travelers' tales of shots fired at the coaches and glimpses of a few horsemen being chased by the military escort, the diligences were in fact unmolested. The more promising target for the bandits was the lumbering caravan of baggage wagons which, within a few miles of both parties starting out, lagged far behind. A few trunks were frequently missing when the next overnight stop was reached, the wagon drivers usually protesting that they must have dropped off without anyone noticing. The Compagnie quietly accepted that the loss of items was the result of some of the drivers and soldiers conniving with local gangs in return for a share in the loot and invariably refunded the value of the stolen goods.

At last, in 1889, the rail track in Bulgaria was completed. Nagelmackers had achieved his dream: the Orient Express was running on the entire route from Paris to Constantinople.

Chapter Six

FULL SPEED AHEAD

IT IS A MATTER OF RECORD THAT THE INITIAL RUNS OF THE ORIENT Express were considered by the railroad managers throughout Europe as mere experiments bound to fail. There was, it was claimed, no demand for a regular transcontinental service; people were quite satisfied to interrupt their journeys at various stages and to change trains provided by the many state-owned or private companies, meekly accepting discomfort as an inevitable price for leaving the comfort of their homes.

From the very start the Compagnie maintained a twice weekly service in each direction, the Orient Express leaving Paris at 7:30 P.M. every Tuesday and Friday, and every Wednesday and Saturday from Constantinople. Ignoring local times—they were different in Paris, Vienna, and Constantinople, with other changes in between—the train took a clocktime of 81 hours 40 minutes on the easterly run. This included the fifteen hours allowed for the maritime passage between Varna and Constantinople. Those occasions when the schedule was not maintained were invariably due to the difficulties of the sea journey. Port facilities at Varna were poor and the ship had to anchor well out to sea. The ferrymen, plying very primitive boats, refused to take passengers out when the sea was rough, though the Austrian Lloyd steamer always left on time with or without passengers.

Within a year, when the railroad authorities had accepted that the Orient Express was a remunerative innovation for them, more powerful locomotives were allocated to the train and efforts made to speed up fueling and watering at the stops. Consequently the westbound train's time was cut by an hour. M. Harand, a one-time joint chief engineer of the French Est Railroad, who recounted in a French journal in 1937 many memories of the early days of the Orient Express, did not mention the time saved on the easterly run, but one may presume that it was much the same as for the other.

The popularity of the train not only confounded its critics but exceeded Nagelmackers' hopes. Naturally, the greatest demand was for fast and comfortable travel between Western and Central Europe. To cater to it a daily service was provided in 1885, with the Orient Express terminating at Vienna on five days a week and the original twice-weekly service right through to the Bosporus on the other two days.

The stretch by road beyond Nish still remained. This handicap was overcome in June 1889 with the completion of the Bulgarian track, and then, for the first time, the entire journey between Paris and Constantinople could be made in the same cars. This shortened the duration of the journey by a further fourteen hours, followed by yet another cut of about two hours in 1894, due to improved tracks and rescheduling of local services, which had hitherto impeded an uninterrupted run in Rumania. That year also saw the opening of the Fetesti bridge across the Danube east of Bucharest, with a railroad direct to Rumania's greatest port on the Black Sea at Constanţa. Although transit from there to Constantinople still meant a sea passage, lasting twenty-seven hours, the land route was more direct than via Giurgiu, and Constanţa was an all-weather port with good harbor facilities.

In 1898 Nagelmackers decided that the time had come to stage a great celebration, and he predated the Silver Jubilee of his enterprise, taking the registering of his very first company in 1873, still in partnership with Colonel Mann, as the date of the founding of the Wagons-Lits Compagnie. He chose Liège, his birthplace, as the "cradle" of the company, although the registration was in fact effected in Brussels.

Thus at the Royal Conservatory of Music—the largest available hall in the sleepy ancient Belgian town—a great gathering of distinguished personages was arranged. More than two hundred guests, brought by special trains from many of the countries served by the Orient Express trains, sat down to a banquet which, even in those opulent days, could easily vie with any royal occasion. The menu sheet printed in gold lettering and preserved in the Compagnie's archives was as follows:

Huitres de Beernham
Potage de la Reine
Truite Saumonée à la Chambord
Selle de Chevreuil à la Duchesse
Poularde Valoise
Chaudfroid de Langouste à la Parisienne
Truffes au Champagne
Bécasses à la Monaco
Parfait de foie gras
Plombière Impératrice
Glaces Wagons-Lits
Fruits—Desserts

After oysters, turtle soup, smoked trout, saddle of venison, capon, lobster in aspic, truffles, woodcock, goose liver—everything lavishly garnished with choice vegetables and salads—and various desserts, a splendid concoction of ice cream was served in replicas of wagons-lits made of marzipan and nougat. All the elaborate catering was performed by the Compagnie's chefs, and the meal was served by the Compagnie's waiters in their traditional uniforms of velvet tails, breeches, silk stockings and buckled shoes.

There was an almost interminable succession of after-dinner speakers, led by the Compagnie's president Neef-Orban; the English vice president Davison Dalziel; the Marquis de Ségur, member of the Academy and grandson of Napoleon's marshal at the siege of Moscow, Comte de Chastel; and other distinguished guests from several countries. Each offered a toast in praise of the celebrated director general Georges Nagelmackers, who sat beaming and was moved to tears. He had indeed every reason to be proud of his achievements. In the same year the entire rolling stock of sleeping cars was replaced by new models, with toilets placed between each pair of compartments of two beds. Most of the restaurant cars had also been replaced by new salon dining cars with metal bogies of special suspension. Two years later, in 1900, a new timetable was introduced by which the Orient Express ran daily from Paris to Budapest, three times a week to Constantinople via Belgrade and twice weekly via Constanţa, and special connection was opened via Salonika to Athens.

Nagelmackers did not live to see the Silver Jubilee celebrations of the inauguration of the Orient Express in 1883; it took place in 1908 in Paris. He died of a heart attack, on July 10, 1905, two weeks after his sixtieth birthday, when taking a brief rest at his château at Ville-preux-les-Clayes, after visiting the International Exhibition at Liège, which he had helped to finance and organize in a tribute to his birth-place. At the exhibition he saw the Wagon-Lit No. 1000 and the restaurant car No. 999 being admired by tens of thousands of visitors. In that year the Compagnie had a thousand sleeping cars running not only all over Europe but also across Asia and North Africa. Nagelmack-ers had obtained a contract from the Czar for a Wagons-Lits service on the Trans-Siberian Express, and the inaugural journey of the sleep-ing and restaurant cars took place on June 17, 1898; thus the cars were running from Calais (for the London connection) and Paris to Port Arthur on the Pacific (and after the Russo-Japanese war in 1905, to Vladivostok). The service in Africa had already begun in 1889 in Algeria, and by 1902 it was expanded along the entire shore of North Africa. Even when the great differences in the value of money are taken into consideration, the supplementary charges for the Wagons-Lits cars were most reasonable. The price for the entire Trans-Siberian journey, which lasted eighteen days and seven hours was £69 or $280.

Nagelmackers' sudden death at a comparatively early age was a sad blow to the Compagnie and, indeed, to the world's railroad system which, within two decades, he had revolutionized and equipped with undreamed-of comfort. But he left the Compagnie in capable hands. In 1893 Davison Dalziel, a thirty-nine-year-old English entrepreneur, had joined the Compagnie's board. He was the owner of a London evening paper and a Sunday journal and had manifold business and financial interests; a few years later he established in London the first taxicab company in Europe. Nagelmackers was particularly eager to attract English travelers, not only to the Orient Express but also to the many other expresses in Europe and overseas on which Wagons-Lits circulated. Dalziel had become the managing director of the British Pullman Car Company and thus Nagelmackers' only rival. Eventually the two companies combined, and after Nagelmackers' death Dalziel became the president of the Wagons-Lits Compagnie while remaining the chairman of the Pullman Car Company. In 1910 he was elected a Member of Parliament, and in 1921 created a Peer of the Realm as Lord Dalziel of Wooler.

The partnership between Nagelmackers and Dalziel was cemented by a matrimonial linking of their families. Nagelmackers' only son, René, born in 1878, married in 1903 Dalziel's only daughter, Elizabeth. Until his death in 1928, Lord Dalziel greatly expanded the business of the two companies in many directions. The *trains transatlantiques* provided excellent and comfortable connections for the ocean liners to America, and were much appreciated by American visitors to Europe. One was the New York Express for the North German Lloyd's boats from Hamburg and Bremen; two other Wagons-Lits expresses ran between Paris and Cherbourg and Paris and Le Havre for French boats sailing to New York. Another of Dalziel's innovations was the Anatolian Express, which connected with the Orient Express to cross Asia Minor. A year after Nagelmackers' death Wagons-Lits service was also extended to the Manchurian Express from Irkutsk to Changchun and connected with Peking, and eventually to the South Korean port of Fusan, where passengers could embark on ships to Japan. And already in 1898 two sleeping cars and a restaurant car of the Compagnie were running from Port Said to Cairo, the service being developed in 1903 as the Wagons-Lits's Cairo-Luxor Express.

At the 1908 celebration banquet guests from all over the world stood in silence in tribute to the memory of the Compagnie's founder, whose death had undoubtedly been caused by sheer overwork. The Compagnie issued a memorial brochure, written by Albert Flamented.

Only seventy-five copies were printed, and the brochure is now a collector's item.

In 1906 the Simplon tunnel under the Swiss Alps had been opened for traffic to Italy. Almost immediately thereafter the Compagnie organized a Wagons-Lits service between Paris and Venice via Lausanne and Milan. In 1912 it was extended to Trieste and provided a very fast service, the trains sometimes consisting of only one or two cars and a fourgon, in order to keep down the weight for the fierce gradients in the Swiss section. The outbreak of war in 1914 meant at first the termination of the service at Venice and later, with the country around Paris a battlefield, the Simplon Orient Express ceased to run.

In the first weeks of 1919, following the negotiations of the Treaty of Versailles, the Compagnie was asked to plan an express train to link France and Italy with Eastern Europe without running through the territories of Germany, Austria and Hungary. This train, which made its inaugural run on April 11, 1919, was available to the public in the normal manner. It followed the prewar route of the Simplon Orient Express as far as Trieste, and then passed through Zagreb, Vinkovci, and Subotica to Bucharest, with a section of the train separated at Vinkovci to serve Belgrade, where it again divided with one section for Athens and the other for Constantinople. Another train, restricted to military and diplomatic personnel, was also inaugurated at the same time. It avoided Germany by running south from Paris through the Belfort Gap into Switzerland, then through the Arlberg tunnel to Salzburg, Linz, and Vienna, and thence to Budapest and Bucharest.

Tacit and, frequently, even open hostility toward the Wagons-Lits had always been shown by German railroads, which, for the most part state-owned, pursued the policy of protecting German monopoly of rail services within national territories and combating any trespass on German influence in neighboring states. But the Allied victors of the First World War included in the clause of the Versailles Treaty a condition that Germany had to provide running facilities over German railroads for Wagons-Lits trains. Thus on September 6, 1919, Britain, France, Belgium, Rumania, and Poland, in conjunction with the Compagnie, drew up the route for a deluxe express to run from Paris to Warsaw and Prague with a western extension to Boulogne, and separation at

Table 32

ORIENT EXPRESS

	arr.	dep.		arr.	dep.	
S	..	2145	Paris (Est) 172............	8 15		
	2 52	3 8	Strasbourg	2 26	2 50	
FS	3 20	3 45	Kehl 🚉 172.................	1 37	2 13	6
	4 35	4 39	Karlsruhe 🚉	0 40	0 44	
	5 53b	..	Stuttgart (Hbf.) 670a......	..	2326	F6
D105	..	6 24	Stuttgart (Hbf.)	2253		
	9 29	9 44	Nuremberg 678.............	1933	1946	
E205	1133	1148	Marktredwitz..............	1745	1748	
	12 5	1225	Schirnding 🚉 688.........	1655	1731	D106
64	1249	14 7	Cheb 🚉	1529	1634	
	16 5	1615	Plzen	1320	1329	
	1810	..	Prague (Main) 812.........	..	1120	63
FS	..	6 5	Stuttgart (Hbf.)	23 2	..	
	7 13	7 15	Ulm 670	2145	2147	
	8 6	8 7	Augsburg	2046	2047	
	8 48	9 0	Munich (Hbf.) 670.........	1952	20 5	
Ex	1040	11 0	Salzburg 🚉 684...........	1748	18 8	F4
122	1239	1242	Linz	16 7	1610	Ex
	1455	..	Vienna (West) 750.........	..	14 0	123

Connecting service by 🚌, 1, 2 cl. with 🍴 Vienna–Budapest and v.v.

TS	..	1520	Vienna (West)	1335	..	TS
125	1633	17 0	Hegyeshalom 🚉 746......	12 0	1225	124
	1924	..	Budapest (East) 806......	..	9 36	2

Daily: 🚌 1, 2 cl. Paris–Vienna and v.v.
    🚌 1, 2 cl. Paris–Salzburg and v.v.
    🚌 1 cl. Paris–Stuttgart (for return, see Table 61).
    🚃 Paris–Prague and v.v.
    🚃 and CC. 2 cl. (French) Paris–Vienna and v.v.
    🚃 Stuttgart–Prague and v.v.
    🍴 and 🚃 Stuttgart–Vienna and v.v.
    🍴 Bar-le-Duc (dep. 5.34)–Paris.
    🍴 (Czech) Cheb–Prague and v.v.
Mons., Weds., Fris. and Sats.: 🚌 1 cl. Paris–Stuttgart.
Tues., Thurs. and Suns.: 🚌 1 cl. Paris–Prague.
Mons., Weds., Fris. and Suns.: 🚌 1 cl. Stuttgart–Paris.
Tues., Thurs. and Sats.: 🚌 1 cl. Prague–Paris.
b—Passengers may remain in the 🚌 Paris–Stuttgart until 7.45.

Table 35

SIMPLON EXPRESS

For journeys beyond Zagreb, see Table 28 (🚂———).

	arr.	dep.		arr.	dep.	
	..	11 0	London (Victoria)..... } G	1935	..	
	1847	..	Paris (Lyon) 50 .... }	..	1047	
S	..	1928	Paris (Lyon) 151..........	9 25	..	
	2230	2237	Dôle	5 57	6 6	
SE	0 7	0 22	Vallorbe 🚉 158...........	4 27	4 41	6
	0 57	1 0	Lausanne 251	3 48	3 51	
	2 36	2 39	Brigue 🚉	2 8	2 14	
	3 15	3 35	Domodossola 🚉	1 14	1 29	
	5 20	..	Milan (Lambrate) 351	..	2322	ES
2S	7 40	5 25	Milan (Lambrate)..........	23 3	..	
	9 6	7 53	Bologna	2033	2041	
RS7	1255	9 16	Florence	1913	1923	
	1553	1330	Rome (Termini) 374	1510	1535	26
		..	Naples (Cent.) 392	..	1253	RS6
SE	..	5 37	Milan (Lambrate)	23 8	..	
	7 16	7 20	Verona (P.N.) 390.........	2124	2127	
	8 51	9 34	Venice (S. Lucia)	1934	1952	
	1141	a12 3	Trieste 390	1713a	1725	ES
SE	a1235	a1255	Poggioreale Campagna 🚉..	1621a	1641a	
	a13 3	a1333	Sežana 🚉	1547a	1613a	
	a1420	a1430	Pivka 791	1456a	15 6a	ES
	2410	a1428	Pivka	1453a	..	
	a1540	..	Rijeka 795................	..	1325a	2421
SE	a16 5	a1640	Ljubljana	13 8a	1323a	
	a1845	..	Zagreb 791................	..	11 3a	ES

At Paris, only takes passengers for stations beyond Milan (in 2 cl. couchettes, only for Verona and beyond; in 2 cl. seats, only for stations or ports beyond Venice), and v.v. Other passengers should use the Lombardy Express leaving Paris (Lyon) at 21.10.

Daily: 🚌 1, 2 cl. and 🚃 Paris–Rome and v.v.
    🚌 1 cl. Paris–Naples and v.v.
    🚃 Paris–Zagreb and v.v. (Paris–Trieste from Nov. 1). •
    🚃 and CC. 2 cl. (French) Paris–Vanice and v.v.
    CC. 1, 2 cl. (Italian) Paris–Trieste and v.v.
    🚃 Trieste–Rijeka and v.v. (to Oct. 31).
    🚃 Trieste–Zagreb and v.v. (to Oct. 31).
    🍴 and 🍴 Paris–Dôle and v.v.
    🍴 Bologna–Rome and Rome–Milan.
    🍴 Rome–Naples and v.v.
    🍴 Venice–Milan.
    🍴 Verona–Trieste and v.v.

G—GOLDEN ARROW Pullman train—See Table 11. Passengers change at Paris (Lyon).

a—May 27–Oct. 31 only.

Table 28

DIRECT-ORIENT EXPRESS

Day	arr.	dep.		arr.	dep.	
A	..	1530	London (Victoria) 50....	1 50		
A	32	19 0	1925	Calais (Maritime) 🚢....	1113	12 5	
Y		2243	2253	Paris (Nord) 50	7 25	8 9	9
A	S29	2319	d2350	Paris (Lyon) 151	6 2vf	6 59	
PO	6 0	6 25	Vallorbe 🚉 158	2354	0 8	S20
	7 0	7 7	Lausanne 251	2349	2357	
	7 32	7 34	Montreux	2310	2322x	
	9 19	9 27	Brigue 🚉 251	2014	2047x	OP
	10 5	1025	Domodossola 🚉	1915	1935	
PO	1220	1318	Milan (Cent.) 351	1636	1715	
	17 1	1735	Venice (S. Lucia) 370 ...	1210	1238	
	20 0	2010	Trieste 390	9 10	9 52	OP
Y	21 0	2130	Poggioreale Campagna 🚉..	8 8	8 36	
B	PA	2130	2225	Sežana 🚉	7 0	8 0	
C	0 38	..	Ljubljana 791	..	4 22	AP
B	D41	..	1559	Munich (Hbf.) 684	1335	..	D45
E		1753	1813	Salzburg 🚉	1139	1150	
735	2020	2024	Badgastein	9 30	9 34	E
	22 5	2225	Villach 🚉 759	7 30	7 50	734
B	907	2312	2340	Jesenice 🚉	5 39	6 20	
C	0 53	..	Ljubljana 793	..	4 18	908
C	PA	..	1 15	Ljubljana 791	4 0	..	
	3 20	3 35	Zagreb	1 36	1 51	
	8 46	9 36	Belgrade 791	1930	2030	AP
	1253	..	Crveni Krst	..	16 3	
	PA	..	13 0	Crveni Krst 792	1548	..	
		1620	1632	Skopje	1210	1222	
Y	402	1947	2022	Gevgeli (Yug. T.) 🚉 ...	8 35	9 5	AP
	2133	2215	Idomeni (Grk. T.) 🚉 ...	8 50	9 30	
C	2	2331	0 20	Thessaloniki 897	6 35	7 25	401
D	10 0	..	Athens 897	..	21 5	1
C	PA	..	1318	Crveni Krst 802	1540	..	
		1522	1550	Dimitrovgrad (Yug. T.) 🚉	1377	14 7	
Y	4	1733	1810	Dragoman (Bulg. T.) 🚉 .	1345	1417	
C		1849	1925	Sofia 821	12 0	1255	
B	546	a0 43	a1 20	Svilengrad 🚉	4 20b	6 10	3
S		a4	6 a5	0	Pithion 🚉	0 25b	1 30b	
Y		a5 20	a6 10	Uzunkopru	2317c	2357c	
Y		a1245	..	Istanbul 901	..	1630c	6

🚌 1 cl. and CC. 2 cl. Calais–Milan and v.v.
🚌 1 cl. and CC 2 (🚃) Paris–Brigue and v.v   ⎫ See Note x
CC. 2 cl. (Swiss) Paris–Brigue and v.v   ⎭
(🚃) and CC 2 cl. (French) Paris–Milan and v.v.
🚃 Paris–Trieste and v.v.
🍴 Trieste–Belgrade and v.v.
🚃 Munich–Belgrade and v.v.
🚃 Munich–Athens and v.v.
🚃 Dortmund–Athens and Athens–Hagen.
🚃 Belgrade–Athens and v.v.
🚃 Jesenice–Belgrade and v.v.
🚃 (Warsaw)–Belgrade–Sofia and v.v.
🍴 Calais (Nord) and 🍴 Paris (Nord)–Calais.
🍴 Lausanne–Brigue and Domodossola–Lausanne.
🍴 Milan–Trieste and v.v.
🍴 (Yugoslav) Belgrade–Gevgeli and v.v.
🍴 Tithorea (dep. 7 11)–Athens and v.v.
Tues. and Sats.: 🚌 1 cl. and 🚃 Paris–Belgrade.
Mons., Weds. and Fris.: 🚌 1 cl. and 🚃 Paris–Athens.
Thurs. and Suns.: 🚌 1 cl. and 🚃 Paris–Istanbul.
Mons. and Thurs.: 🚌 1 cl. and 🚃 Belgrade–Paris.
Mons., Thurs. and Sats.: 🚌 1 cl. and 🚃 Athens–Paris.
Tues. and Fris.: 🚌 1 cl. and 🚃 Istanbul–Paris.
Mons., Weds., Fris. and Suns.: 🚌 1, 2 cl. Munich–Athens.
Tues., Thurs. and Sats.: 🚌 1, 2 cl. Munich–Belgrade.
Tues., Weds., Fris. and Suns.: 🚌 1, 2 cl. Athens–Munich.
Tues., Fris. and Suns.: 🚌 1, 2 cl. Belgrade–Munich.
a— Weds. and Suns only.
b— Weds. and Sats. only.
c— Tues. and Fris. only.
d— Depart 23.53, June 27–Sept. 13 (as train 519).
f— Arrive 6 20, June 29–Sept. 15.
x— From July 21 to Sept. 16, the Brigue–Paris cars will depart Brigue 20 7, Montreux 22 2 and Lausanne 22 34 (Train 45).

NOTES FOR TABLE 27—continued.
    🚌 1, 2 cl. Hook of Holland–Villach and v.v. (extended to Klagenfurt, June 29–Sept. 8, returning June 30–Sept. 9).
    🚃 Cologne–Athens and v.v.
    🚃 Munich–Skopje and Vienna–Skopje and v.v.
    🚌 1 cl. and 🚃 Belgrade–Thessaloniki and v.v.
    🚃 Vienna (dep. 9.35 arr. 20.55)–Athens and v.v.
    🚌 1 cl. (Yugoslav) Ljubljana–Skopje and v.v.
    🚃 (Ostend, Table 64)–Jesenice–Belgrade and v.v.
    🍴 Hook of Holland–Cologne and v.v.
    🍴 Munich–Villach and v.v.
    🍴 (Yugoslav) Ljubljana–Belgrade and v.v.
    🍴 Thessaloniki–Athens and v.v.
Daily to July 5 and from Sept 2: 🚌 1, 2 cl. Hook–Mannheim–Basle and v.v.—see Table 78.
Daily, July 6–Sept. 1: 🚃 Hook of Holland–Lindau–Innsbruck, returning one day earlier.
V—VORARLBERG EXPRESS, Ulm–Innsbruck and v.v. Runs July 7–Sept. 2 only. Conveys 🍴 Ulm–Lindau and v.v.
k— Arrive 20.36 to June 17 (20 50 on Suns.).

GREECE   NOMIKOS LINES
See Table 1403

62

Strasbourg, with one section running via Nuremberg to Prague and the other via Munich and Vienna to Warsaw.

The Compagnie, with Allied approval, worked out a timetable so that this train could also operate as a feeder for the Orient Express, passengers making a convenient transfer at Vienna. But the German government, in spite of the treaty, created problems and objections to delay matters, citing, for instance, track repairs that were prohibitively costly, lack of locomotives, shortage of coal, and inadequate signaling for fast trains. On one pretext or another they managed to prevent the running of any train until June 1920. Even then there were problems, this time genuine. Austria, cut to one-eighth the size of the old Austro-Hungarian Empire, was in economic and financial chaos; coal for the locomotives to haul the new train had to be sent by freight train from the French coal fields, much of it being pilfered en route. Hungary, after two revolutions and the loss of three-fifths of her former territory and two-thirds of her population, had to be written off as providing a viable route, no matter what aid in the way of motive power and fuel was given. A roundabout route to reach Bucharest was adopted from Katowice, southwest of Warsaw, running through Lvov and Snyatin (now both in the USSR) to Bucharest, thus avoiding Hungary. This was a tedious and difficult service to maintain, instituted only because of the need to link Western, Central, and Eastern Europe.

Whichever route was taken by the two main versions of the Simplon Orient Express, there were many short reverses and junctions, as well as divisions or additions of cars. Vinkovci, in the new kingdom of Yugoslavia, was one busy junction, with sections of the train taken off (or joined on the westward journey) for Belgrade and Constantinople, for Subotica and Bucharest, and for Athens. The last terminus was the most important development for the Wagons-Lits service in those chaotic years after the end of the war. It was made possible by the completion of the line from Salonika to Larissa built for military purposes during the war. Then much of the planning and organization to provide a regular and reliable service with the Simplon Orient Express crumbled in January 1923, when French and Belgian troops occupied the Ruhr as retaliation for Germany's failure to pay war reparations. Germany refused to handle the train on any part of her territory. As a result, a new route was adopted through Basle and Zurich in Switzerland and using the Arlberg tunnel into Austria.

Thus was born the Arlberg Orient Express. It immediately became very popular, first with Swiss businessmen who could reach every important capital in Central and Southern Europe in a matter of hours, and secondly with the delegates and their armies of aides attending the League of Nations sessions in Geneva. In the latter instance British needs for fast travel resulted in one section of the Arlberg Orient Express starting from Calais and Boulogne, joining the main part outside Paris.

On November 30, 1924, the last of the French and Belgian troops were withdrawn from the Ruhr, whereupon Germany agreed to accept the Orient Express, but the Arlberg and Simplon expresses had proved so successful that for some time the Orient Express itself ran only on three days a week. Transit facilities within the borders of Germany were in any event offered by the Reichsbahn only at the cost of restriction of Wagons-Lits cars on German internal services, which ran cars belonging to the Mitropa Gesellschaft, formed in 1916 with the declared intention of breaking the Compagnie's monopoly of sleeping and restaurant cars at first in Germany and Austria, and, after the war was won by the Kaiser, throughout Europe. But although Germany was defeated, and despite the Versailles Treaty clauses intended to prevent restrictions on the Compagnie's business, Mitropa continued to compete and hinder, with German government support, throughout the interwar years. After the Nazis took power, open and contrived resistance to the Wagons-Lits trains became one of Hitler's taunts, causing deliberate delays by "track repairs," special customs checks, and so on.

In spite of growing political tension in Europe and the impact of the worldwide economic depression, the early 1930s saw Wagons-Lits carrying more passengers and with faster and more frequent services than ever in their history. Long-distance travel in Europe by automobile was still comparatively slow and uncomfortable; air services were in their infancy and were unreliable. By 1932 the original Orient Express was restored with through cars from Paris to Istanbul (the new name for Constantinople since 1930); the Arlberg Orient Express maintained the service to Athens; the Simplon Orient Express was routed to serve Belgrade and Sofia as well as including a section for Bucharest; and another service, the Ostend-Vienna-Orient Express, both linked the Belgian seaside resort with Vienna and connected the Austrian capital with the Orient Express for Bucharest and Istanbul. Thus, by one route or another, there was a daily Wagons-Lits service between Western Europe and the Balkan capitals.

This superb multitrain service came to an abrupt end when, on March 11, 1938, German troops invaded Austria and the country was declared part of the German Reich. Immediately all contracts with Wagons-Lits for running facilities were broken and the facilities handed over to the German Mitropa company. When the Second World War broke out in September, only the Simplon Orient Express continued to run during the winter of 1939–40. Mussolini, still luke-warm about his "pact of steel" with Hitler, resisted German pressure to ban transit of the Simplon Orient Express through Northern Italy, while Yugoslavia, Rumania, Bulgaria, and Greece were still undecided about throwing in their lot with the Axis or the Allies. It all came to an end when the "phony war" became a blitzkrieg, with the trains of Mitropa advancing as Wagons-Lits was forced to retreat.

After the war the Arlberg Orient Express became the first trans-continental European express to be restored. It made its first run on September 27, 1945, from Paris via Zurich to Innsbruck, which was as far as the track had been adequately restored. A military band and a U.S. Army guard of honor greeted its arrival. Two months later repair of all railroads on its route enabled the Simplon Orient Express to be restarted. On the inaugural run it went as far as Trieste, later was extended as a daily service to Belgrade, and, finally, three times a week via Sofia to Istanbul.

That these trains continued to run at the height of the cold war and penetrated the Iron Curtain was testimony to the strict neutrality of the Compagnie's policy. There was also, of course, the benefit to the Soviet Union and her satellite nations in sharing a means of communi-cation and transit with the West; it was easily supervised at innumera-ble security and customs checks. But periodically the outbreak of local-ized hostilities brought route changes and cancellations. In 1952 the border between Turkey and Bulgaria was closed, and conditions in the latter country were so fluid and unsafe that the Simplon Orient Express schedule was advertised with alternative termini according to conditions on the relevant day—Sofia or Svilengrad. The frontier was not reopened until March 10, 1953, and more than two months elapsed before the service could be extended to Istanbul. In that year a sleeping car on the Simplon Orient Express was again running through Salonika to Athens. Previously, while the Yugoslav-Greek frontier was closed, an eastern section of the Orient Express route was partially covered by running the train only between Istanbul and Salonika twice weekly. It must have been a memorable and somewhat alarming experience, with bands of rebel fighters roaming the country. For safety's sake the train did not move at night, stopping in the comparative security of the station at Alexandroúpolis, close to the Turkish border.

These minor successes in restoring the services of earlier and happier times had been marred by a crisis in Czechoslovakia. After a Communist purge in March 1951 all Wagons-Lits offices in the country were taken over by the Czech state travel organization Čedok. This meant that the Orient Express had to end its run at Nuremberg, and incidentally end the connection for Warsaw and Moscow. The sudden authorization by the Czech government of running rights to Prague and elsewhere within their country was said to be on direct orders of the Soviet Foreign Minister, Andrei Vishinsky, who had found it impossible to travel comfortably and quickly for conferences in the West and to the United States when Wagons-Lits services were stopped in Czechoslovakia and Poland. Their restoration might have been useful also for westbound Soviet espionage agents.

In spite of the widespread development of highways for automobile traffic by-passing villages and allowing for high speeds over hundreds of miles, the rapidly growing network of air routes, and, above all, the steady isolation of the Soviet satellite countries from Western Europe, the Compagnie still continued to link the West with the East. New expresses either extended or connected with the Orient Express services. At the height of the cold war the Tauern Express between Ostend and Athens began running in May 1953, and two years later the Balkan Express inaugurated a service between Vienna, Belgrade, and Athens. Both these services were timed to allow Orient Express passengers to change trains at a convenient station, usually Vienna.

In 1956 the Orient Express once again ran farther east—to Budapest. It had to avoid Czechoslovakia, so it missed Bratislava and was routed into Hungary via Hegyesalom. The Arlberg Orient Express ran daily from Paris to Bucharest until May 1962, when it was terminated at Vienna, and then being renamed the Arlberg Orient Express. In the same month the Simplon Orient Express ceased to run as far as Istanbul, the Direct-Orient Express taking over as the train link between Paris and Istanbul.

The heyday of these great trains was nearly over, but the finale was still some years away. The sad but glorious last runs of the Orient Express belong to another chapter.

The unique place of the Wagons-Lits cars of the Orient expresses in the history of trains and railroads was earned primarily by the tireless work of Nagelmackers and of those who followed him in activating routes to cover the principal cities and towns of Europe on a wide front from the English Channel ports to the rim of Asia. The plan became a profitable reality thanks to two other contributions: the excellent cars of the trains and the personnel that manned them.

The Compagnie did not, of course, supply traction. The locomotives to haul their Orient expresses were the responsibility of the railroad companies concerned, and at the outset there had to be loans of locomotives from the large companies. Innumerable problems about motive power to maintain the tight schedules of cars far heavier than those of many of the Eastern railroads had to be overcome. The desire for prestige deriving from advanced locomotive development prompted the Compagnie to trade with engineering works in Britain, France, Germany, and Austria, all competing to construct more efficient and more powerful locomotives.

Notable among the locomotives that transformed the journey times were, originally, the outside cylinder 1–2–0's of the French Est Railroad, followed by that company's De Glehn 2–2–0 compounds (high-pressure and low-pressure cylinders) in the 1890's; the giant Austrian 0–4–0's, not fast but of tremendous power as their spark-arresting smoke stacks sent swirls of burning lignite smoke over the cars while the train tackled the formidable gradients in the Tyrol; the 4-cylinder compounds built in Hungary at the turn of the century; the first 2–3–0 express locomotives in service in Europe, built by Italy in 1884 and used for decades afterwards; and the superb 2–3–1 compounds supplied by Maffei of Munich to most of Europe's railroads after 1908. Technique developed so rapidly in this early period that later locomotives were largely modifications and improvements on these pioneer machines which, in many cases, continued to work on east European railroads until the advent of the diesel and the diesel electric engines. It can be said, and the Compagnie always acknowledged the fact, that the many railroads involved in hauling the Orient expresses served them well.

The problems over efficient traction power during the first sixty years were as nothing compared with those prevailing after the Wagons-Lits resumed service after the war. Locomotive sheds had been a primary target for Allied bombers and freedom fighters for six long years. In Germany and in the countries liberated by Soviet forces operable locomotives had virtually ceased to exist. In France, the traditional source of supply, fourteen thousand locomotives had been destroyed or removed to Hitler's Reich during the war; the remainder were in a bad state of repair. After France was liberated the United States was asked to supply locomotives. The Baldwin Locomotive Works, of Philadelphia, designed a massive 1–4–1 to be built simultaneously by Baldwin, Lima, of Ohio, and Alco, of Schenectady. In July 1945 the first 141R was ready at the Lima plant. It steamed out of the workshops through a paper barrier adorned with the Cross of Lorraine and the colors of the Free French, and was named *Liberation*. The three American plants supplied twelve hundred of these locomotives, and a hundred and forty more were built in Canada by the Montreal Loco Co. and the Canadian Loco Co. They were able to haul the Orient expresses on the first leg of their run through France at 65 mph with up to eight hundred tons of payload. On the lines further east, particularly in Yugoslavia, Vulcan 1–4–0 engines became available in 1946. They were designed after collaboration with engineers of seven countries and built at the famous British locomotive works at the Vulcan foundries at Newton-le-Willows in Lancashire. These locomotives became for years the mainstay of the 260-mile run between Zagreb and Belgrade as well as the difficult stretch of the Belgrade-Nish-Skoplje track.

Except for the enthusiasts who regarded the locomotives honored with the job of hauling an Orient Express as the focal point of interest at every stop—many stations making special arrangements for inspection by locomotive spotters—most people were more impressed by the spectacle of the "hotel on rails," whether they were ever able to travel in it or not. With the possible exception of the Pullman Company, Wagons-Lits produced cars with a standard of comfort and luxury hardly exceeded even by the few "super trains" running today. And rarely a year passed without some improvement.

Over the years since the first sleeping cars were built in 1876 the Compagnie constructed or ordered more than four thousand vehicles in some 385 different types. It constantly advanced designs, to be imitated all over the world. Through gangways first appeared in 1880, with open-air vestibules on the American pattern. They were followed by cars with mixed sleeping and ordinary compartments. After 1883 the comfortable ride provided by the first bogie-mounted cars meant that no more six wheelers were built.

At that time special cars became the status symbol of royalty, statesmen, and plutocrats, which were quite regularly attached to an Orient Express. In 1893 the Compagnie built one special car (No. 501) with a day *salon*, two bedrooms, two sleeping compartments for the suite, and a servants' compartment. It could be hired by anyone with the necessary cash who could meet the undefined but rigorous standards in the social scale that the Compagnie always maintained when hosting special clients.

The most famous of such Wagons-Lits cars was car No. 2419, built just before the outbreak of the First World War. In October 1918 the French War Office asked the Compagnie to supply a special car for the mobile headquarters of Marshal Foch, supreme commander of the Allied forces on the Western front. He was already working from a Wagons-Lits train of three cars, with trucks at either end to minimize the risk of sabotage. No. 2419 was converted into a conference salon car, with the stove removed from the kitchen to make room for wireless signalers and typists. Completed as a rush job at the Compagnie's workshops at St. Denis, near Paris, the car was kept at Chantilly until 5 A.M. on November 11, when a locomotive crew was ordered to take it to Compiègne, twenty-five miles to the northeast of Paris.

It was then still dark, and the long-range guns mounted on railroad trucks in the sidings were in action. No. 2419 was shunted in order to be coupled to Marshal Foch's train. As dawn broke, the amazed locomotive crew saw a French locomotive approach on the up track drawing German coaches. When the train stopped, a group of German officers alighted and entered the Wagons-Lits car. Four hours later, at 11 A.M., the German surrender was signed and the First World War came to an end.

This historic car, with commemorative plaques, was subsequently exhibited in Les Invalides, France's national shrine in Paris. In 1927, thanks to the generosity of an American, Arthur H. Fleming, of Pasadena, California, No. 2419 was restored to its original immaculate state and taken to a covered building erected on the site of the signing of the armistice at Compiègne. It was visited by tens of thousands every year until June 1940, when a German panzer regiment arrived, blew up the walls of the exhibition hall, and then hauled the car to the precise spot on which it had stood on November 11, 1918. On June 22, Adolf Hitler, accompanied by Goering and the Nazi general staff, arrived to dictate surrender terms to the French delegation. The Führer allowed no discussion, giving the French ten minutes to sign. Afterwards he executed a brief dance of joy before returning to Berlin; Hitler's clowning was preserved on film. From his headquarters he issued a proclamation: "The historic German [sic] car and the monument to French triumph will be brought to Berlin. The rails on which it had stood in 1918 will be destroyed so that no trace of Germany's defeat in 1918 shall remain."

After much difficulty, the car was taken to Berlin on a tank transporter and exhibited beside the Brandenburg Gate. When Allied raids began on the German capital, it was removed to the Anhalter Bahnhof for safety. Intelligence sources reported its exact location to London and, it is said, on the personal request of General de Gaulle, the station was selected as a target during a mass raid in 1944 which utterly destroyed the Anhalter Bahnhof. But the Germans had reckoned on such an attack, and along with other treasures in the capital, car No. 2419 had been taken to a rail siding at Ohrdruf, 180 miles southwest of Berlin. When General George Patton's armored divisions were thrusting deeper and deeper into southern Germany, Hitler gave orders that No. 2419 "must never become a trophy of the Allies once more" and must be destroyed. An SS unit blew up the car, burning everything combustible and removing the metalwork.

AFTER THE END OF THE FIRST WORLD WAR THE FIRST STEEL SLEEPING cars were put into service, with blue paint and gold lines compensating for the absence of the luxurious varnished teak. No wooden cars for the Orient expresses were built after 1924. Further indications of the modern trend was the introduction of cars consisting solely of second-class accommodation, with the fares greatly reduced, bringing long-distance travel in an Orient Express within the means of the growing market among middle-class tourists. The more modest but still very comfortable sleeping berths were so successful that subsequently third-class sleepers were also introduced. They had either four berths per compartment or were modified from existing cars with three berths. Some—perhaps snobbish—doubts about the acceptable behavior of passengers in these second- and third-class cars resulted in an instruction to the train conductors to pull down the blinds during the summer while the Orient Express ran alongside the river Varda in Salonika so that these passengers should not see the local girls bathing naked in the water. This sightseeing remained the prerogative of the Wagons-Lits upper-crust customers. A novelty introduced in the Simplon Orient Express in the 1930s was a bath car, built in a converted truck. It had thermostatically controlled showers in a curtained section, beyond which was a washbasin, hot towel rail, and radiator.

The rapid expansion of war in Europe after 1940 left Wagons-Lits cars stranded all over the Continent. East of Vienna cars simply disappeared, allegedly destroyed by bombing or sabotage but, as often, actually stolen and broken up for the materials in them. Those cars which had been brought back to France were requisitioned by the Germans and parked in sidings as stationary accommodation for troops or as control bureaus. After the end of hostilities a search was made for

845 vehicles listed as missing. Police and military authorities were supplied with photographs, details of identification marks, and other information in an attempt to locate cars that had not been accounted for as having been destroyed by military action. A few cars were located in this way and were useful, whatever their condition, for repairing other cars. By 1947 the Compagnie had sufficient rolling stock to restore virtually all the prewar services where running facilities could be obtained.

Apart from the modernization of equipment such as lighting, heating, and upholstery, major changes were rarely made after the war. An exception was the P-type, which was introduced in 1951 to mark the seventy-fifth anniversary of the Compagnie and henceforth served the vastly increased tourist traffic. With an exterior in aluminum and blue, it had single berths for twenty second-class passengers on two levels, thus ensuring privacy for each passenger.

The facility of traveling thousands of miles by train without the need to sleep overnight in a hotel was the original and primary attraction on which the success of the Orient Express was based. A close second was the exceptional comfort and service available during the waking hours of daytime travel. The policy of emulating in a restricted space the luxury of a first-class hotel and restaurant transformed a rail journey from a boring and often tiresome necessity to a memorable experience.

At first baggage trucks were often modified to include a kitchen, though after 1913 most restaurant cars were built with a kitchen at one end. Great ingenuity was shown in the layout, and in the luxury cars normally used on the Orient expresses forty-two people could sit down for a meal at one time; when second-class passengers were also carried, the tables and chairs were slightly smaller, enabling fifty-six people to be served at one sitting.

The dishes and wines of the country were always a feature of the menu, though as an alternative there were always dishes of universal appeal. Compagnie offices in the capitals of the countries through which the train passed ran a section concerned with ensuring that supplies were ready at every main stop, particularly fresh bread, milk, vegetables, and fruits. But Paris inevitably became the main supplier.

In the final decades of operation the Maison Raoul Dautry had kitchens, a bakery, and freezers. At the zenith of the train's popularity in the 1950s and 60's this plant produced a hundred thousand cakes and pastries every month, and five thousand portions of cold meats and poultry. Uncooked foods, brought in from every part of France, were checked, cleaned, and dispatched to the Orient Express' Paris terminal in fleets of trucks, along with blocks of ice for the storage rooms in the kitchen car to augment the refrigerators. Although buffet cars were introduced on some of the Wagons-Lits trains on shorter routes, the Orient Express, the Simplon Orient Express, and several of their sister trains retained the service of complete meals served by waiters.

Ultimately, the evidence of the organization and ingenuity put into the operation of Wagons-Lits expresses depended on the trains' personnel. Each sleeping car had its own *conducteur,* supervised by at least two superiors who regularly inspected the cars. The *conducteur*—usually with the help of an attendant—was responsible at the start of each journey for checking the equipment and the chores such as cleaning and bedmaking performed by the attendants of lower rank.

A *conducteur* was expected to be able to understand and speak three languages—French, English, and German; most had at least a smattering of several more, including even Serbo-Croat and Greek. He was trained in first aid, and in each car had a small cupboard containing simple medicines, toiletries, towels, and face cloths. He was handed a diagrammatic list of passengers and the berths allotted to them, often with confidential notes about their status. When his passengers arrived he supervised the porters handling the hand baggage, and firmly but courteously restricted the number of bags to be taken into the sleeping compartment. He checked the tickets and took charge of the passports. Orient Express passengers were rarely disturbed at frontiers, and customs examination of the baggage was normally made in the *conducteur*'s presence. He informed the passengers about customs and visa regulations and assisted them in the event of any hitch. Most passengers were generous: many members of the Wagons-Lits staff in the golden years of the Orient Express were able to retire with sufficient money to buy a hotel or open a first-class restaurant in a city of their home countries.

Chapter Seven

THE MAN
IN COMPARTMENT
SEVEN

IN 1885, TWO YEARS AFTER THE INAUGURAL RUN OF THE ORIENT
Express, a young-looking man boarded the eastbound train in Vienna.
Dressed in a brand-new, flashy suit of English cut, wide-brimmed hat
tilted rakishly to display his silky hair, heavily perfumed and with a
complexion so bland that lotions had obviously been applied, he gave
a first impression of a Western dandy. Only his dark eyes and a certain
yellowish tinge to his skin hinted that this was an Eastern European
trying to emulate a Western man of the world.

He was older than he looked—possibly thirty-six but probably
thirty-four. Neither then nor in the many years of his life which lay
ahead did he precisely reveal his birth date or, for that matter, his
birthplace.

But on this momentous day in Vienna—momentous for the world
as well as for the man striding slowly across the platform clutching an
expensive and brand-new document case—the Orient Express played
the first of its many roles in a fantastic career of ruthless intrigue,
fortune hunting, bribery, and corruption—plus one strange incident of
romantic melodrama.

ZACHARIE VASILOU ZACHAROFF, OR ZAHAROFF BASILE, OR BASIL ZOHAR, or Zacharias Basileos Sahar—the names are as varied as the birth date —was born according to his own statements at different times, in four different places. A birth certificate he presented when in middle age claimed he was born in Mouchliou (now Muǧla) in southwest Turkey and baptized there according to the rites of the Greek Orthodox Church. Much earlier, when unable to conceal his youthful period, he was regarded as a child of the slum area of Constantinople—Tatavla, where the country's persecuted Greeks lived in a ghetto. In his late sixties, when he acquired the Grand Cross of the Légion d'Honneur from France, and the Grand Cross of the Order of the British Empire and the Order of the Bath from King George V of England, he changed the locality of his birth to Phanar, the district of Constantino-ple where an exclusive coterie of wealthy and aristocratic Greeks had withstood Turkish oppression for centuries. The fourth reported birth-place was Kishinev in Moldavia, where the Zohar family—Jews— sought refuge from persecution by the Turks. The circumstantial evi-dence for this strange flight from one anti-Jewish country to another just as vicious came from a man, Haim Manelewitsch Sahar, who claimed to be Basil Zaharoff's son, born on April 15, 1868, at Vilkomir (Lithuania). The life of this "man of destiny" will always remain ob-scure; Zaharoff delighted in spreading fictional stories of his early career.

What is certain about Zaharoff's life is that he spent his childhood in the seething melting pot of Constantinople. As a member of the repressed Greek community he had to live by his wits or starve. In all the varied stories of those formative years circulated by Zaharoff him-self in later years, one occupation is invariably mentioned: he became a "guide."

In the mid-nineteenth century the number of conventional tou-rists visiting Constantinople to see the sights was minimal. The stran-gers in the sprawling city were for the most part sailors on shore leave from the ships of a dozen nations. Few indeed were interested in the Blue Mosque or the Roman ruins. They wanted to sample the notori-ous delights of Oriental sex. Every conceivable—and to the Western imagination almost inconceivable—sexual pleasure was for sale in the alleys and courts of the web of buildings around the Golden Gate. To further this lucrative trade was the sole objective of hordes of boys euphemistically known as guides. As a sideline they acted as money-changers, sellers of fake antiques and spurious gems, pickpockets, confidence men.

In his late teens Zaharoff is believed to have combined his guide activities with membership in the Constantinople fire brigade. If contemporary stories can be accepted, the brigade attracted every rogue who could bribe or cajole his way into it. Fires were a lucrative source of salvage and robbery, with the profitable sideline of protection rackets. Periodically the scandal of the brigade brought about a cleanup with dismissals and arrests. There was a major fire in the city in 1865 followed by some arrests and executions. It was in this year that Zaharoff hurriedly left Constantinople, not returning for five years.

He is next identified as a young man named Manel Sahar working in a tailor's shop in Vilkomir, a small Russian town in what was later to become Lithuania. Manel went through a form of marriage to a Jewish girl named Haja Karolinski in 1867. She was already pregnant, and in April 1868 gave birth to a boy, Haim, who during his adult life called himself Hyman Barnett Zaharoff.

The young father—if indeed the Vilkomir story is true—lived by his wits in Russia until he felt it safe to return to Constantinople, which he did in 1870. There he got a job with an uncle, a general merchant, who was a semi-invalid and left the running of the business largely to his enterprising nephew. One may well believe Zaharoff's assertion that the business greatly prospered through the deals of the firm's one and only salesman.

But enterprise did not bring the rewards young Zaharoff considered he deserved. One day he was missing—along with, according to his uncle, 25 cases of gum arabic and 169 sacks of gallnuts, worth £1,000. The merchandise was sold and Zaharoff fled to England, where he found a haven, with odd jobs to maintain himself, in the Greek colony in London.

The irate uncle eventually learned where his erring nephew was living and went to the considerable expense of having Zaharoff prosecuted on a criminal charge of embezzlement. Zaharoff was arrested and tried in the Central Criminal Court of Newgate in January 1873. His name on the charge sheet was given as Zacharia Basilius Zackaroff, and his age as twenty-two.* Eventually, at a deferred hearing the prisoner pleaded guilty and was released on his own recognizances of £100 and a promise to come up for judgment if called upon.

He next appeared in Athens, in 1874, where he was reported as working as a shop assistant, barman, and—a practical role for him— "guide." It was through the third occupation that he apparently met Stephen Skuludis, a wealthy man dabbling in politics and an acquaintance of King George I of the Hellenes. The meeting ground was in the vice and gambling enterprises of the Greek capital; the mutual regard arose from the appreciation of the help each could give the other. One of them was to become prime minister of Greece and the architect of the Greek king's plan for a Balkan league directed against Turkey. The other would furnish the sinews of war to help make that league an effective force.

French and British newspapers later reported that in the period when Zaharoff left Eastern Europe and had his brief but unpleasant sojourn in London, he worked his way to and from the West by getting menial jobs in the French arms factories of Le Creusot and the German plant of Krupp in the Ruhr. If so, the glimpse of the money being poured into modern armaments must have whetted his appetite. These massive firms took no notice, of course, of a youthful Greek laborer, in temporary employment.

But fate took a hand. Skuludis had a carousing companion, a Swedish ship's captain who had been appointed part-time agent of the British arms firm of Nordenfelt. The job had proven sufficiently rewarding for him to give up the sea and devote all his time to selling arms, and his success brought him promotion to a larger agency to cover Central Europe. His employers asked him to recommend his successor for the Balkans.

The gallant captain asked Skuludis if he knew anyone suitable— intelligent, energetic, good at languages, and not too scrupulous. Skuludis did—his clever young friend Zaharoff. That he was sponsored by

*The London *Times*, January 17, 1873, and February 4, 1874.

one of the richest men in Greece and the power behind the throne was good enough. Zaharoff got the job. The objective: in return for a handsome commission and a nominal salary of five pounds per week, to get orders for arms from governments in the Near and Middle East which had sufficient cash to pay the bill.

The merchandise he was at first directed to sell represented a challenge which a less confident salesman would have regarded as unreasonable for a new and inexperienced agent. It seems probable that Torsten Veilhelm Nordenfelt, his employer, gave Zaharoff the commission as a test, without much confidence that anything would eventuate. Nordenfelt had designed a submarine. The sales angle was that this novel device would be an asset to small nations unable to afford a battleship. But every naval expert in every country believed that Nordenfelt had a commercial failure on his hands. A prototype had been built and demonstrated in the Kattegat between Denmark and Sweden. Not a single order had resulted from the lavish entertainment and numerous test submersions, which seemed to show that the vessel was just a technical curiosity. Nordenfelt had virtually abandoned his sales campaign, and concentrated on his quick-fire gun. If there were orders to be picked up for the submarine, it would be on a small scale to minor nations.

Zaharoff, thoroughly aware of the frantic efforts of the Balkan countries to outdo one another with offensive and defensive weaponry, convinced himself that he had a viable proposition. He had obtained Nordenfelt's rather unwilling agreement that the submarine could be sold to Greece at below cost and on easy terms at that. Zaharoff was certain that if he could persuade Greece to buy the vessel, one or two of her potential adversaries would follow suit.

Within a week of Zaharoff stepping off the Orient Express in Athens the deal was signed and sealed. He immediately took the train to Constantinople, and waited till the news of Greece's acquisition reached the Turkish government. He then got orders for two of the vessels from the Turks.

Russian spies quickly learned of the deal. The Czar's personal naval aide rushed to London to negotiate the purchase of submarines from Nordenfelt—the same Russian who had rejected the idea when a guest at the Kattegat demonstration.

Zaharoff, back in Athens, somehow learned of the highly secret deal with Russia completed in London. He wrote to his employer asking for commission on the transaction—and got it. Submarines became not only the first, but one of the most lucrative war merchandise that Zaharoff handled. Up to and during the First World War few submarines were built anywhere in the world without Zaharoff taking a commission on them. He had grown up in a semi-Oriental culture where bribery was a normal facet of business. His instant and spectacular success as an unknown salesman, but one representing a powerful and wealthy manufacturer, can only be explained by the readiness of his prospective clients to be amenable to financial persuasion. The stories of his skill in this field of delicate operations are numerous. One method of ingratiating himself was to make a bet, in a social situation, which he was bound to lose; an instance was his pretense that he had mistaken the date—for example, betting on a Wednesday that the next day would be Friday, and backing his view with a wager of ten thousand rubles. Such "bets" were frequently made aboard the Orient Express on his numberless trips in the company of government officials and politicians. He was a heavy smoker and preferred the then novel cigarette. For patently venal officials, due to be turned into allies so that Zaharoff could reach a cabinet minister, his practice was to invite them to try this newfangled product of Turkey by offering his cigarette case —each cigarette was wrapped in a high-denomination banknote.

Still more profitable was Zaharoff's magnetic power over women. Wives and mistresses of ministers were assiduously wooed, rewarded for their infidelities with cash, and persuaded to divulge the secret weaknesses of their husbands and lovers. He had a penchant for red-haired women, even though the one and only genuine love of his life was black-haired. A Viennese pimp had a permanent order to have a redhead available for dispatching to the Orient Express on its run to the Balkans should Zaharoff send a message. The girls were generously treated and sent back in a first-class sleeper which, however, was never to be compartment No. 7.

In less than a year a man who had lived, often precariously, on his wits, had become one of the most prosperous and ruthless men in the armaments industry. His forays into the field of high politics continually took him from one European capital to another. He then had no home and did not want one. He lived in hotels—at the Ritz in London and Paris, the Imperial in Vienna, the Grande Bretagne in Athens, the Gellert in Budapest, the Athenee Palace in Bucharest, the Perma Palace in Constantinople, most of them huge, sprawling piles of bizarrely mixed Oriental and Neo-Gothic architecture, with palm courts, heavy velvet curtaining, marble staircases, glittering chandeliers, and fake Louis XV furniture. But on his wanderings through Europe and the Balkans he spent literally weeks on the Orient Express. In an age when the railroad provided the sole means of comparatively speedy transit over long distances, the Orient Express became his temporary home. Since that initial journey in 1885 he had come to regard the train as his good-luck symbol. He reveled in the efficient and loyal service of the train's staff. No longer was he rigorously questioned at stations and frontier posts. He had become the train's most regular and distinguished patron. When he boarded the train, he expected—and received—preferential treatment.

Consequently, Zaharoff was put out when, arriving at the Gare de l'Est in Paris for yet another journey to the Balkans, the stationmaster hurried forward to inform him, with profound apologies, that there would be a few moments' delay. By specific orders from the Quai d'Orsay, priority was to be given to a couple of travelers closely connected with the Spanish royal house.

Zaharoff displayed the cold anger that invariably terrified anyone forced by circumstance to thwart him. Brusquely he told the *chef de gare* that he did not intend to be delayed and sit in his fiacre until some royal nonentities deigned to enter the train. He brushed aside the station officials and, with his bodyguard, boarded the train.

Usually he immediately drew the blinds on the platform side of his compartment. But on this occasion he sat so he could watch the arrival of his notable fellow passengers. A small crowd of Spanish residents in Paris had collected beside the barrier. The couple arrived in a coach belonging to the Spanish ambassador. With much ceremony they moved to the train, servants carrying their luggage to the wagon at the rear of the train.

A connoisseur of nubile women, Zaharoff was impressed by the dark beauty of the young lady—as much as he was contemptuous of the stumbling weak-faced young man beside her. But Zaharoff was not sensitive enough to realize that the almost ethereal beauty of the girl's pale face came from a poignant sadness. She walked to the train, eyes downcast, hardly aware of the bowing diplomats and railway officials wishing her a safe journey.

The lady in distress was in fact on her honeymoon—the period popularly supposed to be the happiest in a woman's life. But not for this seventeen-year-old girl, brought up in the isolation of the convent and with the fervid protection afforded the well-born daughter of a Spanish count. She was completely ignorant of what are now known as the facts of life and, more tragically, unaware of the degenerate insanity of her bridegroom.

She had been born Doña Maria del Pilar Antonia Angela Patrocínio de Miguero y Berente, daughter of Count Fermin de Miguero y Azcarate. Negotiations for her marriage began shortly after Maria's sixteenth birthday in January 1885, her parents besotted with excitement when approaches were made by officials of the Spanish court to propose marriage of their daughter with a cousin of Alfonso XII.

The prospective bridegroom was Don Francisco Príncipe de Bourbon y Bourbon, son of the Infante Sebastián. He was twenty-four years old, and had just been made a grandee first class of the Kingdom of Spain. By birthright he was Duke of Marchena, to which title another one was added when he was six months old: Knight of the Order of the Golden Fleece.

Whether Maria's father knew the facts about the duke and was prepared to ignore them, or whether as a rather unimportant Spanish aristocrat, the truth had been effectively hidden from him—as indeed it was from most people outside the inner circle of the duke's family and the Spanish court—no one can say. The reality was that this young man, embellished with all the aura of nobility, was in childhood a simpleton and began in adolescence to show signs of permanent and dangerous insanity.

Whatever qualms Maria's parents may have had at the two or three formal meetings which preceded the engagement, they were probably reassured by servile officials and doctors of the court who insisted that all the young man needed was to settle down in the security of marriage, and would doubtless respond to the affection and care of a pure young woman. At the very worst, the doctors indicated, the union would be a formality: persons suffering from mental defects were sexually cold and, among males, invariably impotent.

So with great pomp and ceremony, plus a special blessing from the Pope for the fruitfulness of the union and the happiness of the newly-weds, the marriage took place on January 7, 1886. The bridal couple left the same day for Paris, en route for Vienna, where they were to be guests of the Emperor Franz Josef.

According to subsequent gossip by servants, the marriage was, contrary to the experts' expectations, consummated in Paris. It was noted that when the bride walked from her carriage along the platform of the Gare de l'Est to board the Orient Express on the following evening, she acted like a frightened child.

As the train crossed the French frontier Zaharoff was dining in his customary place on the side of the carriage with tables for two; the table alongside him, for four, was, he was told by the steward, reserved for the ducal couple.

"But we have been told that they will not be availing themselves of the restaurant car, m'sieu. A repast was taken earlier to their compartment. It was not eaten," the *maître* of the restaurant car informed his favorite guest.

Zaharoff made no reply. He had more important matters to think about than the lack of appetite of some young couple, probably with no wealth worth talking about but masquerading as important personages because they happened to be close to the Spanish throne.

The Spanish throne . . . He began to have second thoughts. Spain was, as usual, in the throes of political troubles. Alfonso XII was dead, and the country was waiting to see if the unborn baby he had fathered would be a boy or girl. In either event, the future looked to be one of unrest and power politics. Arms would be needed.

It was possibly an incidental result of the melodrama to come within a few hours that two months later Zaharoff obtained arms orders from Spain worth £30 million ($120 million), plus introductions to the war ministers of the Spanish republics in South America. But all that was a pattern of future events. Not even the scheming brain of Zaharoff could have envisaged how his life was to be inextricably tied, for decades ahead, to Europe's most ancient regal family.

Meantime there was much thinking to be done before the train reached Vienna. Hiram Stevens Maxim* was demonstrating his new machine gun to officers of the Austro-Hungarian Imperial General Staff, and his gun was all too obviously better than the Nordenfelt gun. Either the Maxim demonstrations in Austria and Italy would have to be sabotaged or Maxim would have to be persuaded to unite with the Nordenfelt company. The certain prospect was that, one way or the other, Zaharoff would be on the winning side. A few hours of hard thinking, scheming, and plotting in the quiet compartment No. 7 would ensure that profitable outcome.

But the night, for once, was not free from disturbance. As the train reached the vicinity of Salzburg a long, piercing scream reverberated along the corridor, far louder than the rhythmic tattoo of the wheels on the rails. Zaharoff took little notice. He was reassured by the sound of Raoul Aslanian, his personal bodyguard, opening the door of his adjoining compartment. Brandishing his six-barreled Colt revolver, bought for him by Zaharoff—who regarded it as America's finest contribution to civilization—Aslanian gently tried the door of his master's compartment. It was, as usual, locked. The corridor was deserted. The *conducteur* must have fallen asleep at his desk at the far end; he remained unaware of the scream. Aslanian, reassured that his master was safe, returned to his bunk. He had hardly settled down when there was a high, agitated voice right outside Zaharoff's compartment: "*Socorro . . . Dios . . . Salve!*"

Zaharoff, annoyed at the fuss at a time when he expected, and paid for, peace and quiet, laid aside the papers he had been studying and moved to the door, not to hurry to someone's assistance but to com-

*An American engineer, born in 1840 in Sangerville, Maine. He died in 1916 in London as a Knight of the Order of British Empire.

plain to the *conducteur.* Before he could reach it there came a frantic knocking. As he released the bolt the door was torn open. In front of him stood the girl he had seen on the platform of the Gare de l'Est. She was wearing a mauve peignoir over a lacy nightdress, which was ripped from the neck to her breasts. A deep scratch marked her throat. She seemed oblivious of her seminakedness and the blood dripping down her chest. He raven-black hair covered her shoulders and almost concealed her eyes. She half slid to the floor—only her arm gripping the door handle prevented her falling prone.

Aslanian had rushed out of his compartment and bent down to grab the woman by the arms. To his surprise, Zaharoff waved him away.

The girl looked up at the bearded man. "Please forgive me, m'sieu," she said in singsong French, which betrayed her Spanish origin. "But please save me. He is mad . . . mad. He will kill me!" She was trying to maintain decorum, even though she trembled and obviously suffered from shock. Then, with the sound of a compartment door at the end of the carriage crashing open, her hysteria returned. She began screaming in terror. Like the mere child that she was in experience and self-control, she began stammering in Spanish: "Please save me! He is mad, raving mad. He wants to kill me if I won't submit . . ." She forced herself past the indignant Zaharoff into the safety of his compartment.

Down the corridor Aslanian, hindered rather than helped by the *conducteur,* was wrestling with a man. The Duke of Marchena was clad in only a nightshirt. In his hand, gripped at the wrist by Aslanian, was a jewel-encrusted dagger. His face, mottled with fury, was half crushed by the bodyguard's other arm, forcing the Spaniard's head against his chest. His mouth, fringed with spittle, was distorted. A stream of incoherent words came from his throat, more like an animal's growls than a human voice. Then suddenly his body went limp and he slithered toward the floor. Released from Aslanian's grip, he looked up as if bewildered by everything. Without any resistance he allowed the two men to carry him back to his compartment.

Zaharoff turned to the girl, standing like a cornered mouse against the far side of the compartment. "Perhaps, madame," he said, "I may have the honor to invite you to rest for a little while until I can make arrangements for you to be accommodated in a vacant compartment and adequately guarded against any further upset."

The calm voice of someone who seemed mature and safe reassured Maria. She moved to the damask-covered fauteuil and sat down, drawing her peignoir around her. She was in shock and could not express any conventional phrases of gratitude.

Such, in brief, was the first meeting of Zaharoff and the Duchess Maria, as she described it to a close woman friend years later. What she and the middle-aged stranger said to each other during the remainder of the night as the Orient Express pounded its way to Vienna she never revealed. The cynical student of this glutton for wealth and the power which came with it is justified in believing that Zaharoff would have used all his talent to ingratiate himself with someone who— despite her youth and the situation in which she found herself by rebelling against her husband—had family connections that could be exploited in business deals in Spain. It is indeed probable that Zaharoff, accustomed to buying women's charms, did consider the girl merely as a puppet to be manipulated for reasons of business. At first, that is. By the time the train reached Vienna this man, who had always scorned sentiment as a sign of weakness, had fallen head over heels in love with the young duchess and had forgotten all about his scheme. At the Ostbahnhof he led her toward the vice chamberlain and the lady-in-waiting Emperor Franz Josef had sent to receive the Spanish noble pair. The bridegroom was discreetly taken to a private nursing home.

The Emperor—like Queen Victoria—was not amused. The rigid etiquette of the Hapsburg Court had been badly impaired. In honor of the Spanish ducal guests a ball was to take place at the Schönbrunn Palace. It had to be canceled, with the duke under sedation in a private asylum and his bride still in a state of shock. Empress Elizabeth, a woman of great humanity and intelligence—a few years later she was to fall victim to a crazy assassin's dagger—took care of Maria and put her up in apartments next to her own.

Somehow Zaharoff and Maria maintained a tenuous contact. The arms salesman was on familiar ground in bribing servants to act as go-between; his experience told him that no one lived who was not amenable to a combination of money and threats. Thus in the six weeks or so that Maria remained in Vienna, on her abortive honeymoon, with her husband in close confinement and officially described as recuperating from a dangerous infection, she probably pined for a meeting with the kind gentleman on the train who had saved her life.

Don Francisco returned to Madrid accompanied by two male nurses. His insanity could no longer be concealed, but his murderous attack on his bride was kept secret. The scion of the Bourbons was taken to an asylum near La Granja, staffed by nuns pledged both to devoted nursing and to complete secrecy. Maria Christina, widow of Alfonso XII and archduchess of Austria, was acting as regent on behalf of her infant son, the new Spanish king. She protected the throne with all the fierceness of a mother, and for seventeen years, until her son was declared of age, she ruled in a dictatorial manner. She regarded Don Francisco's marriage and his attack on his wife on the Orient Express —stories of which eventually leaked out—as involving the Spanish monarchy in a scandal which encouraged anarchist and republican movements. Maria became a "nonperson" in court circles, the hapless girl being blamed for her husband's insanity.

She was sent into exile. This was in fact fortunate for her because it enabled her to join Zaharoff and accompany him on his interminable journeys across Europe. The scandal did not impair his business. The chancelleries of Europe were only too aware that to cross swords with the Levantine armament tycoon—who had appointed himself Maria's protector—would be tantamount to jeopardizing the security of their nations by not getting the best bargains in new weaponry. Thus Zaharoff was still welcomed in all European capitals. But his young ladylove was expected to be discreet. At hotels their suites were always on different floors; Maria never accompanied him to official receptions. Europe's rulers and cabinets were careful not to offend the Spanish court. Zaharoff remained discreet, also. On the Orient Express he occupied, as always, compartment No. 7; Maria had compartment No. 8.

Their liaison produced three daughters. One died in childhood; of the other two, one married the American shipowner Leopold Waldorf, and the other Count Ostrorog, a Russian, who became Zaharoff's resident agent in Constantinople and accumulated a large fortune.

There was, of course, no divorce in Catholic Spain, and Zaharoff and Maria could not marry. But Spanish law and precedent provided that the children of a married woman would be regarded as legitimate, in the absence of any legal action by the husband on a charge of the wife's adultery (which in Spain remained a criminal offense, punishable by imprisonment). Ostensibly, therefore, Zaharoff's and Maria's daughters were legally the offspring of the insane duke, fruit of a travesty of marriage. Yet the two surviving girls, with their dark eyes, short stature, and Oriental facial contour, proved without doubt the inheritance of their real father's Levantine blood.

The famous Zaharoff wallet—made of fine morocco leather and regularly replaced once it lost its shape, the abandoned one being invariably a gift to the *chefs de train* of the Orient Express, one of the few favors ever bestowed on them—contained visiting cards, check forms certified up to a million pounds each, and a photograph. It was a sepia-colored picture of a woman with three little girls leaning affectionately against her: Maria and her three daughters.

The liaison with the aristocratic Maria brought with it the transformation of Zaharoff from a highly successful but uncouth arms hawker to a refined international financier and industrialist. The cornerstone of his power was his financial holding in the British armaments firm of Vickers, which bought out the Maxim firm in 1897 from Zaharoff and Maxim, partly with cash and partly with shares.

Zaharoff's sales campaigns were invariably based on a "bilateral" policy, as he called it, meaning that he always promoted arms sales to both sides of any potential war. And it was a time rich in opportunities for such an enterprise. Cruisers, torpedoes, heavy guns, shells, rifles, machine guns, ammunition—whatever the generals needed Zaharoff could supply, and it mattered little where they bought, for some percentage of the profit would almost certainly accrue to the man from Turkey. Through nominees, holding companies, and intricate share deals, he disguised his interests in companies that seemed to be fervid competitors. He spread his tentacles far beyond the Vickers firm, with profits taken from French, German, and Russian armaments manufacturers pouring into his bank accounts. It has been said with some truth that the ten million casualties among the armed forces in the First

World War represented a profit to Zaharoff of a little over £1 in gold per every dead soldier.

Meantime, Don Francisco, although forgotten by everyone but his wife and Zaharoff, lived on. The storms of his mania subsided into the deceptive calm of schizophrenic withdrawal, the outburst of insanity becoming rarer and rarer. Indeed, there was danger for the two lovers that Maria's husband could be released from confinement and demand from his wife the restoration of conjugal rights. Maria, a devout Catholic, shunned the thought of a legal action, which might have had a chance of obtaining her divorce abroad, on the grounds of her husband's insanity. Nor would she agree to Zaharoff's suggestion to petition the Pope for an annulment of her marriage, though this might have been within the realms of possibility, given her lover's money and great influence.

Zaharoff kept in touch with the discreet asylum on the outskirts of Madrid. His agents managed to enter the place, and they were paid to make reports, month after month, year after year. In any fictional story of a man like Zaharoff, frustrated by the continued existence of a husband, no doubt there would be an exciting account of the paid killer. It is an interesting glimpse into one facet of this complex character that a man who had no compunction whatever in scheming to foment wars, in which hundreds of thousands of deaths occurred through his sales of weaponry, was never known to arrange for a violent removal of a rival. To achieve the utter financial ruin of an adversary or competitor, to expose him to disgrace, to drive his victims to the brink of suicide—yes, those were the methods of this business warrior. To extinguish competition by the crudity of murder—no.

Early in 1922 he had reason to believe that his marriage to Maria would not be long delayed. The monthly report stated that Don Francisco, now sixty years of age, was physically as well as mentally ill. By coincidence, Zaharoff himself was ill at that time. He was by then in his early seventies, and the bout of sickness—soon overcome—increased his sense of urgency to prove his adoration of Maria with a token that probably no other man of his time could emulate.

During the war he had bought a luxurious villa at Beaulieu, the "little Africa" on the French Mediterranean coast between Nice and Monte Carlo. Maria loved the place, which had the warmth and sun reminiscent of her native Spain. From the terrace of the villa, perched on the southern slopes of the Alps, Zaharoff would gaze at the town clinging to the edge of the sea below the steep mountainside: Monte Carlo. What a wedding gift it would be—this mecca of luxury and wealth. And Monaco was an independent country; whoever owned the casino and ancillary enterprises—the country's sole source of revenue —would be its monarch, his wife his regal consort.

In May 1923 he bought the Monte Carlo Casino for one million pounds, using his London bank account with funds mainly derived from war profits of his Vickers shareholdings. The Monegasque holding company, the Société Anonyme des Bains de Mer et Cercle des Etrangers, was in practice the revenue department of the Grimaldi family, the rulers of Monaco. Zaharoff reveled in the knowledge that while the Grimaldis were known as princes, he would in practice be the king.

Six months after the Monte Carlo deal Don Francisco died, thirty-eight years after his wife had left him. Maria explained to her lover that etiquette demanded that a year should elapse before she remarried. But nine weeks before the period of mourning was due to end, Zaharoff persuaded Maria to legitimize their union. They were married quietly in the *mairie* of the small French town of Arronville. The date was September 22, 1924.

For eighteen months the couple lived in great happiness. As a journey into nostalgia rather than a honeymoon, Zaharoff took his fifty-five-year-old bride to Paris, and then on the Orient Express to Vienna, compartment No. 7 at long last openly shared by day and by night. The trip to the Austrian capital was not a success. Maria had too many sad memories of her previous honeymoon with a degenerate husband thirty-eight years earlier. The couple returned to France for a short stay in their Château Balincourt, near Pontoise, and then when spring came, went to Monte Carlo. There, on February 25, 1926, Lady Zaharoff, uncrowned queen of Monaco, died after a brief illness.

Two days after the funeral, her deeply sorrowing husband—the first occasion his servants had seen him registering any visible kind of gentle emotion—left Monte Carlo for Milan. As usual, his car was passed through the customs and passport controls on the border at Menton without hindrance. The car traveled at a carefully scheduled speed over the 220 miles so as to reach Milan fifteen minutes before the Simplon Orient Express left on its eastbound run.

As usual, sleeping car compartment No. 7 had been reserved for Zaharoff. Few people apart from the stationmaster at Milan and the staff of the Orient Express took any notice of the wizened, frail old man who walked slowly from his car to the train. The moment he was aboard compartment No. 7 was locked and the blinds drawn.

Zaharoff was bound for Athens. Two months earlier, thanks to his negotiations, the Great Powers had finally agreed to share out an oil concession with an estimated value of $4 billion—the oil of Mosul, first tapped a year later. The area of Mosul was taken from the Turks and handed over to Iraq—a profitable victory for the man who had for years intrigued with nations large and small as he crouched like a spider in Athens and Monte Carlo to manipulate his agents, spies, and venal politicians. It was his first personal contact with his only rival—Calouste Gulbenkian.

As the train gathered speed through the bitterly cold February night toward Venice, Zaharoff conferred with his secretary, apparently already consigning his bereavement to the fading past. To the surprise of the secretary and the train's chief steward, Zaharoff ordered an evening meal to be served in his compartment—a salad, some yoghurt, and a bottle of champagne. The simple meal had hardly been touched when Zaharoff rang the bell to have the tray taken away. An attendant asked if he could make up the bed.

"I shall not require a bed tonight. Send my secretary."

The secretary hurried from the restaurant car, where he was dining on the expensive dishes that had been intended for his master.

"I do not require you any more tonight. See that I am not disturbed until morning."

As the secretary moved to the corridor Zaharoff called him loudly. Reentering the compartment, he stood waiting.

"What is the exact time?" Zaharoff asked.

The secretary told him. There was no reaction, and once more he stepped into the corridor and closed the door of compartment No. 7. It was after the stop at Salzburg that the bell and indicator beside the car attendant's desk again demanded attention.

The attendant opened the door of compartment No. 7.

"You rang, your Excellency?"

Zaharoff was sitting erect, staring straight ahead. "The time, the exact time," he demanded.

The attendant took out the pocket chronometer supplied by the Compagnie.

"By the empire's time it is now exactly half past two, your Excellency."

"Switch off the lights—all of them—and leave me instantly," murmured Zaharoff.

At 2:32, on the same stretch of line thirty-nine years earlier, there had come that frantic scream and call for help, followed by the sight of a distraught woman clawing at the door of compartment No. 7.

Perhaps this man, who seemed bereft of any sense of the spiritual and had based his life solely on the standards of worldly power and wealth, half hoped for a reverse of time itself with a replica of that melodramatic incident in 1886. But there was no psychic phenomenon. The closed door of compartment No. 7 shook gently with the train's motion. In the corridor was the silence of the night.

When the secretary cautiously gave the usual triple knock just after dawn and, getting no reply, risked reprimand by entering the compartment, he found Zaharoff still sitting erect, with eyes half closed and no movement beyond the involuntary tremor of his thin yellowish hands. And the compartment was very cold. Zaharoff, inveterate addict of semitropical warmth in his office and home, had turned off the heating.

He never again traveled on the Orient Express. He returned to Monte Carlo by sea from Athens to Naples and then by train via Rome to Monte Carlo. There, in his suite at the Hôtel de Paris diagonally opposite the Casino, he prepared to get rid of the glamorous property he had given to his wife as a wedding present. Would-be buyers, believing that, at long last, sentiment was prevailing over business acumen, envisaged a bargain. They were wrong. Within two months the sale was completed—to the banking firm of Dreyfus et Cie. The price was $14.5 million. Zaharoff's profit from an acquisition held for a mere twenty months was nearly $10 million and he retained the ownership of the Hôtel de Paris, so that he could stay there without charge.

One tangible reminder of his beloved Maria had thus been erased. But he was unable to withstand the lodestone of the dreamlike visions that still haunted him awake and asleep, as they had on that last journey on the Orient Express. He left Monte Carlo for the Château Balincourt.

No matter that the huge house, 53 avenue Hoche in Paris, crammed with art treasures, was more convenient for the treatment he now constantly needed for the rheumatic disease that was remorselessly paralyzing his limbs. The great château was redolent with tokens of Maria's day-to-day existence. He spent more and more time just lying in the vast golden bed that had once been the property of a mistress of Louis XIV and was his own nuptial bed—and the deathbed of Maria.

On fine days he moved slowly around the château park in an electrically propelled bath chair. At eventide he was half carried to the room that had been his office. The great desk was now bereft of papers. All that remained on its polished surface were tiny models, in solid gold, of the merchandise that had made him one of Europe's richest men: a toy howitzer, a Maxim machine gun, a flamethrower. Standing alone and apart from them was the only studio portrait of Maria he ever publicly displayed.

As the days and nights passed painfully and slowly, Zaharoff became more and more of a recluse. The secretiveness that had been a business policy became near mania. The number of servants was reduced, and few were ever allowed to see their master.

Rumanian newspapers reported his death in August 1933. London financiers claiming to be "in the know" insisted that he had died on September 16 of that year. The rumor was duly reported in the London gossip columns. Next morning an allegedly official statement was issued in Paris to the effect that Zaharoff was alive and still enjoying his daily drive in his electric invalid chair around the paths and driveways of the Château Balincourt.

An American news agency sent reporters and cameramen to try to get an interview with Zaharoff. They were unable to penetrate the guarded gates of the château and were warned off by armed patrols of strong-arm men wearing the green uniforms of gamekeepers. Many other newspapermen tried their luck, but always failed to get even a glimpse of the old man in his hideout. In a way, the last years of Zaharoff's life bear a similarity to those of Howard Hughes.

For three years after the spate of death rumors in 1933 Zaharoff's name rarely appeared in the press. A new and more ruthless arbiter of power was striding the map of Europe: Hitler.

No one learned that one winter day in 1936 a small convoy of cars left the Château Balincourt and took route nationale 7 for the long journey to Monte Carlo. Nor did the ever-discreet management of the Hôtel de Paris, accustomed to protect the world's most distinguished people from any incommodation, announce that the man who had once owned Monte Carlo was back again.

Zaharoff died in his hotel suite on November 27, 1936. Before any announcement was made, the body was taken back to Balincourt. The local mayor identified the body and issued the death certificate. At a private funeral in the château grounds Zaharoff's body was laid beside his wife's. His two daughters, a son-in-law, and his secretary were the only mourners.

The following evening, obeying the last order from his master, his loyal bodyguard boarded the Orient Express at the Gare de l'Est. He carried an envelope containing the photograph which for nearly fifty years Zaharoff had carried in his wallet. As the train ran toward Salzburg the servant tore up the photograph and scattered the pieces out the window of compartment No. 7 into the wind at exactly 2:32 A.M.

Chapter Eight

THE ROYAL TRAIN

THE GLAMOUR THAT BATHED THE SLEEK CARS OF THE ORIENT EX-
press in its heyday was a unique feature in railroad history, unlikely ever
to be repeated and certainly never excelled. Not only did this remarkable train make a fast and easy communication between palaces and
chancelleries, or between one marketplace and another, a matter of
easy routine, it also became the symbol of the privilege that the exalted
travelers aboard the train regarded as their right as well as a means of
displaying their power to the masses. For untold thousands of Europe's
toiling and exploited peoples the sight of the train was a glimpse of
another world and of human beings entirely different from themselves.
Peasants in half a dozen countries would pause in their work in the
fields and gape at the glittering cars and the supercilious faces behind
the windows. Stops at stations were a free spectacle attracting crowds
to marvel—and perhaps sometimes to hate. Wealth, luxury, warmth,
food were but an arm's length away, yet as inaccessible and unattainable as the way of life these strange travelers enjoyed.

Perhaps even more significant, in the long run, was the erosion of
privilege which the Orient Express paradoxically brought about. The
train was a commercial proposition, and anyone with money and leisure

could travel on it. The social changes were creating a comfortable middle class anxious to become socially acceptable by those their forebears had regarded as higher beings. In theory there was no restraint on anyone traveling in the luxury of the Wagons-Lits trains and partaking of the lavish meals in the restaurant cars. Passports, visas, identity papers, and similar restrictions were either nonexistent or a mere formality. The Colonel's lady and Judy O'Grady could sit side by side—always providing they had the money to pay for the ticket and supplementary fare. Only a few could.

The people who could afford to patronize the services of the Orient Express were of the sort that business tycoons, movie and television stars, and pop singers are today: personalities whose every activity, however trivial, provide the masses of "ordinary" people with a glimpse of an inaccessible world of glamour and adventure. Newspapers and magazines reported the comings and goings of these very special people. Today we read the gossip columns with a mixture of admiration, envy, and contempt. But in the heyday of the Orient Express its passengers were regarded as representing the *beau monde,* the upper crust of society, which was supposed to reflect the virtues of their superior status. By and large the theory was that the more exalted or more wealthy the person, the more enviable and commendable was his or her way of life. The Orient Express was in fact a mobile exhibition of social tradition. That the probity and practices of many of these privileged passengers belied their image was very rarely commented upon.

Paul Morand, the French diplomat and author, whose duties took him to most of the capitals served by the Orient Express, produced well-observed descriptions of his fellow passengers:

Prior to 1914 the passengers were a microcosm of our world. I recall my first journey to Constantinople, guarding my diplomatic valise. Turkey was retreating from Europe, but the Orient Express still remained the umbilical cord which attached her . . . and in the corridors one could still encounter the rich old Osmanli seigneurs—they were mortally offended if described as Turks —who were soon to disappear, along with the fez and Sultan Abdul Hamid. They kept their veiled wives, guarded by eunuchs, firmly locked in their compartments, to which not even the train's *contrôleur* was admitted. They travelled with their *cafedji bashis* who prepared their coffee in special vessels because even on their travels their masters would not touch the "bad coffee" served on the train. There were the elderly diplomats sorrowfully discussing the "Eastern Question" and the decline of the Crescent; they still kept their yachts on the Bosphorus. And the *phanariotes,* the wealthy Greek merchants from the Hellenic district of Constantinople never ceased to talk about war and rebellion and the changes in Byzantine traditions. Prince Ferdinand of Bulgaria—not yet a king—often travelled between Sofia and Vienna locked for a few hours in the toilet, anxious to avoid assassins. Government officials and experts travelling to and from one of the sixty-nine conferences some-where in Europe to confer about the status-quo and to postpone some war. Austrian aristocrats each owning a score of castles and a hundred villages; English 'mylords' enjoying the riches of their Empire, clad in tweeds, return-ing after shooting wild fowl or bears in the Maramuresh and clutching their Holland & Holland sporting guns like mistresses. Hungarian counts and Rumanian boyars making for Vienna or Paris to spend the rich profits of a good harvest; the boyars no longer wearing their voluminous pantaloons and high boots of morocco leather, but dressed in impeccable suits tailored in London's Savile Row, having long since shaved off their long beards. Everyone still referred to them as "these Moldavians." There were sometimes two or three pale, hungry-looking young French tutors, like escapees from a novel by Dostoievsky, on their way—the tickets paid by their future masters—to teach the son of those Moldavian hospodars at their Transylvanian castles. A few Americans, then quiet and well-groomed, like figures from a Henry James story, their portmanteaux stuffed with gold coins for bribes in exchange for some new oil concession. Now and then there were Indian maharajas, praying in their compartments to Vishnu or Allah, and their wives with a red high caste dot or a diamond between their eyebrows. And mysterious financiers on some errand to fix yet another loan for the Tsar of Russia.

The first world war inflicted the first but not yet fatal blow to the Orient Express and afterwards the scene changed somewhat. The train's staff were now younger and no longer as deferential as before, although not less efficient. The Russian grand dukes and Austrian arch dukes had disappeared but there were still the Balkan landowners on their way to "Gay Paris," like the one I remember who, after a long night at the card tables, hired an entire Wagons-Lits and invited all his gaming partners for a joy ride to Paris; in the end he found himself without a *sou* and with a terrible hangover on the boulevard. There was Prince Bibescu, a friend of Proust, who talked of his many estates and proudly told us that the Orient Express had been waiting for three-quarters of an hour in Bucharest for his arrival from his castle. There were now the Levantine merchants and Greek shipowners, behind their backs dubbed as *rastracueros,* a Spanish word meaning that they obtained their wealth by trading in furs and leather, although in fact it came from daring speculations; the stockbrokers and concessionaires, the heroin smugglers, the great impresarios and famous operatic tenors, the fat Jewish bankers from Vienna in the restaurant cars insistently demanding, "Introduce me to the beautiful countess over there . . ." and the demi-mondaines who had been a pleasant distraction for the passengers since the earliest days of the Orient Express. The diplomatic couriers were still travelling, always in pairs like turtle doves, one chained to his valise while the other took dinner, and the secret agents and spies, more numerous than before, but no longer very secret, and easily identified by most of us. And there were even more diplomats, the free-masons of the Little Entente, and clumsy Soviet emissaries, carefully avoiding the gaze of their fellow-passengers.

I recall once having as a compartment companion a German economist who produced most comprehensive but false statistics to submit to some Balkan government, needing to falsify the figures of its budget; and on another occasion I talked to an Armenian whose grandfather, he told me, had scattered sugar in the Champs Elysées to prove to the Parisians that snow really did glitter in the sun. One played poker; one drank champagne with the charming ladies; and at the station of Feleggyhaza the passengers were still awakened by a Hungarian gipsy band, when the train stopped for three or four minutes . . . But in the end the Orient Express was dying a slow death, killed by the airplane. The society for which it had been created was dying out too. The passports and visas had erected long stretches of modern Great Walls of China —or Iron Curtains. The great international train had been dismembered into a succession of short-running national trains, with bleak second and third class cars attached to them, and its speed and its luxury had been transferred to the jet airplanes . . . One day, when the *Compagnie des Wagons-Lits* celebrates yet another jubilee, I hope it will not forget to mention all those exotic birds of passage in their mobile cages—the pugnacious hawks, the horizontal nomads, who had remained loyal to it for so long . . .*

Thus Morand, who in his own evening of life had become one of the Forty Immortals, elevated to the rank of a member of the Acadé-

*Excerpts from Morand's books, listed in the Bibliography.

mie Française. All quite innocuous and, perhaps, a little disingenuous —a nostalgic glimpse by a man faithful to, and tolerant of, the Establishment, and only slightly critical of the often reprehensible incidents occurring in those compartments reserved for the very best people. He probably never heard of the Eastern Church bishop—known to the Compagnie's staff as His Reverence the Archimandrit Cyril—who for years traveled on the Orient Express between Sofia and Belgrade for the sole purpose of enjoying the company of *poules de luxe,* usually Western European girls imported to appear in the Balkan cities' night clubs as pseudodancers and chanteuses. He usually took the train leaving Sofia at 12:55 P.M. and arriving in Belgrade at 2:30 P.M., with the ladies of easy virtue boarding it on the journey in one direction and returning by another in the opposite one. Thus the venerable gentleman could rest confident of escaping the prying eyes of his brethren and parishioners, and returning happily to his bishopric of Crveni Krest only to take off again on a pleasant pilgrimage a week or two later. When eventually a newspaper reporter got wind of the bishop's journeys and tried to draw out a Wagons-Lits *conducteur* he was given the stereotypical answer the Compagnie's staff were ordered to make in such cases: *"Il faut être discret, monsieur."*

Indeed, a few of the *conducteurs* enjoyed for years a welcome addition to their salaries by discreetly procuring girls for select and generous passengers. The service—of which the Compagnie's management could not be entirely unaware—was meticulously organized. The *conducteur* in question sent a message by railroad telegraph from one station at which the train stopped to the stationmaster of another an hour's or so distance away, and when the train arrived there, the girls came aboard, spent the time required for the passengers' diversion in their compartments, and disembarked at a convenient stop to return to their town by a local train. That many passengers traveled in the company of ladies to whom they were not bound by matrimony was accepted as a matter of fact, and neither the Compagnie's staff nor, in later periods, the passport control officers made any fuss about it.

The earliest royal patron of the train, whose activities eroded the lily-white image the Compagnie ostensibly upheld, was Leopold II of the Belgians. Naturally, as a friend of Nagelmackers and an important if bothersome client of the family banking house, with his fictional investment in the Wagons-Lits Compagnie, he was able to go whenever and wherever he wished without payment. He had been a great traveler—usually accompanied by his current mistress—before the advent of the Orient Express, and his interest in Nagelmackers' project had been prompted by his experience of the discomfort of ordinary train services on his journeys around Europe. He had been gloating for a long time over the idea of having a luxury train at his disposal.

Leopold was notorious for his chronic meanness. He would reprimand his valet for changing his underlinen more than once a week and wore the same shirt for days on end. He rarely tipped the attendants and waiters, and if he did, it was with small coins. His negative attitude about spending money was in contrast to his lust for making it. Lured by the stories of gold, diamonds, and other illimitable natural resources of darkest Africa revealed by explorers like Livingstone and Stanley, he formed in 1876 the Association Internationale Africaine to exploit as his personal enterprise more than nine hundred thousand square miles of the Congo. At that time Central Africa was hardly charted and still neglected by the governments of the great nations, which were busily expanding their colonial empires. He succeeded in inveigling financiers, including German and American bankers, to advance substantial funds on a promise of a share in the expected great loot. The most vicious exploitation of primitive natives in modern times, Leopold's Congo enterprise yielded him an immense fortune. Eventually, in the face of worldwide criticism and political pressure by France, Britain, and Germany (whose rulers had only belatedly realized that they had missed a splendid bargain), he was forced in 1908 to hand over his property to the Belgian state as a colony, but not without receiving enormous compensation for his "gift to the nation."

Leopold's business activities kept him constantly traveling across Europe conferring with financiers and visiting his many royal relatives, mainly for the purpose of persuading them to invest in his many enterprises. The Compagnie had to provide facilities on the same train for the mistress of the time, but on some occasions, when the King of the Belgians was compelled to maintain decorum in order not to annoy one of his more puritan royal hosts, the lady in question had to be accommodated in a separate compartment, and additional facilities had to be provided for her servants. His predilection for curvaceous ladies earned him the name of King Popold, a sobriquet which was changed to King Cléopold when the celebrated cabaret star Cléo de Merode became one of his favorites. She was later replaced by a barmaid from Bordeaux, Caroline Lacroix. Although he had many other mistresses during his liaison with her, he had an old man's infatuation for the pretty young woman, whom he met at the age of sixty-eight. He raised her to the style of Baroness de Vaughan, despite the outcries of the Belgian church and society. A few months before his death in 1909 he arranged a solemn marriage with her and left her a fortune of thirty million francs, which subsequently led to protracted litigations when his daughters contested the will.

His marriage, after being a widower for seven years—he had neglected his second wife, an Austrian archduchess, during most of his life —was the ending to a long career of amorous adventures. He had been very proud of his virility, and when reminiscing to one of his few intimate friends Leopold revealed an incident which at the time it happened had caused much puzzlement. On a journey to Constantinople he told his aides that he had some secret negotiations with financiers in the Turkish capital and would return by the Orient Express leaving in two days. The *salon* cars were duly reserved, but he failed to arrive and, indeed, had disappeared. Members of his entourage feared the worst, but twenty-four hours later the king reappeared sound and happy. The story, as told by him, was revealed by his friend only after the King's death.

Leopold had gone to Smyrna (now Izmir) on the promise of the Sultan's governor, a German, that he could arrange for him to sample the delights of a harem in the absence of its owner. The governor's Turkish deputy, Defterdar Ahmed Bey, a devout Muslim, was deputed to arrange matters. Unwilling to dabble personally in such a nefarious and sacrilegious scheme, he paid a Greek restaurant owner to locate a harem of some rich citizen who happened to be absent from his residence. The Greek was promised a good reward and reported that he had found what was required. He escorted Leopold, disguised in a Turkish cloak, to the fine house, explaining that the chief eunuch had been bribed and the servants made drunk.

The ladies proved obliging, but in the early hours the chief eunuch rushed in to say his master had unexpectedly returned. He bundled the royal visitor out of the women's quarters in frantic haste, but Leopold was nevertheless highly delighted. He later told Defterdar Ahmed Bey that he would speak on his behalf to the Sultan and try to get him a more important official appointment in the capital. Unfortunately, Leopold proceeded to boast of his sexual successes in the harem, describing the house, its comfortable furnishings, and also the ladies—to the consternation of the Turkish dignitary, who slowly recognized that it was his own residence that was being described. Unwilling to lose face by conceding that he had been made a fool by the crafty Greek go-between, he made no complaint about the violation of his harem. Only later did he tell the governor of the utter disgrace that had befallen him, and the German gleefully informed Leopold of what had happened. The old roué obviously enjoyed the explanation and found that it made his adventure even more memorable.

The great monarchs of Europe's empires used the Orient Express on rare occasions, and when they did, their own royal cars were attached to the train. Many members of the Hapsburg dynasty were frequent passengers in the special *salon* cars the Compagnie provided. The hapless Austrian Empress Elizabeth—assassinated in 1898 in Geneva by an Italian anarchist—spent years on foreign travels, estranged from her stone-hearted husband. Their son, Crown Prince Rudolph— who shot his eighteen-year-old mistress, Baroness Maria Vetsera, and committed suicide in the famous Tragedy of Mayerling—was another of Nagelmackers' exalted customers, as was a horde of Austrian archdukes and archduchesses of that numerous family.

Queen Victoria, who during her long and mournful widowhood spent many winters at her villa in Cimiez in the South of France, had her own royal train—the first built in 1869—several cars of which were kept at Calais to be used for her travels in Europe when required. Edward VII had several royal trains, one built in 1883, when he was still the Prince of Wales, and the last, much more luxurious, in 1903, soon after his ascent to the throne. Several *salon* cars of his royal trains were also stored at Calais and used for his frequent official journeys in Europe—such as those for his usually acrimonious meetings with his nephew Kaiser William, his trips to Paris to clinch the entente cordiale, or his visit to the aged Emperor Francis Joseph at Bad Ischl near Salzburg.

As Prince of Wales, however, Edward did travel on the Orient Express and its subsidiary trains when making many discreet sorties to Paris, the South of France, and Central Europe, invariably in the company of beautiful ladies. Usually one of his *salon* cars was attached to the regularly scheduled express. He became a familiar portly figure as the "Duke of Lancaster" on his many trips to and from the health spa of Marienbad in Bohemia, where he took the waters, supposedly for the cure of his obesity, and where he enjoyed the sociable interludes generally disapproved by his family.

Most members of the British royal family were devoted to the concept of the sea as the highway linking the British dominions and colonies and to the faith that "British was best"; they traveled by sea whenever they could and in British-made royal rolling stock when they could not reach a country by ship. The younger generation, however, journeyed on many occasions along almost the entire route of the Orient Express. Thus the Duke of York—later, King George VI—attended, in 1922, in Belgrade the marriage of King Alexander of Yugoslavia to Princess Marie of Rumania, and a year later, shortly after his own marriage, the Orient Express carried him and his wife (the present Queen Mother Elizabeth) again to Belgrade for the christening of Crown Prince Peter.

Closely related to the Greek, Yugoslav, and Rumanian dynasties, the British "royals" were frequent visitors to the Balkan capitals between the two world wars. In the 1950s and 1960s Prince Philip, the Duke of Edinburgh, visited his mother in Athens, and she, disliking journeys by air, traveled on the Orient Express—until its demise—when coming to London. Before 1939 all the Balkan rulers used *salon* cars, coupled to the express, when calling on their English relatives.

The most tragic and also most regular Orient Express passenger among British royalty was Edward VIII, who later became the Duke of Windsor. The complete discretion afforded to distinguished passengers on the Orient Express was never better exemplified than in his case. Between the two world wars, as Prince of Wales he made frequent trips between London, Paris, and Vienna. His visits to the Austrian capital were explained as necessary for consulting a famous Viennese physician who treated him for a chronic ear problem. But the prince combined them with social distractions; with his friends, particularly with his equerry, Major Edward "Fruity" Metcalf, he became a familiar figure in Vienna's night spots, such as the Chat Noir and the Cocotte. That was before he met Mrs. Bessie Wallis Simpson, when, at forty, he was still "the world's most eligible bachelor." By the time of Edward's journeys prior to becoming king in January 1936, the world's press—outside Britain, where an unofficial censorship prevailed to the extent of stories in *Time* magazine being torn out of all imported copies—was reporting his close friendship with Mrs. Simpson. Circumstantial accounts, impossible to confirm thanks to the wall of silence surrounding the train and the Viennese authorities, stated that the lady sometimes accompanied the Prince. More sensational were the rumors that as well as consulting medical advisers, Edward had met socially prominent Nazis. Stories later circulated that Mrs. Simpson had been friendly with Joachim von Ribbentrop while he was German ambassador in London. Then there were allegations of his unconstitutional activities, after he ascended the throne, in promising unemployed Welsh coal miners that "something would be done about their poverty." Not a few historians believed—and still believe—that the insistence of Baldwin's Conservative government that Edward VIII must choose between marriage to Mrs. Simpson and abdication was dictated by political motives.

Immediately after his abdication on December 11, 1936, the ex-king—now the Duke of Windsor—no longer having to adopt an incognito, took the Orient Express for Vienna; a few weeks earlier Mrs. Simpson had left England for Cannes in the South of France. In Austria Edward was staying in seclusion as the guest of Baron Eugène de Rothschild at his castle in Enzesfeld. He had traveled in the company of his secretary and with one valet. The train's *contrôleur*, Roger Tibot, recalled in his retirement this pathetic journey. The Duke had

ordered an ordinary first-class compartment, and being anxious to escape newspaper reporters who might have discovered his secret departure, he did not wish to take the meals in the restaurant car and asked
that they be served in the curtained compartment. Tibot described
how one of the waiters, sworn to secrecy, accompanied him with the
trays to the compartment, and how the meals—most of the dishes
remaining untouched—were served on trays balanced on top of two
suitcases spread over the gap between the seats. "It was a sight that rent
my heart," Tibot said, remembering when he had supervised the splendid meals served to the same passenger when he dined in state in his
salon car—the king of Great Britain. Six months later the Duke of
Windsor and Mrs. Simpson returned by the Orient Express to France,
where they were married at a simple ceremony at the Château de
Condé near Tours, after a few days as guests of the American C. E.
Bedaux, the inventor of the "system of productivity" lampooned by
Charles Chaplin in *Modern Times*. After living through the war as
governor of the Bahamas, the Duke of Windsor and his wife settled
in their self-imposed exile in France. There was also a pathetic sequel
to their travels on the Orient Express. The sleeping car No. 3538, built
in 1929 and converted by the Wagons-Lits Compagnie for the then
Prince of Wales' personal use, with a *salon* and shower room, was
confiscated by the Germans after the fall of France in 1940 and used
by Nazi leaders and German generals until it was destroyed during an
attack by French maquis fighters.

Accustomed as were the royal travelers to regard the Orient Express as their personal means of locomotion whenever they deigned to
patronize it, the occasional inconsiderate demands made by some of
them and their often infuriating interference with the normal running
of the train had to be endured by the Compagnie and its staff. After
all, these "royals" and their large retinues provided a lucrative source
of revenue and the prestige they conferred on the Wagons-Lits was
invaluable. The worst offenders were the Balkan rulers, whose every
wish had to be fulfilled, because they could make things difficult for the
Compagnie on the routes passing their domains.

Some of the Balkan kings could claim that but for their cooperation there would have been no properly maintained railroad for the
expresses to run on, or even no track at all. Ferdinand I of Bulgaria,

for example, had made possible the construction of the line between Nish and Plovdiv, thus ending the anomaly of the diligence service by road. For more than thirty years he constantly reminded the Compagnie of the fact.

Ferdinand, the youngest son of Prince Augustus of Saxe-Coburg and Princess Clementine of Bourbon-Orléans, and therefore doubly suitable to be put on any vacant throne where Victoria of England and Bismarck of Germany each considered it of potential value, was twenty-five when he was presented with a career ruling over what he called "a ridiculous country." He rapidly developed into an astute and cunning intriguer, ideal for a nation where plots and counterplots were rampant. By playing off the politicians and the army generals against one another, he secured his position internally. The same policy of being all things to all men worked well on the international front. Innumerable trips on the Orient Express took him on visits to such potentates as the Sultan of Turkey, the Emperor of Austro-Hungary, the German Kaiser, and the King of Greece, plus private sorties to his baroque residence in Vienna, maintained just in case the need for a refuge as a royal exile became abruptly urgent. However, that emergency did not arise until he inadvisedly threw in his lot with Germany in the 1914–18 war. Long before then he had managed to get Turkey to recognize his sovereignty, had married in turn two ladies of royal and ducal antecedents and assumed the title of Czar of Bulgaria. The Compagnie acceded to his command for a special *salon* car, appropriate to his new dignity, to be attached to the Orient Express whenever he made one of his international trips.

But the comfort of the royal *salon* was not enough. Ferdinand also liked to drive the train. Shortly before the first Balkan War of 1912 Ferdinand was returning to Sofia from conferences in Paris and Vienna. Macedonian terrorists, members of the Internal Macedonian Revolutionary Organization (IMRO), were rampaging on and within Bulgaria's borders, and when the train came to a sudden halt in the middle of the night, passengers and train staff suspected that either the track had been ambushed or sabotaged. In fact Ferdinand, unable to sleep, had decided he would drive the train himself and had applied the emergency brakes on the bogies of his *salon* car. The alarmed engineer did his best to protest, but Ferdinand was adamant. The train was just within Bulgarian territory and he could do as he wished. Rain was falling in torrents, and Ferdinand's inexpert use of the emergency brakes had locked them in position. Releasing them took some time and the Orient Express was delayed for four hours. Thereafter the Compagnie came to an arrangement with the King that whenever he wished to drive the train within Bulgaria he would take over only at a scheduled stop. He observed the letter of the agreement—but not the spirit. Came the day when the Orient Express bound for the Turkish frontier was laboring up a steep gradient. The engineer saw a horse-drawn carriage standing across the track. The train pulled up just in time when a tall, burly officer left the carriage, leisurely strolled to the locomotive, and informed the driver: "I am the Czar of Bulgaria, and as the train is on my territory I desire to drive it." After some half-hearted protests the *chef de train* and the engineer agreed. Ferdinand, in his resplendent uniform, happily mounted the locomotive, gave a couple of blasts on the whistle, and got the train in motion. The engineer subsequently reported that he had got on very well with his royal partner, who willingly heeded his advice; he added that with more experience the King would make a good train driver.

Ferdinand had a son by his first marriage, Boris, who was born in 1894 and of whom he was very fond. In order to stabilize his succession to the throne, he had the boy converted from his own Catholic faith to the Eastern Orthodox Church—to please Russia. By the time Boris was four, and Ferdinand a widower, he was traveling time after time with his father on the Orient Express. In 1904 Ferdinand took Boris on one of his many visits to Vienna, traveling in reserved compartments instead of a *salon* car. In the evening the King and two adjutants went to the restaurant car; the Crown Prince was alone asleep in the compartment, with two armed bodyguards sitting in the adjacent one. The train staff was told that the King had instructed his son to keep all shades and curtains drawn so that no passenger passing in the corridor could peer through the door and inside windows.

In a report by the *chef de train,* preserved in the Compagnie's archives, it is stated that before leaving for dinner, the King told the attendant who had been placed in the corridor to prevent anyone lingering: "It will be your responsibility to see that my instructions are implicitly obeyed by the Prince." Hardly had the King gone than the boy pulled up the shades, and with his little nose pressed to the glass pane looked into the corridor, gesturing at anyone passing by. The attendant first waved a warning finger at the boy, who sulkily drew the shades only to pull them up again after a few minutes. The attendant had to decide between ignoring a King's command or committing a minor *lèse majesté*. He chose the latter. Removing one of the slippers he always wore at night so as to avoid disturbing sleeping passengers, he entered the compartment. "I applied my slipper briskly but firmly to the Prince's posterior," he later reported. From then on the shades remained closely drawn. The boy complained to his father, but the King summoned the attendant the next morning and told him: "You did the right thing, that's the way to deal with a naughty boy!" It seems that Boris never forgot this incident, but bore no grudge. He often recounted it to the Wagons-Lits staff on his many journeys in later years when he grew to love and patronize the Orient Express as enthusiastically as his father had.

Boris, at the age of twenty-four, succeeded to the throne after Ferdinand's abdication, which was forced by the Allies. He developed into a politically unscrupulous opportunist. Yet he still found time and leisure to indulge the passion for railroads he had inherited from his father. During his rule the network of lines in his country was greatly improved, despite chronic economic crises, and extended to make the running of the Simplon Orient Express smooth and reliable, even though the train had to carry detachments of armed soldiers to protect it from attacks by Macedonian terrorists, who repeatedly attempted to assassinate the King and his ministers. With relatives by marriage in Italy and France, Boris made frequent trips on the Orient Express. Bent over timetable schedules and armed with a stopwatch, he would spend hours checking speeds on different sections and sharply criticizing any delays, ignoring explanations from stationmasters, *chefs de train,* and locomotive engineers. To find out faults he often manned the locomotive cab himself. He thus gained a genuine skill in driving a train, practicing at first on local lines. Inevitably the cab of the Orient Express locomotive drew him like a magnet. When, one winter evening, he arrived at the Gare de l'Est in Paris clad in tailor-made white overalls and demanded to be allowed to ride the French locomotive as an observer, the *chef de train*, after a frantic call to the Compagnie headquarters, had to agree, hoping that after a chilly run through France to Lausanne in Switzerland the King would have had enough fun and would then retire for the night to the special car he had booked for himself and his adjutants and bodyguards.

On that occasion, and on several more, Boris did tire of standing for hours in the locomotive cab and changed back to his *salon* car. The reports stated that gradually he began returning to his observer's duties every time the locomotive was changed, and then, that he was no longer satisfied with remaining just an observer but took over the controls. Horrified officials of every railroad between Paris and Vienna issued a warning that any engineer allowing Boris to drive the train would be instantly dismissed. Boris himself was diplomatically informed that he could not be allowed to intimidate railroad personnel in no position to deal with a king's capricious orders. Grudgingly Boris agreed that henceforth he would drive the Orient Express only within his own country. That proviso ought to have warned the Compagnie that their troubles were not over. Time after time, as soon as the train crossed the frontier into Bulgaria, Boris, already clad in his white overalls, would emerge from his private car and drive the train to Sofia. As the railroads in Bulgaria were state-owned, which in the King's view meant that they were his property and the railroad staff his personal servants, nothing could be done about it. The climax came when, the train being late, Boris ordered the protesting and frightened fireman to go on stoking the fire until the steam-pressure pointer reached the red danger line. The engineer, demoted to assistant, was able to avoid an explosion by blowing off surplus steam, but the inferno in the firebox was another matter. The draft system blew back a wall of flame just as the fireman was shoveling on yet more coal. Instantly his clothing was ablaze and he leaped screaming from the swaying cab, fatally injured. There was no chance of bringing the train to a stop for at least half a mile, and in any event, Boris did not intend to do so. He brought the Simplon Orient Express into Sofia ahead of time and strode up and down the platform in expectation of the passengers' admiration for avoiding any delay despite the regrettable mishap. How the problem was actually handled after this incident was not explained. But it was effective. The royal railroad engineer thereafter confined his speed-record attempts to trains running entirely within his kingdom.

The outbreak of the Second World War, of course, put a stop to the King's playing with trains. He did not survive the war. When, in the summer of 1943, he secretly tried to contact the Allies in the hope of resisting the growing Nazi oppression, his double-dealing was discovered by Hitler's military intelligence. He was summoned to the Führer's headquarters, and a few days after his return to Sofia, was found dead in his palace. His death at the age of forty-nine was never satisfactorily explained, but there was little doubt that he had been poisoned by Gestapo thugs in conspiracy with pro-Nazi officers of his palace guard.

The advantages derived by the Compagnie from its earliest agreements with the monarchs and governments of the Balkan countries through which the Orient Express ran were on occasion two-edged, involving Nagelmackers in delicate political moves which he wished to have no part of. The train provided the opportunities for both a sure and rapid entry to a country by a would-be conspirator and as safe and speedy an exit for some unfortunate victim of rebellion. With border security systems a pale shadow of today's efficient guardians, there was always the risk that the train would be banned by the eventual winners in these frequent crises in southeastern Europe.

From 1885 the train ran once weekly via Budapest to Belgrade, the capital of Serbia. On the shaky throne sat Milan I, who had succeeded his cousin, murdered by assassins. He had grandiose ambitions, and apart from having ordered to patch up the Serbian rail track to take the Orient Express, he decided to equip his palace with electric lighting, as a cultural example to his subjects. The royal summons went out to the English contractor serving all the best people—Colonel Rookes Evelyn Crompton, founder of the great firm of Crompton Parkinson, which pioneered electric lighting throughout the world. The firm had installed generators and lamps in a string of royal palaces, as well as in the residences of British aristocrats and American millionaires, such as Lord Randolph Churchill, father of Winston; the railroad tycoon Jay Gould; John D. Rockefeller; and Andrew Carnegie. What most impressed the Serbian king was that Crompton had done the same in the palace of the Dalai Lama at Lhassa. If electric lighting could work well high in the Himalayas it could certainly work in Belgrade. After prolonged negotiations Colonel Crompton and his engineers arrived on the Orient Express on March 6, 1889, only to find that their royal client had that day fled on the west-bound Orient Express for exile in Paris.

Belgrade was in the throes of a revolution, with fighting in the streets. The intrepid colonel tried to make his way to the palace, which was under siege by the rebels, with Milan's queen and their thirteen-year-old son Alexander imprisoned in it. Crompton recounted his experiences thus: "I and my colleagues were in the crowd and near us was a German diplomat who had arrived with me on the Orient Express. We all had a narrow escape, for of the forty or fifty people killed in the firing some fell close to us. One woman fell at my feet, her brain scattered over my clothes. I ran to take shelter in a doorway and there I saw a copper disc about four feet in diameter. It was, as I later learned, an antique dinner tray, looted by the rebels, and I used it as a shield."*

When the rioting quieted down, Crompton managed to gain entry to the palace and helped the queen to escape from Serbia, after hiding her in his hotel room. Her young son was proclaimed king, although the leader of the rebellion, Colonel Ristic, became the real ruler. Ten years later Crompton did install the electric illumination of the Belgrade palace, but the twenty-three-year-old King Alexander did not enjoy it for long: in 1903, in another revolution, Serbian officers hacked him and his wife Draga Mashin to pieces with their sabers in the well-lit bedroom.

Once, the Orient Express carried a dethroned emperor and king, who tried to regain a part of his former realm, which he lost in 1918 after a rule of two years, having succeeded his great-uncle, Kaiser Francis Joseph of Austro-Hungary. Ex-Emperor Charles left his Swiss exile at Prangins on the Lake of Geneva on March 27, 1921, was smuggled across the frontier disguised as a gardener and, with a few of his aides, took the Orient Express to Vienna, traveling second class and completely unnoticed. From Vienna he was driven to Budapest, where he called on Admiral Miklós Horthy—who in 1919 had suppressed the

*Reminiscences, Constable, London, 1928.

Communist regime and proclaimed himself regent—to give up his power. But the Hungarian National Assembly voted against Charles's restoration and he was obliged to return to Switzerland. During the summer his supporters assured him that a second attempt would be more successful. This time, on October 21, Charles and his wife, Zita, arrived by air at Sopron (Ödenburg), where the garrison joined them in support. Charles set forth at the head of a few hundred soldiers on a march on Budapest. Czechoslovakia and Yugoslavia mobilized their armies, and in the face of a warlike conflict with Hungary's neighbors, Horthy ordered his troops to surround the imperial rebels; Charles was captured and narrowly escaped death. He and his wife were rescued by the British ambassador, who took them aboard the British minesweeper HMS *Glow-worm* on the Danube. They were eventually transported to Madeira, where Charles died a year later at Funchal at the age of only thirty-five. His last journey in disguise aboard the Orient Express in 1921 must have revived happier memories of his many travels in state on this train before the war when, as a young archduke, he visited European capitals.

One of the last, and perhaps the most unpredictable, European royal devotees of the Orient Express was Carol II of Rumania. All his life he made the headlines, and the train was the vehicle for his final bizarre adventure. Born in 1893 at Pelishor, near Castel Peles,* to Crown Prince Ferdinand and Princess Marie, he was thus related to both Victoria of England and Alexander II of Russia. From his infancy he was accustomed to rail travel, and caught his father's enthusiasm for trains. By the time he was four he knew what it was like to play, eat, and sleep on the Orient Express on the regular journeys he made with his mother for vacations in England and on the French Riviera. Those childhood impressions of a means of escape from the rigid life in the Rumanian court never faded: escape to the West was his policy in crisis after crisis.

During the First World War he secretly married Zizi Lambrino, a union he was forced to concede was null and void even though Zizi

*Where his granduncle and grandaunt, Carmen Sylva, entertained About and Opper on the inaugural journey of the Orient Express ten years earlier.

was pregnant. His solution was to put Zizi on the Orient Express for Paris, accompanied by his mother. Then began the liaison that intrigued the world for more than thirty years. Ordered by his father to devote his time to active service in the army so that an eye could be kept on him, Carol became friendly with a young officer named Tempeanu, and more so with his wife, Elenitza, a twenty-four-year-old redhead. Her origins have remained a mystery. Her mother was a Viennese Catholic and her father a Russian Jew named Wolff, who took the name of Lupescu. The enigma was that Wolff-Lupescu was able to marry a Catholic and prosper as an apothecary in a country that was violently anti-Semitic and normally forbade marriages between a Catholic and a Jew. One of the many rumors was that his wife was in fact not Austrian but Rumanian, and was the daughter of a schoolteacher who had been seduced by King Charles after his marriage to Elizabeth (Carmen Sylva) became a façade. That possibility, even probability, became a dominant factor in the horror about Carol's intimacy with Elenitza, who could have been a blood relative.

Always insatiable in his desire for women, Carol's affair with Elenitza (whom he always addressed by the Westernized name of Helena, but who became known to the world as Magda) was at first deliberately broken by his father, who, having managed to terminate his son's marriage to a commoner, sent him out of the country. The ostensible reason was that Carol had to escort Prince George of Greece from Lucerne for an arranged marriage with Carol's sister, Elizabeth. The royal Greek family included two pretty girls, Princesses Helen and Irene. Helen had been advised that the handsome young Rumanian Crown Prince would be an ideal husband for her. The mission was organized with maximum ostentation. *Salon* cars of the Orient Express were embellished with the royal insignia of Rumania, and Carol traveled in state to Switzerland, bringing the Greeks back in the same cars. He married Princess Helen in March 1921. A son, Michael, was born. By then Carol was seeing Magda Lupescu regularly again. Her husband, in return for the promise of advancement in his army career, did the gentlemanly thing and provided grounds for divorce, and she resumed her maiden name of Lupescu.

For months Carol and Magda had to devise brief and secret meetings for a few hours. The chance to be really together came when he was ordered to represent the Rumanian throne at the funeral of Queen Alexandra of England in November 1925. He took the Orient Express with his aides from Bucharest. Magda, to the relief of the police deputed to watch her, had left for a visit to friends in the country some days before. In fact she had crossed the border into Hungary. She joined Carol on the train at Subotica and shared his sleeping compartment as far as Paris. The duties at the London funeral over, Carol left for Milan, where Magda was awaiting him. They had a few pleasurable days together until increasingly vehement orders from Bucharest forced him to catch the Simplon Orient Express back to his unfortunate wife and his court duties.

Tension developed rapidly. Refusing either to resume cohabitation with his wife or to give up Magda, Carol renounced his right to the throne on January 4, 1926. That summer he once more boarded his beloved express for Paris, where he took a house for Magda and himself in fashionable Neuilly. His first wife, Zizi, living only a few miles away in comparative poverty, found this blatant insult too much. She sued Carol for desertion, claiming ten million francs' alimony.

Carol's father, King Ferdinand, died in July 1927, creating a constitutional crisis for Rumania which put an end to the idyllic life Carol had been enjoying in Paris. Infatuated as he was with Magda, whom he called his green-eyed goddess, he was also enthralled with the potentialities of kingship. With what he rightly considered the trump card of royal heredity in his hand, he gave his terms for rescinding his renouncement of the throne: divorce from his wife and no harassment of Magda. He got the first but was refused the second. Resigned to the inevitable, and calculating that Magda need never be more than a train journey's away, he agreed. She was established in a villa at Vitznau, a Swiss lakeside village near Lucerne, and easily reached from the Simplon Orient Express stopping place at Basle.

When Carol, as king, arrived in Bucharest by air—a spectacular descent from the clouds, which appealed to him and had been enthusiastically approved by his ministers as a certain way of ensuring that

Magda did not accompany him—it seemed that the notorious liaison had been successfully hidden from the new king's subjects. Just to make sure, every minor station and every road on Rumania's Western frontier were manned by secret police checking everyone coming from Hungary and Yugoslavia. They had been given photographs of the King's mistress, with early versions of identikit pictures showing what she might look like in various disguises. Actually, she entered the country on the Orient Express without any effort to hide herself on August 4. In the usual manner the Wagons-Lits *contrôleur* had ensured that none of his passengers was disturbed at the frontier. The train was authorized to proceed without more than a half-hearted check on passports.

From then on Magda Lupescu became not only the uncrowned queen of Rumania but a powerful political force. She was an ally and friend of Corneliu Codreanu, boss of the rapidly growing Legion of the Archangel Michael, better known as the Iron Guard, a rabidly anti-Semitic fascist organization financed by Hitler and Mussolini—which was at least surprising, considering her Jewish antecedents. Her villa, connected to the palace by a tunnel, cost Carol a fortune. She was alleged to have spent $48,000 a year on clothes, most of them created for her by Chanel, and she phoned Paris daily for the latest news of fashions. The real queen, Helen, was the danger to both Carol and Mme. Lupescu. In the deteriorating political conditions of the country, Helen became the figurehead of the anti-King and anti-Lupescu factions. Once again Carol thought of the Orient Express as the means of solving a problem. Carol forced her out by the heartless ultimatum that if she did not go into voluntary exile she would not be allowed to see her son Michael. On a night in 1933, when the Orient Express from Istanbul bound for Paris was due, all lights at Bucharest station were extinguished and the station personnel withdrawn. Lines of police surrounded the station precincts. Queen Helen arrived in a car and was escorted to the train by the Bucharest chief of police carrying a torch.

Fearful for his mistress's safety, Carol subsequently had to agree to Magda Lupescu leaving Bucharest to live in Paris. He went to her as often as he dared to leave his country, until in February 1938 he appointed himself virtual dictator of Rumania. With what he believed was absolute power over army, police, and parliament he telephoned Magda and told her it was safe to return. For a time they both managed to survive. But the demoralization of both King and country was soon complete. In the summer of 1940 Hitler and Stalin grabbed whatever Rumanian territory they required, and on September 6 Carol was forced to abdicate and leave his country.

A pale shadow of the prewar Orient Express still struggled to maintain some sort of service in territories that were not actually at war or had accepted Hitler's terms. Just after midnight on September 8 three cars—two *salons* and a sleeping car—were shunted into the freight yard outside the Bucharest main station. Carol and Magda Lupescu arrived in a car followed by a truck carrying more than a hundred pieces of baggage and crates. Their contents included El Greco masterpieces removed from the palace walls, Carol's vast stamp collection, dozens of valuable first editions of books, and—in Magda's personal baggage—a case crammed with dollars and Swiss francs, which she had been methodically collecting for years.

The Orient Express steamed into the station. The three cars were shunted onto the main line and coupled. The journey was uneventful until the train passed between high embankments near Timişoara. Gun flashes in the darkness spurted out from both sides, and some bullets pierced the metal sides of the cars. Carol dragged his mistress along the floor of the sleeping car to the bathroom, where he thrust her into the bathtub, holding her down with his own body. The train gathered speed and, within minutes, passed into Yugoslavia. It was periodically held up and shunted into sidings to give priority to troops and arms trains, mainly in northern Italy, where Mussolini's legions were moving into France. The Orient Express did not reach the safety of neutral Switzerland until the following morning.

Carol would never again travel on the Orient Express. Eventually he left with Mme. Lupescu for Portugal, where he acquired a splendid villa at the seaside resort of Estoril, the ultimate refuge of several eclipsed kings and royal pretenders, including ex-king Umberto of Italy and Don Juan of Spain. In 1947 Carol married Magda Lupescu in Brazil—where his divorce from his ex-queen was recognized—when she was thought to be on her deathbed, bestowing on her the fictional title of Princess Elena. In the event, the notorious woman, who had been compared with courtesans of the style of Madame de Pompadour and Madame du Barry, survived her lover by twenty-four years. She died at the Estoril villa on June 30, 1977, at the age of eighty-one, insisting to the end on being addressed as "your Highness."

By then the royal train was no more and all its royal passengers had departed forever.

THOUGH ROYAL PATRONAGE CONFERRED THE CACHET OF GLORY AND grandeur on the Wagons-Lits, France—the bastion of republicanism —was no less enthusiastic about providing the highest standard of luxury travel for her presidents. In 1887 when President Sadi Carnot took office, Nagelmackers was required to provide him with specially built *salon*, sleeping, and restaurant cars. It was when Carnot stepped from his *salon* car on March 24, 1894, at Lyons station that he was assassinated by the Italian anarchist Caserio. His successor, Jean Casimir-Périer, was in office for only six months; he never made use of the splendid train. The next President of the Republic, Félix Faure, was a great railroad enthusiast and he frequently used the presidential cars. But when the new—and last—Czar, Nicholas II, and the Czarina were due to pay a state visit to Paris, the President decided that even his luxurious *salon* cars were not splendid enough to carry the ruler of All Russia. Nagelmackers was asked to provide three new *salon* cars, three new sleeping cars, and one restaurant car, all to be furnished and decorated in a way that would "prove to the Russian imperial pair and their entourage the spirit of true French elegance." It was a tall order: the visit was only six weeks away. But the Magician of the Wagons-Lits did not disappoint the President. At the Compagnie's workshops at Saint-Denis, work to rebuild and redecorate seven of the best existing cars was carried out without interruption day and night by the best artisans the manager, Jean Saint-James, could muster. He had a very personal ambition to produce a superb job: his uncle, De Montebello, was France's ambassador in St. Petersburg. Within thirty-five days the seven cars were completed and stood in the station of Cherbourg when on October 6, 1896, the Czar and Czarina and their large suite arrived aboard a warship.

Car PR1—the initials stood for *Président de la Republique*—had been turned into a large bedroom with a huge double bed surmounted by a canopy of costly tapestry, with two bathrooms next door—containing tubs of Italian marble, gold-plated taps and pipes, and two toilets —and two compartments for the Czar's chamberlains or bodyguards. Car PR2 included two *salons,* a study for the Czar and his ministers, and a boudoir for the Czarina and her ladies-in-waiting. Car PR3 had a smoking room, a recreation area with card tables and a miniature billiard table, a dressing room, a bathroom, and a compartment for court officials. A restaurant car was modified to take a large banqueting table with seating for thirty-six. The other cars were luxuriously refurbished to accommodate the Czar's court functionaries and army and naval adjutants and secretaries. It seems that one result of all the splendor was that Nagelmackers received from the Czar, who expressed his great satisfaction, the promise of a contract to operate Wagons-Lits on the new Trans-Siberian Express. The cars he built for this train's enormous journey of nineteen days in each direction began to run in 1898. They had to be specially designed, had a double skin to insulate them from the cold and many facilities to ensure an enjoyable journey; they included a barber's shop, a gymnasium, and a steam turbine driving a dynamo so that all cars were lit by electricity.

The special PR cars used by the Czar during his visit in France were subsequently used by the Presidents of the Republic, and were known as L'Elysée sur Rail. The most enthusiastic user was Raymond Poincaré, who was President throughout the First World War. He frequently conducted secret negotiations with monarchs and political leaders from other countries in the moving train, when "courtesy" visits were the pretext for alliances or secret parleys. Roger Commault, the remarkable *chef de train,* held at that time only a very junior job, but he recalls the despair of the *chef de cuisine* when the PR train was due to take King George V of England from Cherbourg to Paris. President Poincaré and his cabinet waited at the quay, while aboard the train a gargantuan dinner was being prepared. The menu is preserved in the Compagnie's archives and was as follows:

Cantaloup glacé au Marsale
(Iced Melon with Sicilian wine)

Truite de rivière meunière
(River Trout grilled in butter)

Poulet de grain grillé à Diable
(Chicken baked in breadcrumb batter)

Selle de Pré-Salé Marie-Louise
(Saddle of Lamb fattened on aromatic pasture)

Pointes d'asperge à la crème
(Asparagus tips in cream)

Chaud-froid de Caneton
(Duckling in liqueur-flavoured aspic)

Salade Catalane
(Salad of Aubergines and Tomatoes with
safran-flavoured rice)

Cheese Board of fifteen French cheeses
Soufflé Palmyre
(Soufflé of Anisette with Kirsch)

Corbeille de Fruits
(Fresh Fruit)

The finest champagne, vintage wines and choice liqueurs were, of course, kept ready, and assuming that the English king might desire tea instead of coffee, there was a selection of Indian, Assam, Ceylon and Chinese leafs in the pantry.

But there was a heavy storm in the Channel and the Royal Navy cruiser bringing the English guests was badly delayed. To the utter despair of the *chef de cuisine* and his staff, there was only twenty minutes available for the meal, and most of the elaborately prepared dishes remained untouched.

Poincaré's successor, Paul Deschanel, was the victim of one of the most bizarre mishaps ever to be recorded in the Wagons-Lits annals. On May 23, 1920, he left Paris on the presidential train to unveil a monument to a French aviator at Montbrison, near Lyons. The train also carried several Cabinet members, including the foreign minister, Pierre-Etienne Flandin (during the Second World War, as a member of Marshal Pétain's Vichy regime, he became a Nazi collaborator), and traveled overnight. An early breakfast was served at which the *chef de train* politely asked to be allowed to count the number of the passengers because, as he explained, the railroad telegraph had transmitted a message that someone had been seen to fall out of the train as it passed through Saint-Germain-des-Fossés, some twenty miles back. All the officials and secretaries had been accounted for, and all the ministers and high functionaries enjoying the honor to take breakfast at the presidential table were present when the count was taken. But one member of the group was missing: the President of the French Republic. No one was unduly worried—the President was obviously still sleeping in his fine bedroom. But when eventually someone dared to open the door of Deschanel's sleeping car, the alarming truth became known: the President was not there, and it now seemed certain that his was the body seen falling from the speeding train. Nobody ventured to decide what to do, and the train continued to Lyons.

Meantime the unfortunate man, then sixty-four years old, bruised, shivering in his soiled pajamas and with one slipper missing, had managed to reach the hut of a level-crossing keeper. "I am the President of the Republic," he stammered, and the reply of the simple railroadman was a sarcastic "Oh, really, then I am the Emperor Napoleon . . ." It took Deschanel some time to convince the man that he was indeed the First Citizen of the French Republic and not some escaped lunatic. A frantic exchange of telegrams followed, and the President was collected by the prefect of the neighboring town. The ceremony of the monument unveiling duly took place without him, but one can imagine how disconcerted the ministers were while listening to the long speeches.

A belated official bulletin explained to an intrigued nation that the President, feeling unwell, had left his sleeping car and tried to open a window in the corridor to get some fresh air; by mistake he opened a door and fell headlong, fortunately suffering no injury. Inevitably, rumors spread as to the real cause of the accident. Had the President been drunk? Or was he mentally deranged? Or had some foreign assassin somehow got on the train and pushed the President out? Satirical ballads were featured in every Paris cabaret and night club. *Canard Enchainé,* the famous satirical journal, had a field day with cruel caricatures and libelous insinuations. Attempts to protect the hapless President's good name by insisting that the lock on the door had been defective were discarded amid the babel of criticism. The Compagnie indignantly announced that there were no defective locks in its cars and that accidental opening of the door was impossible. Deschanel endured for four months the aspersions cast on his character and mental stability. Then he resigned.

During the Second World War only one of the PR cars was used by Admiral Jean Darlan for a few journeys in unoccupied France before 1942; the others were seized by the Germans and at times used for journeys by generals and Nazi leaders. After the liberation in 1945 the Compagnie retrieved three cars, but they had been stripped of their contents, probably looted by German officers and SS commanders. The Compagnie once again refurbished the cars and the first President of the Fourth Republic, Vincent Auriol, made thirty-six journeys in the newly assembled special train, entertaining aboard it General Eisenhower, the king of Cambodia, the king of Iraq, and also the then President of Vietnam, Ho Chi Minh. René Coty, who was President from 1953 to 1959 made fourteen journeys. General de Gaulle preferred to travel by air, particularly by helicopter, but on official occasions he did use the presidential *salon* cars, for instance, during visits of Chancellor Konrad Adenauer of the German Federal Republic. President Georges Pompidou never used the PR train at all, he invariably traveled by air. On the one occasion when he went on a state visit to the Netherlands, he asked for a separate Wagon-Lits car for himself and his aides, and it was attached to a scheduled train from Paris to The Hague. President Valéry Giscard d'Estaing, a well-known connoisseur of *haute cuisine,* used the presidential cars on only a few occasions.

The famous Elysée sur Rail is today a thing of the past and in the foreseeable future the PR cars may become exhibition pieces in the Transport Museum.

Chapter Nine

THE FAMOUS
AND THE NOTORIOUS

REIGNING MONARCHS AND MEMBERS OF ROYAL FAMILIES WERE OF only occasional trouble to the Compagnie and its staff. They traveled in their own royal cars, attached to the Wagons-Lits expresses, or in special *salon* cars provided by the Compagnie. Invariably they were accompanied by their court officials, secretaries, security guards, valets and maidservants, and usually they had their own dining cars, where the meals were prepared by the chefs and kitchen personnel in their employ.

Sometimes, however, the royal passengers took meals produced by the Compagnie's staff and served by the waiters in the private dining cars. One of the longest-serving and most remarkable gastronomic virtuosos of the Wagons-Lits restaurant cars was a chef named Voisseron. His great days were between 1899 and 1933, and he devised the menus and supervised their preparation for many special passengers. On one of his journeys King Edward VII, well known for his fondness of good food, called him to his dining *salon* and said, "Look here, Voisseron, I have eaten your delicious masterpieces many times, and I have eaten meals prepared by many other famous chefs, but none was better than yours. I want you to be my royal chef. Come to London.

I will pay you anything you ask, certainly much more than the Compagnie. I will get you a nice house and I will look after the education of your children." Voisseron begged to be allowed to think it over. He later wrote to the King that although he was greatly honored, he had to refuse "because Madame Voisseron would never leave France and live abroad." Two months later Madame was dead, but the King, piqued by the chef's refusal, never repeated his offer.

From the very outset of the Wagons-Lits Compagnie, Nagelmackers had taken great care to train his staff meticulously. A special school was established, and the first instructors were maîtres d'hôtel and banqueting managers recruited from luxury hotels, usually from Switzerland. Over the years the corps of the Compagnie employees grew into a hierarchy within which promotion was as strictly regulated as in a government service, army, or police. The *chef de train* was the commander in chief, his deputy the *contrôleur* (distinguished by his wearing a winged collar and black tie); then came the *chefs de brigade* (with stiff white collars and ties), the *conducteurs,* the *brigadier-postiers,* and *bagagistes,* all wearing uniforms with buttoned-up military-style collars, their ranks distinguished by gold and silver piping on their collars, sleeves, and caps, and finally the *bagagistes-nettoyeurs,* the porters and cleaners. The manager of the restaurant car had the title of *maître d'hôtel,* and invariably wore tails. Under him were the *serveurs-receveurs* (headwaiters who supervised the service and presented the bills), followed by various grades of waiters, such as *serveurs* and *aides-serveurs.* Likewise, there was a kitchen hierarchy, from the *chef de cuisine* to humble kitchen help, *plongeurs* (dishwashers), and cleaners.

For many years the most renowned member of the corps was Roger Commault, who served the Compagnie for half a century. A Parisian, he was born in 1904 in a house adjacent to the station of Les Batignolles, from which the first French train made its journey in 1837 from Paris to Saint-Germain. Train-watching became the boy's great passion, made easier because one of his aunts was the level-crossing guard. He enjoys telling the story how in 1917 he had missed a school examination because, enraptured by the sight of expresses steaming away to far destinations, he had stopped on his way to school for an hour on the bridge of Cardinet, near the old Ceinture station, "enveloped by a cloud of steam and smoke like in a dream." Regarded by his teachers as a bright youngster and encouraged to go on to college, he applied instead for a job with the Wagons-Lits Compagnie, starting in the humblest position as a *plongeur.* But his dishwashing did not last too long; his abilities were recognized and promotion was quick. He became a sleeping-car attendant, then soon afterwards a *conducteur,* and eventually, between 1954 and 1968 until his retirement, he was the *chef de train* in charge of special *salon* cars, supervising the journeys of VIPs, including the Presidents of the Republic, royalty, and visiting statesmen.

During his long service he had met thousands of famous personages and accumulated a unique collection of documents, photographs, drawings, timetables, and newspaper clippings relating to the Wagons-Lits Compagnie, and particularly to its Orient expresses. After his retirement the Compagnie appointed him their official historian and he thus became a fathomless source of information for historiographers and writers on railroads in general and the Wagons-Lits in particular. He himself had written scores of articles, published in railroad magazines and newspapers the world over, and several books, including a biography of Georges Nagelmackers* and the history of *Le Wagon de l'armistice.*† His second passion remained music. Self-taught, he had become a distinguished expert on Richard Wagner, and compiled an important bibliography of the composer's works.‡ Although he has helped many writers, he remains, when these lines are written, a spritely septuagenarian who is adamant in opposing all attempts by publishers to persuade him to produce his own memoirs, in which he could describe his encounters with thousands of his famous passengers —he is being true to the Compagnie's tradition that its employees must exercise complete discretion.

The life of the Compagnie's employees was not only subject to exacting demands but, in contrast to the luxury the passengers enjoyed, hard and uncomfortable. Only the top-ranking personnel could hope

---

Editions Capitelle, Paris, 1966.
†Capelle, Paris 1969.
‡Published in *La Revue Paladienne.*

to spend the night in a compartment, provided that sleeping accommodations were not fully booked. Others, when not on night duty—and particularly the kitchen staff—had to be content to sleep in hammocks slung between the racks in the restaurant car. They had to rise at dawn to put the car in spick-and-span condition and prepare it for the *petit déjeuner,* which some passengers preferred to take there rather than in their compartments. The attendants had to be immaculately dressed and pass a rigid inspection by their superiors. On some of the expresses before the First World War, and also for some years after 1919, the waiters wore tailcoats, blue velvet breeches, white silk stockings, and silver-buckled shoes. On their faultless appearance and obsequious behavior depended, after all, the amount of reward they could hope for from the passengers. There was a saying among the personnel that in the first class the passengers abuse the staff, in the second class the passengers abuse each other and—after its introduction in more recent times—in the third the passengers were abused by the staff.

If the "royals" were regarded as easy passengers because their own lackeys looked after them, not so the hordes of princelings, aristocrats, and millionaires—particularly the *nouveaux riches,* who demanded special treatment according to their privileged position. Until two world wars swept away the need to tolerate inconsiderate behavior, the personnel of the Orient Express endured a good many insults and faced innumerable quandaries while pandering to exalted or overbearing passengers; but the attendants also found not a little humor in the bizarre incidents involving some of the capricious clients. By general consent the English and the Americans were the most considerate and least demanding, and the Austrian and Hungarian aristocrats and the Balkan boyars the most difficult to satisfy.

The *contrôleur* Brouet, employed for thirty years on the Orient Express, recorded, for instance, the specious demands of Prince Ernest Rüdiger Starhemberg von Schaumberg and Waxenberg, whose lineage was even longer than his title, going back to the twelfth-century rulers of Styria. Prince Ernest retained his virility to an advanced age, proving it by regular trips on the Orient Express to the bordellos of Paris. With his own ideas about the aphrodisiac properties of food and having the predilection of a gourmet, he refused to touch the meals served on the train. Instead, the chef of the Hotel Sacher in Vienna was always informed of the Prince's departure date and told to prepare special dishes to provide the five meals required between Vienna and Paris. This was in the days before vacuum containers were available, and the food, wrapped and placed in specially made metal boxes, had to be reheated prior to stipulated mealtimes during the journey. The *chef de cuisine,* infuriated by this reflection on his skill and disgusted at the thought of serving reheated food, retaliated by adding quantities of salt, pepper, and other condiments to make the dishes almost inedible. But the Prince, convinced that each dish was a Hotel Sacher masterpiece, ate them all with zest.

Many of these difficult passengers traveled with their pet dogs. Unless the owners were as unyielding as they were exalted, the dogs were usually carried in a special covered wagon; if not, the fare was almost as high for a dog as for its owner. Often these pampered pets got as much attention from the staff as the passengers did. One of the Hapsburgs, the Archduchess Marie Valerie, traveled three or four times a year to Paris to have her poodles trimmed by a canine expert in the Faubourg Saint-Honoré. The Archduchess's dogs, with fare paid on each, had to be fed three times a day on slices of milk-fed calf— Wiener schnitzel—fried in Normandy butter.

The restaurant-car chefs took such culinary problems in their stride. More formidable were the difficulties of observing the religious dietary laws of Jews and Muslims. It was not too difficult to omit any meat dish based on pork, but in the case of Orthodox Jews every utensil used in the kitchen had to be kosher, examined in advance by a rabbi, and kept separate from all other equipment. Invariably this meant a special car. For both Muslims and Jews evidence had also to be given that animals and poultry had been killed and dressed according to the ritual of their religions.

The chefs on the Orient expresses were rarely unable to cater to their clients' special preferences in foods, the Compagnie always taking the precaution when a VIP booked a seat to ascertain his or her likes and dislikes. Very occasionally there was a failure in communication, as happened when Dame Nellie Melba, the temperamental Australian operatic soprano, was making one of her frequent tours of Europe which she always based on the Orient Express routes. En route from

Brussels to Vienna, she demanded a *pêche Melba* with her luncheon. She was inordinately proud of this dessert, invented in her honor by Escoffier, the famous *chef de cuisine* at the Carlton Hotel in London. But the Compagnie commissariat had failed to deliver any peaches. There were pears, however, and with considerable unease the waiter presented this concoction of pears, ice cream, and raspberry purée to the singer. She tasted it and then called for the chef. "Excellent," she said. So was born *poire Melba.*

In more recent times, another chef hit upon a subterfuge to please the Prince of Wales—later Edward VIII and the Duke of Windsor— on one of his private journeys to Vienna. The Prince, perhaps suffering from a bout of homesickness, demanded a grilled kipper for his breakfast. But there was no such fish in the otherwise lavish stock of food stored in the restaurant car, a kipper being regarded as a dish fancied only by the lower classes. The chef discovered, however, that there were some choice smoked trout in store. He sliced the fish and carefully grilled it. The Prince found the "kipper" entirely to his satisfaction.

There is no accounting for taste, and some of the famous passengers remained untempted by the culinary delights created by the Orient Express chefs. Such a one was Sir Ernest Cassel, the English multimillionaire, who was one of the mightiest manipulators of the City of London for forty years—between 1880 and 1920—when the City was the world's undisputed financial center. Cassel's great banquets were for many years the talk of London. Edward VII, "The Corpulent Voluptuary," enjoyed the twelve-course meals created by Cassel's French and Italian chefs, while his host, always worried about his digestion, dined on a small dish of boiled fish. On the Orient Express, which took him to his big business operations in every Balkan capital and Constantinople, Cassel became the despair of every *chef de cuisine:* all he would order was a light soufflé with a dry biscuit and a morsel of English cheese to follow. In contrast, some of his close business friends, such as Baron Ferdinand Rothschild (of the Austrian branch), Alfred de Rothschild, the Paris banker, Sir Basil Zaharoff, Sir Henry Deterding, and scores of other great entrepreneurs, who traveled with a retinue of directors, managers, legal counselors, and secretaries, not only enjoyed the gastronomic delights of the Orient Express but also consumed enormous quantities of vintage wines, champagne, and brandies costing double the price billed in luxury hotels and restaurants of Europe's capital cities.

No one exceeded the Indian rajahs in demands for special treatment, but these were always expressed in a most polite fashion. These Oriental potentates were as fabulously rich and spendthrift as any Gulf oil sheik today, and the Compagnie was more than compensated for the elaborate arrangements it had to make. Notable in the records of these costly journeys was that of the Maharajah of Cooch Behar, His Highness Djiraj Mirza Maharao Shri Sir Khengarji Savai Behadur, whose realm in northeast India, although comparatively small in extent and population, was of great strategic importance to the British Empire. Deciding to come to London for the imperial conference in 1907, he announced that he intended to travel overland from Constantinople, where he arrived aboard his magnificent yacht from Bombay with his seven wives and concubines and twenty-nine retainers. Although he regularly visited Britain because of his enthusiasm for cricket, sailing, and sculling and the Compagnie was well aware of his insistence on train accommodations comparable in luxury to that of his palaces, this was the first time he was traveling in state on the Orient Express.

The two cars assigned to the party were entirely reequipped. Berths in the sleeping car were replaced with divans upholstered in swan's down and decked with gold-embroidered coverlets sent from his own palace. The floor was almost completely covered with large cushions for the wives and concubines. These ladies wore diaphanous silk gowns when in the presence of their lord and master. Because, obviously, extra heating was necessary, instructions concerning the minimum temperature required day and night during the journey were sent to the Compagnie headquarters in Paris. All went well on the outward journey, but on the return during an unseasonably chilly period the heating system in the special *salon* cars broke down. The staff hastily produced reserves of blankets, but the Maharajah angrily told them that neither he nor his ladies would go around like Egyptian mummies. Diplomatic appeals to other passengers on the train yielded the loan of furs and overcoats, with the Maharajah selecting the heavy hunting coat of an English peer.

Through delay while attempting to repair the heating system the train was badly behind schedule, and an additional meal had to be served. But the Maharajah's staple diet was lamb curry, and there was no more lamb in the train's cold store. Risking dismissal for unauthorized stopping of the Express, the *chef de train* ordered the engineer to halt just over the Turkish frontier. The stationmaster was told to rush to the village butcher and buy the carcasses of four sheep. To the relief of everyone concerned, he was back within fifteen minutes with the meat—a speedy errand which delighted the Maharajah, who turned to the *chef de train* and gave him a handful of pearls, rubies, and emeralds, saying "Please give one of these jewels to each of the good men who have obliged me, and keep the rest . . ."

Among the Indian nabobs who used the Orient and Simplon Orient expresses was the immensely rich Aga Khan, the spiritual head of the Ismaili Muslim sect spread over Asia and Africa. He spent most of his eighty years—he died in 1957—in the casinos and on the race tracks of Europe. The owner of world-famous stables, his horses won the English Derby five times. His son Ali Khan was an even more renowned playboy, and when he died in a racing-car crash in 1960, his body was brought in a special *salon* car of the Simplon Orient Express to Paris.

DURING THE EIGHT DECADES OF ITS EXISTENCE THE ORIENT EXPRESS and its sister trains must have carried hundreds of thousands of passengers, particularly after the introduction of the less expensive second-class cars. The Compagnie's archives still preserve many of the booking lists, and some read like pages from the *International Who's Who*. There was Menelik II, emperor of Ethiopia, traveling in state, and many years later his dejected successor, the diminutive but dignified Haile Selassie, on his way to his London exile after Mussolini's army had overrun his country; Cardinal Pacelli—later Pope Pius XII—on an inspection tour of Europe's southeastern dioceses; statesmen and diplomats, such as Pierre Laval, the French prime minister (executed after the Second World War for collaboration with the Nazis), traveling to Little Entente conferences; Sir Robert Vansittart, the head of the British Foreign Office, on futile diplomatic errands to dissuade Balkan rulers from falling into Hitler's lap; Sir Maurice Hankey, the *éminence grise* behind half a dozen British cabinets, who insisted on taking ice-cold baths every morning during his journeys. Theodor Herzl, the founder of Zionism, was bound from Vienna for Constantinople for secret negotiations with the Turks to secure the Jewish homeland, and Chaim Weizmann, later to become the first President of the State of Israel, on similar business, perhaps traveling on the same train as did Shibly Jemal Effendi, who pleaded on behalf of the Arabs with the Sultan to stop Jewish immigration into Palestine.

Before 1914 a young American engineer, Herbert Hoover, was a frequent passenger surveying proposed oil fields from Rumania to Baku —hardly yet dreaming of becoming the thirty-first President of the United States in 1928. After the First World War the Simplon Orient Express carried many noted Americans who had adopted the French and Italian Rivieras as their second homes—Elsa Maxwell, the professional hostess; Sara and Gerald Murphy, the expatriate painter; Scott Fitzgerald, the novelist. Of the train Fitzgerald wrote: "Unlike American trains, absorbed in an intense destiny of their own and scornful of people in another world less swift and breathless, this train was part of the country through which it passed. Its breath stirred the dust from the palm leaves, the cinders mingled with the dry dung in the gardens . . ."

The catalogue of famous stars of the theater, concert stage, cinema, and—in the dying days of the Orient Express—also of television, is long and impressive.

One of the most famous as well as the earliest passengers was Sarah Bernhardt. For some twenty years she frequently traveled on the Orient Express, particularly between Paris, Germany, Vienna, Budapest, and Bucharest. Every *conducteur* of the train willingly indulged the great tragedienne's whims—and there were many—knowing that he was serving "the greatest actress of the century."

Eleonora Duse, the great Sarah's Italian counterpart, was born in a railroad car near Pavia, and all her life found delight in train journeys. With her ensemble she toured central and southeastern Europe, using the Orient Express whenever possible.

An English actor-manager, Edward Stirling, founded in 1920 the

English Players, a company which for the next twenty years toured Central Europe and the Balkans with a repertoire that ranged from Shakespeare to Edgar Wallace whodunnits; on their travels they became a feature of the Orient Express. It often happened that during the long journeys passengers were treated after meals in the restaurant car to improvised rehearsals. Despite language difficulties the English Players always had full houses not only in the capital cities but even in such sleepy towns as Szeged, Timişoara, Constanţa, Plovdiv, or Nish.

Among latter-day stars of stage and music hall, whose names are still well remembered, peregrinating between Paris, Vienna, Budapest, and even Constantinople were Lucien and Sacha Guitry, the immortal Mistinguett, Maurice Chevalier, and Marlene Dietrich. And there was rarely an Orient Express run without a few international cabaret and circus performers, a troupe of Ziegfeld or Garrick Gaieties girls—or their imitators—giggling and showing off their shapely legs; trapeze artistes flexing their muscles by hanging from baggage racks, and frequently also the famous clown Grock, who, as a young man named Adrien Wettach, had been the French teacher to the children of Count István Bethlen, one-time Hungarian prime minister, and became a celebrated acrobat, tightrope walker, and juggler. Circus and music-hall attractions were the most popular forms of entertainment in the Balkan capitals before and after the First World War, and the Orient Express carried the performers on their profitable tours. One of the most frequent passengers was the American-born conjurer Harry Houdini, whose ostensible phenomena of spiritualist séances performed by mechanical tricks kept cabaret audiences in every capital and city between Vienna and Constantinople even more spellbound than those in Western Europe and America.

But the number of famous stars of the world of music and ballet traveling on the Orient Express far exceeded that of the theater and music hall. It seems that every great conductor, concert virtuoso, prima donna, and prima ballerina had at one time or another traveled on the Express in its eighty-year history. Their names, taken at random from the rosters of the Compagnie, read like a dictionary of music. There was Gustav Mahler, who conducted in many European capitals and eventually became the director of the New York Philharmonic, Hans von Bülow, Max Bruch, even Debussy, who made some rare appearances on the concert podium, Wolf-Ferrari and De Lara—the latter best known as the inaugurator of the Monte Carlo Opera—Mascagni, the composer of *Cavalleria Rusticana*, and, in a later era, Richard Strauss, who conducted the *Rosenkavalier* and his controversial *Salome*, and the celebrated exponents of the Viennese operetta, Franz Lehár and Oscar Straus. At the turn of the century the violin virtuosi Eugène Ysaÿe and Joseph Joachim were given, on Nagelmackers' orders, reserved compartments to enable them to rehearse in the train. Another famous violinist was Jan Kubelik, who had been a prodigy at the age of eight. The renowned Austrian violinist Fritz Kreisler hurried aboard the Orient Express and the Simplon Express from one concert hall to another for many years, as did his French colleague Jacques Thibaud, who in later years changed to air travel and died in a plane crash.

Thibaud has a special page in the Wagons-Lits annals. On one of his many journeys he was fast asleep when the Orient Express stopped at the Vienna Westbahnhof and a sharp knock by a conscientious attendant at his compartment door reminded him that he had a concert that evening at Vienna's Konzerthaus. Only half-awake, Thibaud grabbed a small suitcase and alighted, leaving behind a double-case containing his two precious instruments, a Stradivarius and an Amati, worth several million francs. One of the attendants noticed the case, grabbed it and ran along the platform to the station's exit just as the drowsy virtuoso was stepping into a cab. The man had just enough time to throw the violin case into the cab through a window and to run back and jump onto the already moving train. The next morning Thibaud came to the Vienna Wagons-Lits office and asked that an envelope be forwarded to the attendant who not only had rescued the priceless violins but had also saved Thibaud's concert. In the envelope were five 1,000-franc bills and a note: *"Merci cinq milles fois!"* The Compagnie's standing rule was that their employees must not accept rewards "for services rendered in the course of duty"; in this case the attendant was allowed to keep 1,000 francs; the rest was deposited in a special fund benefiting the entire personnel.

Among the famous conductors the most frequent passenger was

Arturo Toscanini, who raised his baton in concert halls the world over. Sometimes he traveled with his family—his daughter Wanda was the wife of the great pianist Vladimir Horowitz—and Roger Commault recalls one in particular of the many meetings he had with Toscanini. In the 1920s the Wagons-Lits management introduced "soft music" to be played on gramophones in the restaurant cars. One day in 1929, it was Commault's turn to be the disc jockey—at that time neither this term nor an electric automatic record changer had been invented— which meant putting a new record on the turntable every few minutes. Sitting in a tiny glass-fronted cubicle, he interspersed dance music with the inevitable "selections" from Johann Strauss waltzes and Viennese operettas until he suddenly spied Toscanini and his companions at one of the tables. Frantically Commault searched through his record cabinet and found a few discs of Verdi's and Bizet's operas. Toscanini was at that time the musical director of La Scala in Milan, and Commault rightly assumed that the maestro would be pleased. After the meal Toscanini congratulated him on his good musical taste.

The passenger lists contained scores of names of celebrated musicians: pianists such as Moszkowski, Paderewski (who in 1919 was briefly prime minister of a reborn Poland); the composers De Falla and Rachmaninoff, among others; singers spanning the great years of opera— Caruso, Melba, Chaliapin (the basso known for his title role in *Boris Godunov*), and in later years, divas such as the tempestuous Maria Callas.

There were many times when entire ballet companies were aboard the Orient and the Simplon expresses, particularly after 1909, when Diaghilev introduced Russian ballet to the West and brought Fokine, Nijinsky, Pavlova, Massine, and Lifar to Paris. The company took the great cities of Europe by storm; after setting up his headquarters at Monte Carlo, Diaghilev regarded it his duty to take the Ballet Russe at least occasionally to his southern Slav brethren. One old headwaiter recalled that on one of the company's tours he served Pavlova, Chaliapin, Sacha Guitry, and the novelist André Maurois at the same table.

At about the time Diaghilev's company appeared in Paris the San Francisco–born dancer Isadora Duncan began to tour Europe. She was a rigid opponent of the classical ballet and dancing *en pointe* and created a sensation by her interpretation of Greek dances which, she claimed, were reconstructions from vase paintings of ancient Greece. For her dancing she favored diaphanous costumes and veils. Her unconventional behavior during her journeys on the Orient Express often enthralled passengers and attendants alike. When strolling from her compartment to the shower cabin at the end of the car she would wear what one *conducteur* described as something "much less than a veil—rather, something in the size of a handkerchief, and in the wrong place, too."

Another celebrated dancer, who traveled the route during the *belle époque* and contributed to the popular designation of the Orient Express as "The Mystery Train," was Margaretha Gertrud Zelle, who achieved worldwide notoriety as Mata Hari, "the most dangerous woman spy." She was born in 1876 in a small town in Holland, where her father kept a store. At the age of nineteen she married an officer of the Dutch Colonial Army, Rudolph MacLeod, whose family was of Scottish descent. For her it was a marriage of convenience; her mother had died some years earlier and her father had become bankrupt. Margaretha was glad to escape poverty and hoped for a secure and comfortable life in Java in the Dutch East Indies, where her husband, more than twenty years her senior, was stationed. But MacLeod was a drunkard, his health was affected, and a few years later the couple returned to Holland and lived on a meager pension. The marriage broke down and Margaretha, a determined young woman, decided to go to Paris in search of adventure. She later told journalists that she arrived there "with half a franc in my pocket but went straight to the Grand Hotel." Soon she had a string of men friends, mostly elderly gentlemen, who kept her in comfort. She might have lived happily ever after as a courtesan if somebody had not suggested that she should try to become a dancer. She had no professional dancing training at all, but in Java she had often watched Oriental ritual dancers; pretending to know all about Hindu and Malayan dancing of the bayaderes, she presented herself to Guimet, the owner of the Oriental Museum, where Indian and Arabian dancing ensembles occasionally staged performances.

What impressed Guimet even more than her art was her offer to dance in the nude—the first woman ever to do so in Paris, as she later insisted. Guimet invented for her the name Mata Hari, which means in Malayan "the eye of day." Her success was instantaneous, even though her dancing routine was entirely improvised. Soon she was the star of the Folies-Bergères and her tours through Europe took her to every capital of the Continent—to Berlin, St. Petersburg, Madrid, Rome. She had also acquired a large number of admirers and lovers among distinguished and influential personages, including the rich German industrialist Kiepert, the French ambassador Cambon, Count Gyula Andrássy (an Austro-Hungarian Cabinet minister), the composer Massenet, and the German diplomat Baron von Krohn, who at the beginning of the First World War became one of the chiefs of the Kaiser's secret service. On the behest of one of her friends, Baron Henri de Rothschild, she went to Vienna and "conquered the Austro-Hungarian Empire," traveling on the Orient Express as far as Bucharest. Her friendship with Baron von Krohn was to prove fatal. In 1916 she was in France and decided to visit Madrid, where Von Krohn had set up a German espionage outpost. Returning from Spain to Holland, she was taken off the ship at Falmouth, suspected of being a German spy. But British intelligence let her go; there was no evidence that she had ever obtained any secrets other than idle gossip. But when she later returned to France, where a spy mania was rampant, she was arrested, tried, and sentenced to death. One of the gravest accusations against her was that she had maintained an amorous contact with the French war minister Messimy and had seduced him into betraying war secrets, which she was supposed to have communicated to Von Krohn. Although some people of influence pleaded for her reprieve, she was executed by a firing squad on October 15, 1917. The Mata Hari myth became one of the classic stories of espionage, but it is extremely doubtful whether she had ever been an effective spy at all, even though she was undoubtedly involved in some sordid intrigues.

In January 1936 the Simplon Orient Express carried another passenger who suffered a similar fate. It was the burly, bemedaled Soviet Marshal Mikhail Nikolaevich Tukhachevski, Stalin's minister of war. With a procession of monarchs and foreign statesmen he was on his way to London as the Soviet representative for the funeral of King George V. He and his suite had arrived by sea in Mussolini's fascist

Italy in order to avoid traveling through Hitler's Nazi Germany. The marshal joked with the train's staff and tipped them generously. In May 1937 the Soviet delegation for the coronation of King George VI was headed by the foreign affairs commissar Maxim Litvinov, who took the similar route. On the train was an attendant who had served Tukhachevski and he ventured to ask Litvinov why the marshal did not come on this occasion. Litvinov told him that "the marshal was otherwise detained," a cryptic but entirely accurate explanation. Tukhachevski, along with seven other generals and many hundreds of high-ranking Red Army officers, had been arrested on Stalin's order during the "great purges," and on June 12 it was announced in Moscow that the marshal and other "traitors" had been sentenced to death and executed by firing squads.

DURING THE HALCYON YEARS OF THE ORIENT EXPRESS BEFORE THE rivalry of the Great Powers of Europe culminated in the First World War, the "Eastern question" and the situation in the Balkans were in the foreground of political intrigue.

Inevitably, the struggle for mastery among the Great Powers led to a vastly increased activity of their espionage services, which were emerging as a powerful instrument of political manipulations and military strategy.

The Orient Express, running on much of its route through Europe's most sensitive areas, became the vehicle for the movements of secret agents of many nations and the channel through which information was passed. Its gratifying designation as the Royal Train was almost replaced by the much less flattering one of the Spies' Express.

Many of the secret agents came to bless the existence of the Orient Express, which made their jobs so much easier and their travels much more comfortable. An excellent cover in those days was to be an English "milord," preferably a real peer, or just being taken for one. From the days of the grand tour—beloved by English aristocrats—Europeans and, in particular, Levantines had accepted that wealthy and pleasure-loving "milords" were devoted to travel for travel's sake. The niceties of the British titular system were lost on these people—any gentleman speaking nothing but English, demanding in his requirements, and generous in his rewards for services could rely on being deferentially addressed as "milord."

Some of the most successful British agents were of German ancestry and thus provided a match for the many German spies who infiltrated the Balkans and the Turkish Empire. Lord Edward Gleichen was the son of the Duke of Hohenlohe-Langenburg, who had married into the British royal family. His memoirs are often quoted because of the hackneyed incidents of spies chewing and swallowing secret messages, a practice now dismissed as the product of thriller writers' imagination. But Gleichen did in fact engage in such indigestible activity. Awaiting the Orient Express at the station of Czaribrod in Serbia, he saw two policemen approaching. In his notebook he had scribbled some coded signals ready for transmission as soon as he could reach the safety of a British legation or consulate; he tore out the pages, stuffed them into his mouth, and swallowed them. But the policemen only asked him politely to give them a match to light their cigarettes.

Another British agent was Lieutenant Colonel Richard Meinertz-hagen, whose family hailed from the Rhineland. Under an assumed name he had served for two years as a private soldier in the German army, and later operated as a spy against the Turks, often traveling on the Orient Express. After identifying spies working for Germany— sometimes doing so by pleasant chats during the long hours on the Orient Express—he would find out their addresses so as to further the new friendship and then send a letter thanking them for their information, enclosing money in payment. Meantime he would arrange it so that the German intelligence chiefs were informed that their man was a double agent. German security men would arrive at the victim's place and find the incriminating note and the money. In vain the victim would protest that he had been framed. Several German spies were shot as a result of this trick.

One of the regular travelers on the Orient Express in the early part of the century was known to the staff as "the trick man" because of his habit of entertaining his fellow passengers at the end of a meal in the restaurant car with conjuring tricks. He was Major Lionel Branson, operating as an agent in Southeast Europe. Appropriately, his code name was Wizard. At one time a vice president of the Magic Circle of professional illusionists, he used his dexterity to strike up friendships with likely sources of information. The identity of another man frequently on the train on mystifying errands was a meek-looking clergyman, who disappeared for weeks on end in Turkey, an unprofitable place for converting people to Christianity. After the breakup of the Ottoman Empire it was admitted that he had been Agent XB9 and a highly successful spy, but it was revealed only much later that he was indeed a man in holy orders, the Reverend John Hawkins—a pastor of the Reformed Church—and, in the crucial years, head of the British Secret Intelligence Service in Constantinople.

One of the characters well known to the personnel of the Orient Express during the last decade of the nineteenth century was a thin, diffident Englishman who was to gain world fame in a very different sphere. He was in the habit of joining and leaving the train at small, lonely stations in Austria-Hungary and the Balkans when the train stopped for just a few minutes to take water and fuel. The sleeping-car attendants usually arranged that this unassuming passenger had a compartment to himself—not because of any bad habits that might have offended another passenger sharing accommodations with him, but because he always insisted on the heating being turned off and the windows lowered even in winter and inclement weather. Inevitably this regular passenger was classified as an English eccentric, a view supported by the paraphernalia he always brought with him: nets on long poles, preserving jars, sketching pads, illustrated manuals—the equipment of an enthusiastic butterfly and moth collector.

Robert Baden-Powell was then in his early thirties. His whipcord-like body and heavy tan were not the result of forays in pursuit of lepidoptera under the summer sun of mountain and valley in remote areas of Eastern Europe, but from his soldiering in Afghanistan and India. After 1887, with the convenient status of "assistant military secretary" in South Africa and Malta, he was given leave by the British War Office to indulge his passion for butterflies—and more utilitarian pursuits. Baden-Powell, famous as the founder of the worldwide Boy Scout movement, was an intelligence agent, or as this down-to-earth man preferred to be known when he wrote *My Adventures as a Spy* in 1915, by the more forthright designation of a "spy." One of his earliest assignments was in Russia. He had been sent there to obtain information about a new type of machine gun the Russian army was supposed to be testing, as well as about the design and performance of an observation balloon, a French invention for which the Czarist General Staff had bought the patent.

As it was clearly inadvisable again to trespass on Russian territory, Baden-Powell then transferred his explorations to Austria-Hungary and the Balkan countries—including Turkey—the lands through which the Orient Express conveniently provided a ready means of entry and, if need be, rapid exit. It was reasonable, as any lepidopterist would have confirmed, to seek new specimens for his collection by exploring those areas forbidden to the general public where the butterflies by day, and especially the moths by night, could flourish without molestation. In short, fortification zones were Baden-Powell's targets on more than one count. He was able to roam around the Dalmatian coast (now part of Yugoslavia) making drawings of naval installations at Ragusa, Spalato, and the Bay of Cattaro, often aided by friendly Austrian police and naval guards, who were intrigued by the hobby of this eccentric Englishman. Many admired the visitor's skillful sketches of butterflies, though all too often he had failed to net them, and some of the interested observers of his artwork may well have wondered why they themselves had never seen the rarities recorded on the pages of the sketch pad. In fact the drawings of blobs, lines, and squiggles of the butterflies' wings formed a color-coded plan of fortifications, to be redrawn to scale later. They proved of inestimable value when the First World War broke out, enabling British and Italian warships to pinpoint their targets.

Many years after Baden-Powell ceased his activities as a spy and stopped using the Orient Express, another colorful agent began patronizing the train. "I have traveled so much on Europe's expresses that the retention of individual railway journeys defeats my memory," Sir Robert Bruce Lockhart wrote discreetly in one of his volumes of memoirs,* the first of which was titled *Memoirs of a British Agent.* Held prisoner by the Russians until an even exchange was worked out with a captive Russian spy, Lockhart and his operations were transferred from Russia to Central and Southeastern Europe, his headquarters

*Retreat from Glory, Putnam, London, 1934.

moving from town to town along the familiar Orient Express route—
Vienna, Prague, Zagreb, Budapest, and Belgrade. Those who demanded to know what his vocation was were told that he represented
the British Trade Corporation and the Anglo-Austrian Bank. Whatever the records of these commercial enterprises may have contained,
there was another file on Lockhart in the British Foreign Office, listing
him as a member of the Political Intelligence Department. His work
on its behalf was at least as conscientious as for the trading company
and the bank. His main interest was Hungary, its social and economic
fabric ripped to pieces by a couple of revolutions. Hungary was in effect
a battlefield on which the new ideology of communism and that of
Western democracy, plus the even newer concept of fascism, rehearsed
the bigger clashes to come. As a bulwark between the West and East,
capitalism and communism, Hungary was a vital source of news.
Friendships struck up on the Orient Express could prove a useful source
of information.

"On one of my journeys from Budapest to Germany I had as
companions in my compartment two Hungarian bankers," Lockhart
recalled, "who in that pleasant semi-Oriental manner which is characteristic of Central Europe conversation became intimate, and in an
hour or two I knew most of their life history and business. They were
taking shares and money, which they had successfully smuggled out of
Hungary, to Zurich and were highly pleased with themselves. They
talked glibly of the new dynasty of robber barons that had grown up
in Central Europe since the war and to which, on their own confession,
they obviously belonged."

The Hungarian bankers left the Orient Express at its first Swiss
station, insisting on carrying their heavy suitcases themselves, which
were probably filled with banknotes and gold and jewelry. "The Wagon-Lit *conducteur* came up to me," Lockhart recalled, " 'Excuse me,
sir,' he said, 'those friends of yours were rich men or poor men?' 'I do
not know them,' I replied, 'but they said they were bankers and from
the contents of the portfolios they seemed to be rich.' The *conducteur*
grunted. 'I thought so,' he said. Then he pulled out two Hungarian
notes. 'There's their tip, and they gave me more trouble than half a
dozen American millionaires.' He threw the money down on the seat

in a passion of disgust. The equivalent in English money was about threepence. It was a curious sidelight on robber-barons psychology."

Such men, by the standards of patriotism and honesty prevailing in Hungary at the time, were quite mild offenders. Defrauding the government, people, and commerce was a way of life. The personnel on the Orient Express were only too well aware of some undesirable passengers who regularly traveled from Budapest to Paris, going first class and tipping lavishly. Some of the women were well-known cabaret artistes, some no more than prostitutes, and many of the men the typically furtive denizens of the crime world. Behind one particular fraud were Count Andrássy, a member of one of Europe's oldest and noble families, and a group of aristocrats, high army officers, and businessmen. Their secret printing presses had produced almost perfect forgeries of French franc bills to the value of several hundred millions. The counterfeit bills were transported on the Orient Express and eventually unloaded on French banks and the public in exchange for genuine francs, U.S. dollars and British sterling. The fraud was uncovered by the French Sûreté, but despite official protests to the Hungarian government, the conspirators received only mild sentences, their defense that their enterprise was really a patriotic move being regarded as extenuating circumstances.

There were always some ladies of doubtful virtue among the passengers of the Orient Express, not necessarily engaged on any ulterior business, but belonging to the pathetic profession of pseudo-artistes, dispatched by dubious impresarios in Paris or Vienna to the Balkan capitals, with promises of remunerative engagements in night clubs and cabarets. Lockhart mentioned these ladies in his memoirs and noted how the attractions of these entertainers decreased the farther one traveled East while their age increased, until by the time they could find a job only in the more sleazy night spots of Constantinople or Cairo, they were haggard and squalid. It was a one-way route, ending in the oblivion of some brothel.

Lockhart recalled the jaded women he saw on this downward path when, with a friend, he visited a night club in Belgrade, where the Serbian view prevailed that "a woman was a woman and a drink a drink, and both had to be bought as cheaply as possible." The place was well patronized by Serbian army officers—potentially useful for information once they had drunk enough to become garrulous—and there were nine or ten *Animierdamen,* dancing partners and available for additional pleasures. The fawning proprietor recommended to Lockhart a girl named Liesl, who, he claimed, had just arrived from a well-known night club in Vienna. On an order from the proprietor she came to the table taken by Lockhart and his friend, and sang some interminable song in a hoarse voice. This dubious entertainment was interrupted when two men came into the smoke-filled room. One Lockhart recognized as a Belgrade police officer; the other he had never seen before.

He looked more like a bull than a man. He seemed to have no neck, and his huge shaven head stood out like a cannon ball on his massive shoulders. He had a chest like a stallion's front. His legs were like tree trunks. His eyes flashed with a villainous fire. But it was his hands that fascinated me. They were gnarled, immensely strong, and as large as hams. He was, I think, the most powerful man I have ever seen. His arrival created a depressing silence. The waiters deserted us. The girls in the corner whispered and shivered. Liesl became suddenly grave. "Be careful," she said. "That is Luna, the famous Komitaji leader. He comes from the Macedonian frontier and fights against the Bulgarians. He is as strong and brave as a lion. When he's in a good temper he's not so bad. When he's angry God help you . . . He's killed twenty-five men with his own hands and is proud of it."

Three years passed before the paths of Lockhart and the Macedonian crossed. Both got on the same Orient Express bound for Nish. This border post was then a checkpoint for the Yugoslav police to search for wanted terrorists. Passengers were ordered off the train to be searched and their baggage inspected. Luna swaggered to the end door of the car and lounged at the bottom of the steps. A police officer ordered him to open his bulky valise, with the predictable reaction from Luna. "You swine," he roared. "You ask me, Luna, to open my baggage? You don't know me? I'll show you!" Whereupon he reached for the policeman's throat. His victim evidently did know Luna, at least by reputation. He managed to draw his pistol and shot his would-be strangler through the heart. The Macedonian's reputation for dealing with those who thwarted him evidently survived him. The unfortunate police officer's reward for killing a madman in self-defense was three years' imprisonment. This incident was, by the way, one of the very few killings that actually happened in or alongside the famous train.

Amid the motley of spies traveling on the Orient Express on spurious business and hiding under false identities there were, year after year, the overt and known bearers of state secrets—the King's (and Queen's) messengers of the United Kingdom and their brothers-in-duty, the *couriers diplomatiques* of France. Since the inception of the Wagons-Lits both governments had contracts with Nagelmackers' Compagnie, which provided reserved compartments once a week on the train, the cost being paid whether the accommodation was used or not. The first reference to a King's Messenger goes back to 1432, when one Robert Asshwell was paid four pence ha'penny a day for his foreign travels. Messengers know nothing of the contents of their diplomatic bags, but are expected to defend them with their lives. They must travel without wife, family members, or companions, but usually an armed escort is provided. One of the old-timers, Major Martin Haworth-Leslie, who wrote his reminiscences in *The Silver Greyhound,* named after the emblem worn by the messengers for centuries as a royal badge, told how on one occasion he was ordered to escort animals for the private zoo of the Sultan of Turkey—including an elephant, a tiger, and tropical birds picked up at the Vienna stop.

Toward the end of the nineteenth century, when the British Foreign Office began to regularly use the Orient Express, about a dozen messengers were employed to carry the elaborately sealed bags to and from the embassies and consulates in all the capitals and principal towns on the route. By 1914 there were six of them making twenty-six journeys a year on the Orient Express. Though modestly called messengers, they were always retired officers, up to the rank of colonel, often with distinguished war records and highly decorated. Sometimes for reasons of diplomacy the British government fulfilled odd requests of Balkan kings. Captain Philip Wynter carried a cage of eight canaries from London, and was told to play to the birds on a penny whistle to encourage them to sing during the train journey so that they would arrive in perfect condition. A messenger's dignity was subjected to more than the usual strain when Ferdinand of Bulgaria, an avid entomologist, put a request to the Foreign Office in London for a clutch of eggs of a rare moth indigenous to Scotland. The eggs were duly collected on the royal estate of Balmoral and packed in a lined box. The warmth of the sleeping compartment resulted in premature hatching, and the messenger spent the last day and night of his journey searching for caterpillars crawling into every crevice of the Orient Express car.

Officers of the French Deuxième Bureau were probably the least conspicuous of the secret agents who used the Orient Express. Always strictly observing old-world courtesy, impeccably dressed, and sometimes accompanied by elegant and beautiful women, they could easily pose as idle tourists on pleasure trips, or as academics traveling to Balkan capitals on lecturing assignments. Indeed, French professors, physicians and surgeons were always being invited by universities or called by wealthy Rumanians and Greeks for medical treatment. Thus agents were able to blend into groups of other French passengers without arousing suspicion. French industrial companies and banks had substantial investments in many Balkan countries, particularly in Rumania and Yugoslavia, where they controlled oil fields and mines and provided managers and mining experts.

One of the most remarkable French agents who commuted on the Orient Express was Leon Wenger. He was the head of a Franco-British team which, in 1916, just before Rumania's entry into the war on the side of Germany, accomplished a devastating sabotage action in the oil fields of Ploesti in order to prevent them from falling under German control. Shortly before the outbreak of the Second World War in 1939, Wenger, by then an elderly man, led a team of sixty French and British secret agents, many of them skilled technicians, in an attempt to duplicate the 1916 sabotage exploit. The French and British intelligence had intercepted Nazi plans for a thrust into the Balkans, which, it was believed, would be executed soon after the inevitable outbreak of war.

The sabotage team traveled in small groups on the four last Orient Express trains that ran in the late summer of 1939. The agents, with the help of some Rumanians, were able to carry out only a partial destruction of the oil refineries at Ploesti and Targoviste. In the event, Hitler did not send his troops into Yugoslavia, Rumania, and Bulgaria until the spring of 1941, but the Balkans were swarming with Nazi spies ever since he came to power in 1933.

Until air travel became reliable and widespread in the 1930s, the Orient Express and the ancillary Wagons-Lits services that provided connections with it—such as the Paris-Stuttgart-Prague-Warsaw Express, started in 1920, and the Nord-Express, which connected Paris, Berlin, and Warsaw—were always the principal means of travel for the secret agents of all the great powers. The Soviet Union, emerging from the chaos of revolution and civil war, created its espionage system within an amazingly short period and built it into the largest and most powerful in the world. Thousands of Soviet spies, political emissaries, and agitators of the Comintern traveled on the Wagons-Lits expresses crisscrossing Europe. In addition, there were Stalin's "traveling executioners," who located exiles and defectors and disposed of them, particularly after Trotsky's expulsion from the Communist Party and his eventual deportation to Turkey, where he was interned on the island of Prinkipo, south of Constantinople, between 1929 and 1933. In order to intercept Trotsky's contacts with his supporters in Western Europe, Stalin ordered special teams to commute between Constantinople and Paris, where in the mid-thirties several of Trotsky's secretaries and his son Lyova were murdered by Stalin's executioners. Soviet agents also used the Wagons-Lits trains to reach Spain during the early phases of the Spanish Civil War. After the Second World War one could still detect the taciturn Soviet agents, in their ankle-length coats and black wide-rimmed hats, on the Direct-Orient Express on their errands to and from the Communist-dominated Balkan countries, but like the spies of other nations, they, too, eventually took to air transport.

Last but not least, American operators deserve a mention. In the decades up to the First World War the United States had no institutionalized secret service at all, and agents of the State and War departments sent to Europe used the Orient Express routes as diplomats and military attachés. But after 1919, following the realignment of power blocs and the enormous development in the oil-producing areas of the Near and Middle East, American finance poured in to exploit mineral and natural resources. The investments needed protection, and Washington began to collate information on both the political and the economic fronts. The intelligence activities were rather haphazard and uncoordinated. Tactics used by the British were adopted, with newspaper men, archaeologists, and missionaries working as amateur but effective operators.

One of the most colorful of these agents was Reuben Markham, a Baptist missionary, who dropped off the Orient Express at various stations in the Balkans and preached his version of Christianity to an uninterested and often hostile population of pious Orthodox Christians and Muslims. To justify his continued presence he later became a *pro forma* correspondent of the *Christian Science Monitor.*

Many of these American agents became high-ranking officers of the OSS when it was formed at the start of the Second World War. Among them were Colonel William Eddy, born in Syria, and a U.S. army intelligence officer during the First World War, and his cousin, Harold Hoskins, born in Beirut. David K.E. Bruce, the distinguished American diplomat, who was successively U.S. ambassador to France, West Germany, and Britain, recounted in his memoirs how he was recommended for espionage service by Allen Dulles after serving as an artillery officer in France in 1918. His duties after the war required him to take on the Orient Express several times, and on some occasions he traveled with a Colt .45 strapped to his hip and a diplomatic pouch to his wrist. Later, as an ambassador, he frequently used the Wagons-Lits expresses, traveling much more comfortably.

American agents, generously supplied with funds, were regarded by the personnel of the Orient Express as "Yankee business millionaires" because of the large tips they distributed. Being dubbed a tycoon was a useful cover, which some of the top CIA operators, such as Colonel Meade (who operated via Turkey in Syria) or Kermit "Kim" Roosevelt, gladly accepted. In 1956 the Hungarian Communists accused the CIA of having sent "scores of agents" to assist in the revolution which for a few bloody days shook the Communist regime.

Now, like the Orient Express, the era of the secret agent following his own hunches and adopting somewhat ridiculous disguises is a chapter in past history. The traditional spy and his spy train are as dead as the steam locomotive; the bugging device, the probing satellite, the kidnap, and the political defection have taken over. But the most elaborate electronic device cannot fully replace the modern spy, who has become a highly trained technician, often indeed a scientist versed in nuclear physics, telecommunications, or complex armament technology and industrial production.

THRILLER WRITERS HAVE FREQUENTLY USED THE ORIENT EXPRESS AS THE scene of mysterious murders, but there is no conclusive evidence that any mayhem was ever actually committed aboard the train, perhaps with the exception of the Karpe case, described in Chapter Thirteen. However, stories of mysterious defenestrations were told on various occasions, and consistently denied by the Compagnie. One that was repeated in various versions and is best known was retold by Martin Page in his excellent book *Great Trains,* published in 1975. In a compartment of the Orient Express were two women and two men, one of them "a diminutive and silent Belgian." When the train entered a tunnel the lights suddenly went out. There was a piercing scream, and when the train emerged into daylight there were only three people in the compartment—the Belgian had disappeared. His body was found some miles further back on the track, the lining of his jacket ripped out. The three people who were with him in the compartment all swore that they had never met him before, had not exchanged a single word with him during the journey, and had neither felt nor heard any commotion until the terrible scream. Page attaches little credence to this story. Had it really happened, police would have conducted investigations, the fellow passengers would have been interrogated and carefully screened, and some official announcement would have been published. The Wagons-Lits Compagnie has no record of the alleged incident, nor have any of its employees ever been questioned about it.

A much more definite claim of foul play—attempted poisoning in the restaurant car, and not one but two murders and defenestrations —was made by two Simplon Orient Express passengers. Even though the stories contradict each other, they cannot be entirely discounted if only because of the solid reputation of the men who told them.

In his book *Guilt Edged,** Lieutenant Commander Merlin Min-

*Bachman & Turner, London, 1975.

shall described how he killed "a beautiful Nazi spy" on the Simplon Orient Express. An officer of British naval intelligence—during the war his operational chief was Commander Ian Fleming, later the creator of James Bond—Minshall was sent by the department to Rumania and was given the rank of vice-consul as cover. He traveled on the Simplon Orient Express with a Walther PPK pistol strapped to his shoulder and a .25 Beretta to his groin. He claims to have survived two attempts by German agents to kill him. During the journey a German agent tried to murder him by dropping poison into his wineglass during dinner in the restaurant car. Minshall relates that he killed the German in the corridor, quickly pushed the body into the toilet and bundled the dead German out of the window. It must have been a very small and thin German agent because the lavatory windows in all Wagons-Lits cars were narrow and could be opened only by lowering one frame of about eighteen square inches.

Minshall's story is disputed by one of his former colleagues, Lieutenant Commander Michael Henry Mason, a well-known author, traveler, explorer, and former commodore of the Royal Ocean Racing Club; he was also a Royal Navy boxing champion in his younger days. Mason stated that the Rumanian assignment Minshall described was in fact given to him and that it was he who had dispatched not one but two German agents by defenestration from the Simplon Orient Express. "Two fellows followed me into the dining car and watched me for half an hour or more," Mason told an interviewer.* "I'd let them think I'd drunk a lot but most of my wine went on the floor. I knew they'd be waiting to jump me in the corridor and there they were. I hit one under the heart and one in the jaw and out they went. I beat them insensible and threw them off through the lavatory window." Sir Alexander Glen, who during the last war occupied a high position in naval intelligence, confirmed Mason's story: "Mickey Mason is being typically modest; in fact, he broke both their necks in turn . . ." So, after all, at least some of the true stories about "Murder on the Orient Express" were more thrilling than fiction.

*London *Sunday Times*, September 28, 1975.

LIKE ANY LUXURY HOTEL IN THE BIG CITIES THE WORLD OVER, THIS hotel on wheels" was a haunt of international burglars, jewel thieves, and pickpockets. There were, of course, many cases of baggage rifling and some ladies lost their jewel cases with contents of very substantial value. On many occasions they themselves were to blame for the loss, having carelessly left the jewelry behind in the compartment when going to the restaurant cars. The Compagnie introduced an elaborate security system and eagle-eyed attendants patrolled the corridors, often locking the doors of the compartments left unlocked by passengers. In order to avoid untoward publicity, the Compagnie discreetly reimbursed the robbed passengers if for some reason the insurance companies refused to pay full indemnity.

More recently, when the Simplon Orient Express remained the only contemporary token of the past glory of the old Orient Express, the Compagnie and police authorities of several countries were faced with a new and much more serious problem: organized gangs of highly professional train robbers operating on French and Italian routes and using chloroform aerosol sprays to render their victims insensible. In January 1976 the head of the French railroad police, Commissioner J.C.Aure, stated that during ten months in 1975 more than two thousand complaints were received from passengers who traveled from Paris to Italy and Yugoslavia, or vice versa, of having been drugged and robbed in their compartments. "This was double the number of such incidents in the previous year and this kind of crime is on the increase," he said. The gangs usually consisted of four or five people and always included one or two well-dressed women, who strolled through the corridors to find the prospective victims. The female member of the gang looked for ladies traveling alone, sometimes engaged them in conversation and appraised the hand baggage. If satisfied with the prospects, she reported to the gang leader; two lookouts took positions at each end of the corridor and one of the robbers entered the compartment. With a flick of the hand he sprayed a strong chloroform spray at the victim, quickly rifled the handbag or hid it under his coat. The gangsters usually robbed no more than two or three passengers and then alighted at the next station to wait for another express train.

A typical victim during the Christmas week of 1975 was the Paris actress Annette Farnoux. She described her unnerving experience to a reporter of *France Soir:* "I was traveling on the Simplon Orient Express from Paris to Venice, having booked a first-class sleeping compartment. At about 11 P.M. I went to bed and was reading before falling asleep. I have only a vague memory as to what happened. I had fastened the movable little bolt on the door. I am a light sleeper and I must have waked up when I heard a faint noise at the door. I only saw a shadow and then I passed out. When I awoke after several hours I felt faint and had a very bad headache and feeling of nausea. My handbag with my jewel case and all the money, traveler's checks and passport had disappeared. Even a gold bracelet and a watch had been taken from my wrist."

The Italian police and the Paris *Police Judiciare* believed there was evidence that the train robber gangs were Algerians and Italians and were sometimes of mixed nationality. Despite greatly increased security and detectives traveling on most of the direct expresses, only one Yugoslav gang was caught on the Paris-Lyons-Turin route; in their possession were found several wallets—still stuffed with bills—several passports and jewelry with a total value of about 480,000 francs (about $100,000) which gives an idea of the enormous booty the gangs collected on even a single journey.

ALL THROUGH THE HISTORY OF THE ORIENT EXPRESS THERE WAS THE serious problem of smuggling. Half a century ago during the chaotic period of currency collapse in Central Europe, the smuggling of gold, jewelry, coins, rare postage stamps, objets d'art, and any valuables that could be exchanged for dollars or Swiss francs in the West was an almost respectable occupation. Compagnie personnel were fully aware that many of the Wagons-Lits's regular passengers were professional smugglers and couriers of finance syndicates. It was the responsibility of the customs men and frontier police to enforce the currency regulations of their countries. But many of these officials—in Austria, Italy, and particularly in the Balkan countries—either accepted bribes or conspired with the syndicates. An even bigger problem was presented by the drug smugglers. Turkey has been—right to the present time— one of the world's largest producers of opium. In the old days of the

Orient Express there was hardly a run without several smugglers carrying considerable quantities of hashish westward. In modern times this fairly harmless drug had given way to morphine, cocaine, and heroin, the smallest packets of which could make fortunes for the pushers who sold them to middlemen and addicts. For years drug smugglers, usually members and couriers of large and powerful syndicates, some controlled by the Mafia, used the Orient Express and its sister trains as virtually safe vehicles for their sordid trade. Many of them were known to the trains' personnel, but the Compagnie observed a neutral attitude. Customs men and frontier guards rarely apprehended the drug traffickers because at least some of them, and often the higher officials, were receiving regular payoffs from the syndicates. However, after the tightening of drug regulations in many countries and, particularly, after the establishment of Interpol, the Compagnie instructed their security guards to provide information on suspicious passengers, and in more recent years quite a number of dangerous drug smugglers were caught.

One of the top couriers of the large syndicates was the elegant and voluble "Slim" Souf, who was on the Orient Express that was snowed in for several days in November 1929 in eastern Thrace.* While all able-bodied passengers tried to assist the staff in digging out the cars buried in huge snowdrifts, Souf refused to leave his compartment, apparently fearing that someone might discover the contents of his bags. A year later, however, justice did catch up with him. On arrival on the Orient Express from Constantinople he was arrested at the Gare de l'Est in Paris, and several small parcels of heroin, weighing nine hundred grams and worth about a million francs on the drug market, were found on him. Within a single year Souf had made twenty trips on the Orient Express.

IN ITS LONG HISTORY THE FAMOUS TRAIN MET WITH SURPRISINGLY few accidents. There were a few mishaps in the early years, which offended Nagelmackers' sense of excellence and perfection, such as the time the train was held for almost twenty-four hours in 1894 at the station of Tchtaldja because of an outbreak of cholera in the region. A German doctor in Turkish service officiously imposed a quarantine

*See p. 216.

Railroad Revolution

Among the rich it was not uncommon to own a railroad car for social purposes. George M. Pullman set the pace with his "P.P.C." (Pullman's private car). It was constructed in 1877 at a cost of about $50,000. Here is the dining room, which boasted, among other things, an organ.

Colonel William d'Alton Mann (*sitting*), the American entrepreneur and adventurer, with Georges Nagelmackers, his partner in the endeavor to introduce sleeping cars in Europe, in front of Mann's "boudoir sleeping car" in 1872. (*Photo Wagons-Lits*)

George Mortimer Pullman, the creator of the "palace sleeping cars" on American railroads. (*Wide World Photos*)

The admission card for Georges Nagelmackers to the Paris World Exhibition in 1878. He was then thirty-three years old, and having taken over Mann's assets, had established the Compagnie Internationale des Wagons-Lits.

Two caricatures in the satirical magazines *Le Cri du Peuple (top)* by G. Julio in 1907 and *(bottom) Le Cri de Paris* by Roubille in 1902 depict him enjoying free trips on the Orient Express. He spent more time abroad than in his capital, Brussels, and was known never to tip conductors and porters.

King Leopold II of the Belgians, a Saxe-Coburg princeling and first cousin of Queen Victoria, was a shrewd business manipulator and a notorious womanizer. He solicited important contacts for Nagelmackers in exchange for generous banking facilities. Note the pretty nude girls in his head and beard in a contemporary satirical portrait.

A cartoon shows King Leopold with his mistress Cléo de Merode. This liaison gained him the nickname of "King Cléopold." (*Cartoon from* Paris Match)

The first office of Nagelmackers' Compagnie in his hometown of Liège, Belgium, was in a small building belonging to a printing works. *(Photo Archives Wagons-Lits)*

Georges Nagelmackers at the height of his success as president of the Compagnie Internationale des Wagons-Lits and des Grands Express Européens, which now ran sleeping and restaurant cars on three continents. *(Portrait by Nadar)*

One of the earliest sleeping cars with one door and open end used in the 1870s on the first services between Paris and Cologne.

Sleeping car No. 75 with bogies, with three double and two single compartments and separate toilets, as used for the inaugural Orient Express journey in 1883.

The inaugural journey of the Orient Express in October 1883 from Paris to Constantinople. The train, consisting of a mail fourgon, two sleeping cars, a restaurant car, and a baggage fourgon, was hauled by a French Est 500-class 2-4-0 locomotive on its two-thousand-mile journey. (*Engraving by Peyot*)

The French novelist Edmond About, another distinguished traveler on the inaugural journey.

Opper de Blowitz, the renowned correspondent of the London *Times*.

King Carol of Rumania and Queen Elizabeth (the poetess Carmen Sylva). (*Photo BBC Hulton Library*)

The bizarre Palace of Peles at Sinaia, where the Orient Express party was entertained by the Rumanian monarch. (*Photo Romanian Tourist Office*)

The Royal Train

The luxurious interior of one of the *salon* cars which Nagelmackers provided for his illustrious passengers. This car was one of three built for the President of the French Republic, Félix Faure, on the occasion of the visit of Czar Nicholas II and the Czarina to Paris. *(Photo Wagons-Lits)*

Some of the destination plaques of the Direct-Orient Express and the Simplon Orient Express.

A ladies' drawing room in one of the special *salon* cars. *(Photo Wagons-Lits)*

Calouste Sarkis Gulbenkian, the Armenian oil tycoon who became famous as "Mr. Five Percent," having negotiated the merger of several companies from which the Shell Co. emerged, and helped to create the BP British Petroleum Co. *(Photo Popperfoto)*

Gulbenkian's son Nubar with his wife. Fleeing from Turkish persecution of the Armenians, he was brought from Constantinople to Paris aboard the Orient Express wrapped in a rolled carpet. Nubar, too, became a frequent passenger. *(Photo BBC Hulton Library)*

The mysterious armament king, Sir Basil Zaharoff, who rescued a Spanish duchess from a murderous attack by her husband on the Orient Express, later married her and gave her the Casino of Monte Carlo as a wedding present. For years Compartment No. 7 was reserved for him on his regular trips on the famous train. *(Photo BBC Hulton Library)*

Sir Ernest Cassel, financier and friend of King Edward VII. He had extensive business interests in the Ottoman Empire and was another famous Orient Express traveler. *(Portrait by Zorn in the Broadlands Collection)*

The young King Alfonso XIII of Spain being greeted in Paris by the French President Armand Faillères in 1908 on one of his Orient Express journeys. *(Photo Collection Commault)*

Many crowned heads of Europe were frequent passengers of the "Royal Train." At the christening, in 1923 in Belgrade, of Crown Prince Peter of Yugoslavia (later King Peter II, deposed by Marshal Tito) were *(from left to right)* his father, King Alexander; Queen Elizabeth of Greece; King Ferdinand of Rumania; the Duke and Duchess of York (later King George VI and Queen Mother Elizabeth). The baby is held by Queen Marie of Rumania. *(Photo BBC Hulton Library)*

A smoking room in a *salon* car of 1899 with heavy leather fauteuils providing the ambience of an exclusive London club. *(Photo Wagons-Lits)*

King Boris of Bulgaria was, like his father King Ferdinand, a railroad buff, insisting on driving the Orient Express through his country and on one occasion causing a serious accident. *(Photo BBC Hulton Library)*

A poster for the Simplon Orient Express of 1929, after a direct route from Paris had been extended to Constantinople (renamed Istanbul in March 1930). The original Simplon Orient Express was inaugurated in April 1919, connecting Paris with Belgrade, Bucharest, and Athens via Brig in Switzerland, the Simplon Tunnel, Milan, Venice, Trieste and Zagreb, and avoiding postwar Germany and Austria.

An advertisement of the Wagons-Lits Compagnie in 1901 for the route of the Ostende-Constanţa run of the Orient Express, providing a connection with London, and another by sea from Constanţa in Rumania to Constantinople. The entire journey from London to the Turkish capital took seventy-one hours. (*Prints from the Archives of the Wagons-Lits Co.*)

One of the earliest restaurant cars equipped with bogies being cleaned at the old Gare de Strasbourg in Paris. The cars were built of teak timber. Although the kitchen was tiny, gargantuan meals were produced and service was impeccable. *(Photo Wagons-Lits)*

Luxury and Gluttony

Some interiors of an early sleeping car. The pantry next to the kitchen contained some of the wine stores; more supplies were in a separate fourgon. The stove produced the heating for the cars. An attendant in each car watched over the passengers' comfort. Lotions and pomades were freely provided in the toilets, and beneath the marble basin was a cupboard containing chamber pots discreetly called "vases." *(Artist's engravings* in L'Illustration, *Paris)*

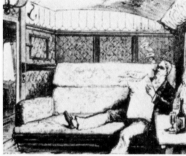

One of the luxurious single compartments where the berth was disguised as a sofa for daytime use.

The rich décor of the dining car included paneling of mahogany and teak inlaid with rosewood, gilded racks and brackets, and original paintings by Delacroix, Schwind, and Seymour. The chairs were covered with hand-embossed leather; cutlery was of solid silver, plates of Sèvres porcelain, glasses of Baccarat crystal. *(Engravings in Wagons-Lits Archives)*

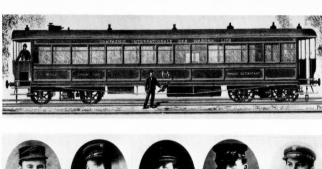

The dining car, No. 148, built for the inaugural journey in 1883. An axle box ran red-hot and the car had to be replaced at Munich by a less luxurious one, but the meals continued to satisfy the most demanding gourmets. *(Engraving in Wagons-Lits Archives)*

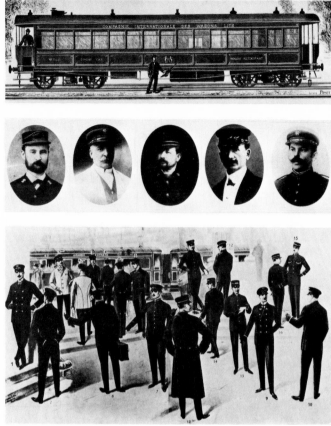

From left to right: conductor in 1883, attendant in 1890, waiter in 1900, *chef de train* in 1914, senior conductor in 1925.

Roger Commault, who served the Compagnie for half a century, starting as a dishwasher and reaching the exalted rank of a *chef de train*. He became the Compagnie's official historian after his retirement in 1964. *(Photos Wagons-Lits and Collection Commault)*

At the height of its operations the Compagnie employed a staff of twelve thousand, organized like an army and elaborately trained in special schools. Maîtres d'hôtel and chefs were recruited from luxury hotels. All those in senior ranks were expected to speak three languages. They were distinguished by different uniforms, caps, and badges: (1 and 2) *Chefs de train;* (3 and 4) dining-car waiters; (5 and 6) maîtres d'hôtel; (7 and 8) porters and cleaners; (9 and 10) *chefs de brigade,* senior attendants; (11 and 12) headwaiters and dining-car supervisors; (13 and 14) sleeping attendants; (15 and 16) conductors and *contrôleurs.*

The dining-car scene during the inaugural journey of 1883, as envisaged in a contemporary engraving.

A contemporary artist's impression of the elegant diners in 1909. (*Picture in* The Traveller *magazine*)

A menu of 1884 listing a dinner of eight courses.

In the halcyon days before the First World War the waiters in many of the restaurant cars wore tails, velvet breeches, silk stockings and silver-buckled shoes. The picture shows restaurant car 1651, with the maître d'hôtel in the foreground.

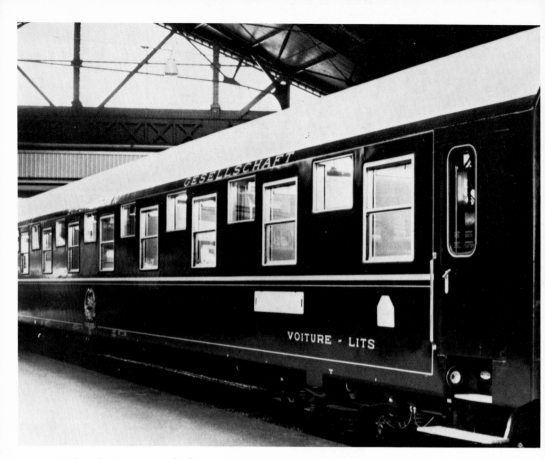

A present-day sleeping car of the Wagons-Lits with second-class tourist compartments, each with two beds, washing facilities, and "all modern comfort." (*Photos Wagons-Lits by J. C. Dewolf*)

The interior of a modern T-2 sleeping compartment of the second-class tourist type. (*Photos Wagons-Lits by J. C. Dewolf*)

Crests of the Compagnie des Wagons-Lits in 1900 and 1930. (*Photos Wagons-Lits by J. C. Dewolf*)

Adventure
of the
Orient Express

The Orient Express suffered very few accidents in its long history. In November 1911 it ran into a stationary freight train near Vitry-le-François because of wrongly set signals. Two members of the staff were killed, but there were no serious casualties among the passengers despite the derailment of several cars.

For the past century the Balkans were a hotbed of political intrigues of the Great Powers. So many secret agents traveled on the Orient Express that in addition to being called "the Royal Train" it came to be known as "the Spies' Express." *Above:* the train in Turkey in 1910.

A rare picture of the Orient Express marooned for six days in February 1929 in huge snowdrifts near Cherkes Keui, some 70 miles from Constantinople. It shows the train after it was partly dug out by Turkish soldiers. The staff had dug a tunnel through the snow and ice to reach a village and collect some food and water for the half-starved and freezing passengers.

In January 1901 the train jumped the rails and ran into the restaurant hall of the Frankfurt-am-Main Central Station. Although the buffet was crowded, no one was seriously injured in this freakish accident. (*Photo Lemmel*)

Lord Baden-Powell, the founder of the Boy Scouts, was in his youth also a secret agent. He regularly traveled on the Orient Express; disguised as a butterfly collector, he sketched Austrian and Turkish forts and naval installations. *(Photo Scout Association)*

Mata Hari, the Oriental dancer and German spy, frequently used the Express when she appeared in Vienna, Budapest, and the Balkan capitals. Lord Kitchener (seen here on an army recruiting poster of 1914) traveled on it when, as a young military intelligence officer in the 1880s, he reconnoitered Austrian, Turkish, and Russian fortifications. *(Photos Musée Guimet, showing Mata Hari as Salome; Imperial War Museum, London)*

A contemporary artist's drawing showing the smoking lounge and library of the Orient Express. On the left is a typical English "milord" . . . or perhaps a secret agent . . . and was the drowsy young Turk drugged? *(BBC Hulton Library)*

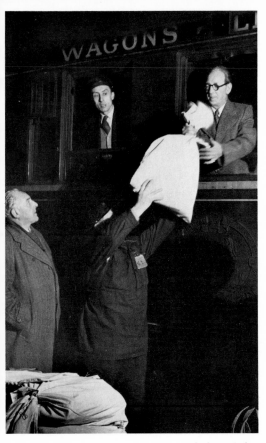

A British Queen's Messenger receives a diplomatic bag of the Foreign Office. The messengers, all former army officers, carried the sealed bags on the Orient Express to Balkan capitals, the bags usually chained to their wrists. *(Photo BBC Hulton Library)*

1. Maréchal FOCH.
2. Amiral Sir R. WEMYSS.
3. Général WEYGAND.
4. Contre-amiral G. HOPE.
5. Captain MARRIOTT.
6. Général DESTICKER.
7. Capitaine de MIERRY.
8. Commandant RIEDINGER.
9. Officier-Interprète LAPERCHE.

11 NOVEMBRE 1918

Marshal Foch, the Allied commander in chief, with British and American officers in front of restaurant car No. 2419, converted into a conference salon for the signing of the armistice in November 1918 at Compiègne.

The German delegation signing the surrender document that ended the First World War. (No photographers were allowed inside the car; the picture is an artist's impression.)

After the fall of France in June 1940 Hitler ordered that the car be taken to the exact spot at Compiègne where the Germans signed the surrender twenty-two years earlier. Accompanied by Ribbentrop, Goering, Hess and General Brauchitsch, he watched General Keitel read the surrender of the Pétain government. The car was then taken to Berlin and exhibited until 1944, when it was blown up by SS men to prevent its falling into Allied hands.

The train figured not only in novels and thrillers and on movie and television screens, including movies by Hitchcock, but also in stage plays, musicals, and vaudeville shows. The picture shows a poster for performances staged in a Montmartre cabaret in 1898 with all the naughtiness of Gay Paree.

The Orient Express in fiction. The train was used by many famous novelists and thriller writers as the background for their plots. The picture shows the jackets of three famous best sellers. (*Photos by courtesy of Paul Elek Ltd., Collins, Fontana Books, and Pan Books Ltd.*)

and insisted on spraying all passengers and their baggage with a disinfectant. Aboard were the British Queen's Messenger Captain Taylor and the French *courier diplomatique* Pierron, both vehemently protesting that their secret documents would be utterly ruined or, at best, acquire a quite undiplomatic odor. A year later the Orient Express was saved from derailment by the presence of mind of its engine driver when a rockfall in Bulgaria blocked the line. In 1901 the train—because of a fault in the locomotive's breaking system—ran into the station buffet at Frankfurt, demolishing a wall and putting diners to flight. But on neither occasion were there any casualties. One serious collision occurred on November 6,1929. The Orient Express was 100 miles east of Paris, en route to Constantinople. It was a wintry night, and by the time the train reached the river Marne thick fog had descended on the track. The signals at the point link before the small station of Vitry-le-François, where expresses did not stop, were set at green and the train was traveling on at full speed. But because of some fatal error a freight train was standing on the same track. The engineer might have seen it at a distance of only twenty or thirty yards, too close to have any chance of bringing the heavy locomotive to a halt. He yelled at the fireman to jump, but he himself bravely remained on the footplate, desperately slamming on the brakes. The engine mounted the rear wagon of the freight train and then toppled down the steep embankment, taking the coal tender, mail and baggage fourgons, and two of the freight wagons with it in a deafening crash of twisted steel and splitting timber, along with the scream of steam escaping from bursting pipes. Miraculously, the coupling between the baggage fourgon and the restaurant car broke when the fourgon was propelled down the embankment and all the cars remained standing on the track. The impact of the sudden halt broke some windows and caused baggage to fall from the racks onto the beds of the sleeping passengers. Except for bruises and cuts no one suffered serious injuries. The engineer who had remained at his post was killed, and his mangled body had to be recovered literally in pieces from the mass of crushed metal. The fireman had jumped, but the fourgon had crashed on top of him and he, too, was killed, as was a *conducteur* who had entered the baggage wagon only minutes before the collision.

It was a narrow escape for the train, but it was as nothing compared with the catastrophe that befell the Orient Express two years later. In our era of skyjacking and terrorist activities a bomb planted on a train would be accepted as almost a matter of course. But in the more tranquil days of 1931 the disaster provided front-page headlines in the world press for weeks and kept the public excited not least because of the mysterious circumstances of the terrible event and its strange sequel.

On September 12, 1931, the train left Budapest at 11:30 P.M. on its run from Istanbul to Vienna and Paris. While crossing the viaduct of Biatorbagy, a few miles to the west of the Hungarian capital, a bomb exploded on the track. The locomotive and nine cars crashed into a ravine to a depth of more than a hundred feet. Some of the cars piled on top of others; those beneath were utterly crushed. Twenty people were killed outright, and rescue teams working through the night extricated from the wreckage a hundred and twenty passengers and train personnel, most of them seriously injured; several died later in hospitals. During the rescue operations thirteen railroad workers, policemen, soldiers, and nurses were injured. Located at dawn were shreds of a canvas bag and splinters of a powerful TNT bomb.

The fascist government of Admiral Horthy immediately blamed "Communist terrorists" for the outrage and produced a note, allegedly found on the track, which read: "Brother Proletarians! If the capitalist state cannot provide work we shall get it by other means. We have plenty of explosives!" Several railroad workers were arrested the same morning, and for several days the police and secret service men rounded up suspects. Admiral Horthy offered a reward of 50,000 pengo (about $10,000) for the apprehension of "the revolutionary terrorists." The outrage was politically embarrassing to the Hungarian regime because so many foreigners were among the dead and injured. Among them were Jean Renard, the director of the Belgian airline Sabena, and his wife; several Austrian, French, American, and English passengers, some returning—like Renard—from a congress of the International Air Transport Association; and a young Austrian honeymoon couple. A Hungarian cabinet minister, Count Joseph Palffy, who was on his way to Paris, had jumped off the train, but had suffered serious injuries.

Aboard the train was the famous Missouri-born cabaret dancer

Josephine Baker, who was then only twenty-six years old but had already taken audiences by storm the world over with her exotic dances, sometimes wearing only a girdle of bananas strung about her midriff. She was returning from a sensational tour to Vienna. She had escaped injury, and calmed the panicked passengers in the Wagons-Lits coaches by breaking into her most acclaimed song: "I have two loves, my country and Paree . . ." Mademoiselle "Bakhair," as she was known to the Orient Express attendants, was very popular with them, not only because she tipped them very generously but because she taught them to make real American double-decker sandwiches.

The police stated that two hundred and sixty informers had come forward, and there were many arrests of "Communist conspirators and murderers," including Janos Leipnik, a known Communist and secretary of the illegal Red Aid. But then a strange silence descended on further investigations. A month later, on October 10, the Austrian police detained a man in Vienna on suspicion that he had placed a bomb on a railroad track near Ansbach in Lower Austria. The man was thirty-nine-year-old Sylvester Matuska, a former Hungarian officer and member of the Arrow Cross League, an organization formed in Hungary on the pattern of Mussolini's Black Shirts and Hitler's storm troops, using as its emblem a slightly modified swastika composed of arrows.

Matuska immediately admitted that he had attempted several railroad bombings before, one at Jüterbog, south of Berlin—during a visit to a Nazi rally—and two or three in Austria. He proudly announced that he had put the bomb on the viaduct at Biatorbagy. He glorified his misdeeds by stating that the Holy Spirit had appeared to him and that three archangels—Saint Michael, Saint Gabriel, and Saint Raphael—had ordered him to undertake missions of derailing trains "to punish atheists traveling on luxury trains and to free the world from Communism." At first it was assumed that Matuska was suffering from religious persecution mania, but leading Austrian psychiatrists declared that he was only simulating paranoia and was responsible for his crimes. He was kept in prison in Vienna for several months, and then the Austrian government offered his extradition to Hungary to stand trial for his crime at Biatorbagy. The Hungarian authorities, extremely embarrassed that the terrorist was not a revolutionary Communist but an ardent supporter of the Horthy regime, at first made no move.

At the Vienna prison Matuska continued to avow his religious and anti-Communist beliefs. A gifted draftsman, he made several hundred sketches of "inventions to benefit mankind," including a plan to navigate the Niagara Falls and to produce artificial gold to stop inflation of world currencies. He signed all his sketches with the words *ad majorem Dei gloriam* (for the great glory of God). Eventually, an Austrian court sentenced him to six years' imprisonment for the abortive bomb attempt at Ansbach. Several governments, whose citizens had been killed or badly injured in the disaster, pressed Hungary to put him on trial for the much more serious crime. It was only three years later that he was picked up by Hungarian detectives and put on trial in Budapest in November 1934 with minimal publicity. The death sentence was appealed, but it was upheld and Matuska was hanged in January 1936.

Another bomb attempt on the Orient Express was made thirty-six years later. Its motives, though obviously political, were never ascertained, nor were its perpetrators ever caught. On July 24, 1967, a plastic bomb was found in a lavatory of the Direct-Orient Express when it arrived in Munich from Istanbul. This happened only three months after the Six-Day War in the Middle East, in which Israel had crushed the Arab enemies and occupied Sinai and the Jordanian West Bank. At first it was thought that the bomb had been placed by Palestinian Al Fatah guerrillas, who had begun to be active. But the attendant who found the bomb noticed a sheaf of leaflets behind the cistern. They were in the Czech language and contained attacks against the Communist regime in Prague, apparently originating from dissident groups.

A bizarre reenacting of the past glory of the Orient Express, complete with wealthy travelers and an imaginary "murder" aboard the train, was staged by the enterprising management of the London tourist agency Concordia in the summer of 1978. A few vintage sleeping cars and a restaurant car were hired to rerun the route from Paris to Istanbul, and an incongruously modern link between London to Paris was provided by a hovercraft. The passengers were charged a ritzy fare for the ten-day holiday; nevertheless the trip was fully booked, mainly by German and American tourists. A number of well-known stage and screen stars were invited, and all passengers were asked to wear period costumes of the 1920s to make the scene as authentic as possible. During the journey a "murder" was enacted by a troupe of professional actors—in true Agatha Christie tradition—and passengers were invited to act as sleuths and solve the crime. One actor played the part of a Balkan monarch, others impersonated some famous passengers of times long past, and there was also the inevitable "spy" to revive the background of mystery.

Chapter Ten

TRAVELS
OF AN OIL TYCOON

IT IS MORE THAN MERE COINCIDENCE THAT THE ORIENT EXPRESS played such a significant—even vital—part in the early careers of two of the richest and most ruthless merchant bankers cum political jobbers of the past hundred years.

Both were of Oriental origin, molded by their race's uncanny ability to survive and fired by ambition for power, which they achieved through wealth and ruthless assault on rivals. And both broke out of the despotism of Turkey into the marketplaces of the West via the road of steel that carried a luxurious train across a continent. Zaharoff was the pioneer along this new route to notoriety and fortune. Calouste Sarkis Gulbenkian came close on his heels.

It is apposite to suggest that the Orient Express provided more than a speedy method of moving between seller and buyer, between politician and industrialist. The train always had a profound psychological influence on even the most sophisticated traveler. In its heyday it typified the brash ostentation of wealth, with its ornate coach fittings and the prestige the Compagnie carefully promulgated. For at least three-quarters of its route it passed through rural areas where the population existed in direst poverty. Wherever the train stopped or even slowed down, men, women, and children stood beside the line with outstretched hands, begging for alms before railway officials chased them away. It is understandable that many of the travelers came to believe consciously or subconsciously that the train was on a treasure route—a symbolic talisman that could confer success on the business deal at journey's end.

For Zaharoff, as we have seen, the Orient Express also brought love into his life—the capacity to deeply love another human being was perhaps the only laudable attribute of this moneymaking and trouble-fomenting man. In the life of Gulbenkian there is not to be found any such redeeming facet of character. His nickname of Mr. Five Percent summed up his life; the acquisition of this commission was patently the sole genuine interest he ever had.

Gulbenkian was born in Scutari (Üsküdar), on the Asian side of the Bosporus opposite Constantinople, the eldest of three surviving sons of a fuel dealer. Although the Gulbenkian family was Armenian, for generations living in Kayseri (the Caesarea of the New Testament), Calouste's father, on moving to Scutari, was wise enough to take Ottoman nationality, and was given a minor government appointment as a sideline to his fuel business. He was able to afford to send his son to the American Robert College in Constantinople, where racial or religious discrimination was virtually nonexistent, the scholars being sons of diplomats and businessmen of a dozen different nations. This education launched the westernization of young Calouste. He left the college with a good knowledge of English and French as well as of the exact sciences. His record was so commendable that he was accepted as a student at the Aix-Marseille University in France, followed by a place at King's College, London, when he was only sixteen. There he read civil engineering and was regarded as a brilliant scholar.

After three years as a student in London, Calouste returned to Turkey and entered his father's business, being given the oil side of the trading as his own responsibility. After a few months his father sent him to Baku to gain firsthand experience of oil production and bulk selling.

Calouste had returned from London to Constantinople on the Orient Express from Paris. He had plenty of time to contrast the speed and comfort of that trip with his journey to Baku. First came travel by sea to Batum in Georgia. Then the new railroad was to take him across Georgia and Azerbaijan to Baku. The rámshackle train went no farther than Tiflis, less than halfway. Among the benefits of civilization that the town offered were good restaurants, a theater, and entertainments to suit for every taste. Although it was hardly a sojourn which Gulbenkian senior would have approved, Calouste apparently stayed in the city for nearly three weeks, drinking heavily and taking part in what a sanctimonious era branded as obscene orgies. That he "grew up" at this time is indicated by the fact that when he eventually reached Baku he had a beard—black and coarse, adding years to his actual age.

When he left Tiflis by a train scheduled eventually to arrive at Baku after innumerable stops, taking twenty-two hours to cover the distance of some 350 miles (along a route which was later to be used for the oil pipeline Gulbenkian financed), he was moving from a town with a certain veneer of civilized behavior to one of unbridled turbulence and near savagery. In Baku he learned—though he needed little tuition—that oil was liquid gold, and with gold a man had power. The ethics of business meant little to the men who had fought and killed to gain possession of the oil wells, and to the men who controlled its transport and its sale. Whatever honesty there was among the oil men of Baku was based entirely on racial ties.

The sprawling town was the home of Azerbaijanis, Russians, Persians, Arabs—and Armenians. The last were by far the most resourceful, with an innate talent for profitable business deals. Calouste was readily accepted by them as a welcome visitor: he was Armenian in appearance and could provide proof of his lineage.

Gulbenkian derived from a foreigner in Baku, a Swede, the real inspiration for the great things to come. Alfred Nobel, then in his fifties, was one of the few outsiders who could challenge the monopolistic attitude of the Armenian entrepreneurs. Thanks to his technical know-how in heavy engineering and his skill in using his newly concocted explosives to blast away rock, Nobel had created for himself a unique position as developer and exploiter of new wells. The huge fortune he amassed and left, on his death, for the annual Nobel prizes came largely from his oil profits. Nobel was nearing the end of his life, and as an older man will do when he meets an intelligent youngster with brains and ambition, he took Calouste with him on his tours of inspection. They watched the endless procession of horse-drawn wagons on the rutted roads and the all too few trucks on the overburdened railroad carrying the barrels of unrefined oil to Baku.

"Given finance by someone in the West and the cooperation of a steelworks in Britain or Germany," Nobel said, "we could cut out this costly and slow method of transport. We would have a pipeline. No problem about a fairly level track—simply lay it alongside the existing railway line. It's just a question of getting the sections of pipe manufactured and delivered. I have all the specifications a steelmaker would need. Plenty of half-starved peasants to do the rough construction work!"

Calouste murmured his agreement. He had no intention of appearing too enthusiastic. This fantastic concept was something he wanted to keep for himself. Soon after he returned to Constantinople in 1890 his father gave him the equivalent of $100,000 as a gift for his twenty-first birthday. The fortune of the future multimillionaire had been founded, though there were setbacks to come all too soon.

With cold-blooded efficiency Calouste began to plan his future both in the personal and business field. He would make the name of Gulbenkian world-famous. That meant he would need an heir, and his son would have to have the blood of a distinguished Armenian family in his veins. And what was the greatest Armenian family in Constantinople? His father told him: the Essayans. Were there any marriageable daughters? Yes, there was a girl, Nevarte, aged fifteen. Gossip had it that she was already promised to a young man belonging to a distant branch of the Essayans. Calouste dismissed this rumor as being of no account. He paid a formal call on the Essayan household. There were introductions over coffee and sweetmeats to members of the family. Nevarte was brought in briefly by a governess, bowed formally, and withdrew after a few moments. But the glimpse of the pretty little girl was enough for Calouste. He determined to marry her.

He learned from her father that the girl was to be betrothed as a prelude to a marriage that had been arranged soon after her birth. Calouste made no comment and talked instead of his minor triumphs as an oil merchant. He took his leave with the deference necessary for an Armenian tradesman to show toward a distinguished leader of the Armenian colony in Constantinople. Calouste had already discovered the benefits accruing from a policy he maintained for the rest of his life: The hand you dare not bite, you kiss.

Frustrated by Nevarte's parents, he set out to ingratiate himself with the girl's governess and with every servant in the household. With an adroit mixture of flattery and bribes he began a steady campaign of courtship by letters, gifts of flowers, and confectionery, while the governess and bribed servants extolled his good looks, wealth, and brilliant future to the innocent girl. Then came an almost incredible stroke of good fortune. Nevarte was to be sent to London to complete her education. No sooner had Calouste learned of this from her governess than he booked a seat on his "lucky transport," the Orient Express. In London he took a flat in Kensington.

The Essayans had rented a house overlooking Hyde Park for Nevarte, her mother, and a half-dozen servants. Calouste called on Mme. Essayan, offering his services as a fellow Armenian thoroughly conversant with London's ways and customs because of his student days in the city. Walking back to his modest flat, he paused in front of the largest house in Hyde Park Gardens—No. 38. "That is where we will live," he said aloud, to the mystification of passers-by. It was no idle boast. A few years later he purchased the house.

What form Calouste's persuasion took to win over Nevarte's family to the idea of Nevarte's marriage to him is unknown. Suffice it to say that all objections were overcome, and the couple was married in 1892. Nevarte brought a dowry of $50,000 in Turkish gold. She was seventeen. There was no real honeymoon. After a few weeks in his small apartment Calouste took his wife to Paris, where she was left alone while he made business calls. Then he abruptly told her that he had bought tickets for the Orient Express leaving at seven-thirty that evening; in four days they would be back in Constantinople. His father would no doubt be able to find them a furnished apartment; it would not have to be large, as he had arranged with a French banker to make an exploratory tour of Mesopotamia (Iraq) in quest of possible oil-bearing terrain and therefore would spend little time in the city.

To finance the expensive trip and his stay in the Turkish capital, he used much of Nevarte's already depleted dowry. The trip yielded no immediate dividends. But, significantly, Calouste in later years often remarked that the great luxury displayed on the Orient Express gave him an incentive for his business efforts: he was determined to accumulate wealth to be on a par with the rich and elegant travelers he observed on the train. In fact his gains were to far exceed their wealth. In Constantinople his schemes for selling oil on behalf of any producer that he could inveigle into an agreement were combined with some trading in his father's business—father and son were always ready to buy cheap and sell dear whatever commodity they could get hold of. For once in his life—perhaps the only time—Gulbenkian experienced a failure. In partnership with his brothers, he used most of what remained of his funds to buy quantities of silks and carpets. The market was slack, and sales did not cover expenses. The rest of Nevarte's dowry became the main source of livelihood. This period of failure coincided with the birth of his first child: a son, Nubar.

Other events brought darkening clouds. Abdul Hamid, the degenerate sultan ruling Turkey from his Yildiz Kiosk Palace, was remorselessly increasing his attacks on all non-Turkish people in the Ottoman Empire. Economically the country was heading for disaster. Calouste transferred all the assets he could realize from his own and his father's business to London and Paris. He tried to persuade his father-in-law to do the same, but Essayan dismissed the warnings as the trick of a fortune hunter. Calouste's money was saved from the ruin that was soon to sweep through every Armenian community. The Essayan family lost everything.

At this time—1896—conditions in Turkey had brought to a zenith the sufferings of the persecuted but resilient Armenian people. Armenian terrorist societies sprang up, the strongest being the Armenian nihilists, emulating their Russian counterparts. In August a group of Armenians rioted in Constantinople and occupied the Ottoman Bank in the city. The Sultan's reaction was typically brutal. Through the issue of a *firman* (a royal edict embodying a religious commandment), he ordered all loyal subjects to ruthlessly suppress the rebellion. For two days Armenian men, women, and children were massacred in the streets, in their homes, and in the boats they tried to escape in. The number killed has never been known even approximately: the figure varies from seven thousand to fifty thousand. The total of the Armenian dead in Turkey as a whole reached three hundred thousand during the following months.

For Calouste Gulbenkian, married, with a newborn son, there was no question of joining the young firebrands organizing their well-nigh hopeless battle against the Turks and the troops of Abdul Hamid. Calouste told Nevarte to collect her oldest clothes, and if they were too obviously of good quality, to exchange some of her own dresses with those of her servants. Little Nubar would have to be stripped of all the costly dress, shoes, and the traditional decorated bonnet of an Armenian child and to be clothed in the tattered rags of a slum baby. Calouste himself obtained an ill-fitting European-style suit. A few changes of clothing for all three were tied in a bundle. But in that bundle he concealed English sovereigns, French francs, Maria Theresa dollars, and gems ripped out of Nevarte's jewelry. He obtained a large Turkish rug, woven by peasants in Anatolia. It was new and of reasonably high quality—an item a carpet seller would take on his travels, but of a size and value that only an impoverished hawker could afford to handle. Calouste's idea was to escape on the Orient Express—that certain means of reaching the serenity and freedom of the West. His aim was to reach London.

The particular Orient Express which he knew he would have to board, if there was to be every chance of escaping from the marauding Turkish troops, left on a Saturday afternoon. To minimize the risk of confrontation, the family left the Armenian colony on the outskirts of Constantinople at midday on Friday, when most of the Muslim population could be expected to be in the mosques. Until the following day the Gulbenkians stayed in the rear room of a friendly sailor's home near the railway station. Shortly after midday the family left their hideaway. Nevarte carried the bundle of spare clothes on her head in Oriental fashion, and Calouste the rolled-up carpet. Inside the carpet, carefully swathed in a sheet and sleeping deeply from a soporific added to milk, was Nubar. Calouste had few illusions about the fate of an Armenian baby if discovered by rampaging Turkish youths on the lookout for an easy victim.

They reached the train without incident. Two o'clock—the scheduled time of departure—came and went. No locomotive appeared. Another hour passed. Passengers were milling about the platform badgering helpless station staff. A mob of onlookers grew steadily. They were clearly hostile toward the passengers, who might be eluding the orders of their sultan. Calouste knew that there was no chance of his son remaining quietly asleep for much longer. Already Nevarte was anxious that the child might be suffocating in the cloying heat of an August afternoon. They left their compartment, Calouste pushing roughly through the crowd outside the station.

The streets were seething with people leaving the mosques. There was no time to lose. At last the train was assembled and shunted. Because of the street riots there were fewer passengers boarding the express than at normal times. The Gulbenkians, with the infant still inside the carpet, reached the carriage without hindrance. Once inside, Nevarte unrolled the carpet and took the panting child in her arms. But Calouste was still worried, and he insisted that as long as the Orient Express was still standing in the station the boy should be hidden under the seats. They breathed freely only when they heard the shrill sound of the *chef de train*'s whistle. The Orient Express—all too slowly at first—steamed out of Constantinople to freedom. The money and jewels came out of the bundle. The Gulbenkians, in their shabby attire, hurried to the restaurant car for badly needed refreshments. But the *maître* at first barred their way; he could not possibly allow them to sit next to his high-class passengers. But waving his tickets and chattering excitedly in both fluent French and English, Calouste convinced him that they were entitled to be properly treated. His explanation for the strange dress was that they had been robbed by marauding rioters and had had to borrow clothes from a poor but honest Turkish friend.

A few weeks later Gulbenkian was once again aboard the express from Paris, but he went only as far as Vienna, from where he proceeded to Trieste to sail to Cairo. A fellow passenger aboard the Lloyd Triestino liner was Alexander Mantachoff, an Armenian by origin but a Russian subject. An enormous man, over six feet four inches tall and very fat, he was uneducated and without principles of any kind. In his native city of Baku he was said to be the wealthiest of the dozens of men who, by luck, enterprise, and ruthless force, had become the first oil entrepreneurs in history. In modern terms he was a multimillionaire. Some of the huge storage tanks he had built on his wharves along the edge of the Caspian Sea were decorated with gold and silver filigree; the distillation tanks were lined with platinum. Illiterate and unable to speak anything but a bastard Russo-Armenian, Mantachoff was nevertheless able to describe to Calouste the fantastic potentialities of the oil business. Knowledgeable as Calouste already was, he saw the fortunes to be made if these uncouth semisavages who were the sole concessionaires and well owners in the Baku area could be brought into a rational business enterprise. He ingratiated himself with Mantachoff, ordered Nevarte to move herself and the baby from their cabin to the deck, and got the oil man to share the cabin with him. By the time the vessel put into Port Said Calouste Gulbenkian knew with absolute certainty where his future lay.

He remained in Egypt for only a week or so. He, his wife, and child then took a ship for Piraeus and thence traveled by the Orient Express from Athens to Paris. The stay in the French capital was brief. Before the end of the year Gulbenkian brought his wife and child back to London. This period marked the major upturn in his fortunes. By the turn of the century he had realized his dream of becoming a resident of 38 Hyde Park Gardens, with such influential neighbors as Herbert Louis (later Viscount) Samuel, Liberal statesman, and Thomas Baring, head of the banking house that had furnished the nation with statesmen for more than a century.

Gulbenkian's daughter, Rita, was born in the house in 1900. Her birth marked the decline of Gulbenkian's determination to appear as a family man. His presence in his London home became less frequent. When in London he often stayed at the Ritz or Carlton hotels instead of under the matrimonial roof. More frequently he was in Paris, where he bought a house on the Quai d'Orsay, because it was convenient for the many hasty trips to the Middle East on the Orient Express.

In 1902, thanks to his contacts, he obtained British naturalization papers as a mere formality. The benefits were immediate. Not only could he now be accepted without much xenophobic protest on the boards of British companies, but his United Kingdom status ensured his safety and freedom of action in Turkey and the Balkans. Thus he was able to negotiate with Haghop Pasha, the personal treasurer of Sultan Abdul Hamid, for the exclusive rights to search for and exploit oil in the Ottoman province of Mosul. Gulbenkian never left his hotel suite in Constantinople, but thanks to payments to traveling merchants and German engineers working on the railway being constructed to Baghdad he obtained a detailed account of terrain that was almost certainly oil-bearing. Haghop Pasha was fobbed off with some personal cash, in return for which he drew money from the Sultan's exchequer to buy drilling concessions over a vast area of Mosul from the local sheiks and emirs. Gulbenkian retained a personal share of any revenues to be derived in the future. Oil was not found until 1927, but it then brought Gulbenkian an astronomical income, for Mosul was by then part of the Iraqi oil bonanza.

Armed with the Mosul oil concession, Gulbenkian returned to London to cultivate an old acquaintance, Marcus Samuel, co-founder of the Shell Transport and Trading Company. Samuel had originally run a small business in London's Houndsditch called the Shell Shop. Its merchandise consisted of boxes and bowls decorated with sea shells, which were to be seen in thousands of Victorian parlors. The more exotic shells were imported from the eastern Mediterranean, collected by middlemen trading in Constantinople. Samuel, visiting the city, noted the growing number of vessels engaged in the oil trade, and he bought a shipload or two. Rapidly his oil business became infinitely more lucrative than the buying of sea shells. It was during this period that Calouste and his father had come to know Samuel, helping him over language difficulties in buying shipments. Young Gulbenkian recognized that this astute businessman from England was someone to cultivate: he was, like his brother, a banker as well as a merchant and ready to finance a viable enterprise.

By the time Gulbenkian had established himself in London the Shell Transport and Trading Company had greatly expanded. In 1903 it became associated with the Royal Dutch Petroleum Company. Together they had a virtual monopoly of oil distribution in Europe and the Far East. Gulbenkian visualized an agreement with this cartel and the Baku oil men. This he advocated first to the Royal Dutch Co.'s directors and then, within a week, in person to the producers in Baku, going to and fro on the Orient Express with proposal and counter-proposal.

The financial reward for the key man in such negotiations was huge. Not only did Gulbenkian expect commissions from both producer and seller, but he surmised that it would arm him for a battle for the worldwide trade in oil with John D. Rockefeller's Standard Oil Company, which controlled 90 percent of America's oil wells and refineries. The most important man to win over for success in his scheme was his old shipboard drinking friend, Mantachoff. He accepted that Mantachoff and his friends in Baku were deeply wary of any move that might erode their independence to trade just as they wished, keeping every bit of profit for themselves. With the fast-increasing world demand for kerosene and the first hint of the coming of the motor age, with its insatiable demand for petroleum, even these billionaire "peasants" living around the Caspian Sea recognized that outside organizations would have to plan and run the intricate business of balancing supply and demand. Their obstinacy in even being willing to come to a conference, let alone signing an agreement, was due entirely to their healthy suspicion of the smart, well-dressed English negotiators, who tried threats and blandishments in equal strength to obtain some kind of concession. They were welcomed as guests, treated regally, and then sent away empty-handed.

The exception was Calouste Gulbenkian. Mantachoff, still the most powerful of the oil magnates of Baku, appointed himself spokesman and sole arbiter of commercial policy. He knew nothing of economics and cared less. He wanted only proof of still-greater profits, with no master to direct his activities. The only person he was prepared to trust was the fellow Armenian, friend from that voyage from Constantinople to Port Said—Calouste Gulbenkian. Even with this advantage of friendship, negotiations were difficult. For the first four months of 1903 Calouste was a regular commuter on the Orient Express, reporting one week to the Royal Dutch–Shell board in London and then to the Mantachoff group, usually in Baku, but sometimes in Constantinople. To flatter Mantachoff, Frederick Lane, organizer of the Royal Dutch–Shell merger and the representative in Britain of the Rothschild financial interests in oil, eventually agreed to accompany Calouste to Constantinople and become acquainted with Mantachoff prior to drawing up a contract.

After many arguments, and with nothing becoming final, all three set off on the Orient Express for Paris and London. Mantachoff quickly became restless at the confinement of a train journey continuing for days on end, and his impatience grew as Lane attempted to discuss involved financial matters.

The discussion—or argument, as it became—was not made easier by the fact that Mantachoff knew no English and Lane no Russian or Armenian. Calouste had to act as interpreter as well as peacemaker.

Late one night, in Calouste's sleeping compartment, Mantachoff took violent exception to Lane's proposal to limit oil output so as to keep prices high.

"I'll rape your mother!" He spluttered the strongest insult an Armenian could use.

"What is he saying?" Lane asked mildly.

"Mr. Mantachoff said that your proposal sounds quite reasonable," Calouste replied.

Months of patient negotiations ensued before Gulbenkian achieved success. With it he had irrevocably thrown in his lot with the British, Dutch, French, and Russians—which meant that he was isolated from any direct involvement with the other major and growing power in Europe, the Germany of Kaiser William II.

In hindsight, it can be seen that Gulbenkian had waged a personal war against Germany for years before 1914. His formation of the Turkish Petroleum Company (its name was changed to Iraq Petroleum Company in 1927) ranged British, Dutch, French, and American oil interests against the German government, which, through the Deutsche Bank, believed it could finance oil exploration in large areas of the Ottoman Empire. Germany owned the Ottoman Railway Company of Anatolia and, with it, all oil rights for 20 kilometers on each side of the track.

Gulbenkian went to stay in Constantinople, where he had persuaded Royal Dutch–Shell to open an office. He turned it into an intelligence center, with spies to watch every German move over hundreds of miles of existing and planned track. He learned with satisfaction that a number of German teams boring for oil in Mesopotamia along the railroad route had failed to find any.

For three years, from 1907 to 1910, Gulbenkian conducted this one-man campaign against German attempts to discover and retain any oil in Turkey and in Mesopotamia as far as Baghdad. Conferences in London and Paris alternated with hectic periods in Constantinople persuading Turkish officials with lavish bribes to impede German engineers and technologists applying for travel permits.

Gulbenkian's firsthand knowledge of the political maneuverings in Central Europe and the Middle East, which was supported by conferences with British and French ministers, convinced him as early as 1910 that a major war between the great European powers was inevitable. He then began to organize his business interests to profit from the polemics of the Central European powers on the one hand, and Britain and France on the other, to gain control of the Middle East oil region. While he did much to thwart the German penetration, he took out insurance by carving a niche for himself in Turkish policy. In 1910, after a journey on the Orient Express during which he shared a compartment with the Turkish ambassador to France, he was appointed financial and economic adviser to the Sultan's embassies in Paris and London. The prestige of this appointment resulted in Sir Ernest Cassel's invitation to Gulbenkian to become a member of the British mission that went to Constantinople to attempt to persuade the Turkish rulers not be dragged into the war on the German side. Through Cassel, a close friend of Edward VII, Gulbenkian obtained entrée into the highest social and financial circles in London.

He achieved his most remarkable coup when, after becoming a director of the British National Bank of Turkey, he closed a deal concerning the British-controlled Iraq Petroleum Company, the Anglo-Iranian Oil Company, and the Royal Dutch–Shell. It is said that the agreement was initialed in the restaurant car of the Orient Express on the back of one of the elegant menu cards. From each of the two main parties to this agreement Gulbenkian received a 2½ percent interest in all future oil deals. It was thus that he became known to posterity as "Mr. Five Percent." He was by now moving into the conglomeration of multinational companies. The crux of the agreement was to get the Ottoman Empire to concede the control of the oil fields of Mosul and Kuwait to the new partnership. The companies already held vast investments in these areas, but it was Gulbenkian who provided them with the ultimate control by disbursing massive bribes to the Grand Vizier, Said Halim Pasha, in June 1914. Whatever the outcome of the war that started a few months later, Gulbenkian's financial interest was secure.

During the war he had to walk a tightrope of diplomacy to ensure that Turkey—by November 1914 fighting on the German side—did not withhold his own profits from oil supplied to Germany and Austria while not appearing to be giving aid and comfort to the enemy. Frustrated from any actual promotion and extension of his interests in the Middle East while the armies fought over the oil-bearing territory of Mesopotamia he looked to the West for more profit. The upshot was the introduction of Royal Dutch–Shell to oil concessions in Venezuela and Mexico.

Gulbenkian inevitably emerged from the war with his financial interests in oil enormously increased in value. His only setback was the confiscation of his holdings in the Baku wells by the new Soviet government of Russia. He never forgot this example of how communism and Russian expansion could endanger his fortune. It was one of the factors that inspired his prolonged negotiations to strengthen the power of the West in Middle East oil lands. He won a triumph when he organized the entry of the United States into the old Turkish Oil Company. In July 1928 American and British politicians and diplomats conferred with Gulbenkian and the oil companies of Britain, Holland, France, and America to carve up the oil concessions in the territories of the old Ottoman Empire.

Within the borders of these ramshackle dominions—before 1918 partly under direct Turkish rule, partly unexplored and uninhabited desert, partly semiindependent sheikdoms—the potentialities of oil production boggled the imagination. The problem was: What areas had originally been an oil monopoly of the old Turkish Oil Company? The politicians wrangled and argued. Exasperated, Gulbenkian called for a map of the Middle East. He took a red crayon and drew a line around the area between the Red Sea and the Persian Gulf, including the territorial waters.

"That was the Ottoman Empire in 1914," he said, ignoring all the finer points of commercial agreements, treaties, undecided tribal wars, and disputed deserts. His red line included a veritable ocean of oil then still to be tapped—in Kuwait, Bahrein, Saudi Arabia, Qatar. The red line was accepted with relief by weary negotiators and without any serious argument. Gulbenkian had thereby guaranteed himself the 5 percent interest in the greatest source of mineral wealth the modern world had known.

Obvious wealth and behind-the-scenes power were his twin gods, and presumably he was well content with the gifts they bestowed on him. But as a human being there was little about him to admire. After 1925 he rarely saw his wife or shared a room with her. His mistresses were numbered in the hundreds, the banal affairs being as routine and emotionless as his daily massage. It was said that at every stopping place of the Orient Express—for all his active life up to the outbreak of the Second World War his favorite means of travel—there were apartments and houses leased in confidential agents' names year after year just so they were available when required for a night or two. The men and women permanently employed as procurers had precise instructions as to their master's sexual pleasures, and girls were carefully groomed and instructed on their duties. Only a few could come up to expectations and thus receive orders for a return visit. But there were one or two exceptions, and these women had to be ready to travel across the continent at a moment's notice. One crew on the Orient Express talked for years about the Kurdish girl found in Constantinople who for three years in the mid-1920s was regularly dispatched first class on the train for one-night assignations in Vienna, Belgrade, and Paris. She was completely illiterate, apparently spoke only in a Turkish dialect, and seemed completely unaware of the high status of her paramour.

Gulbenkian's secretiveness over these affairs was peculiar in that, with his wealth and power, he had no need to consider criticism of his morals. But he always went to enormous lengths to conceal his sexual peccadilloes. At the Ritz Hotel in the Place Vendôme in Paris, where he maintained a permanent suite, the staff was instructed to refrain from greeting or even looking at the black-haired, bearded little man creeping up and down servants' staircases, using the baggage lift, or entering and leaving the hotel through delivery doors. Whenever he stayed at the hotel in this manner, the staff knew that a girl had been taken to his suite. When none was there, he would enter by the main entrance and expect everyone from manager to page boy to be awaiting him.

The most efficient of the employees who sought out the girls, groomed them, and ensured their silence afterwards was Gulbenkian's daughter Rita's one-time French schoolmistress, Elize Soulas, whom Gulbenkian had hired in 1913. She was expert in finding the right kind of girl in a café, cabaret, or some street market, and then persuading her to prostitute herself. Preparation might take many weeks—with tuition in etiquette and speech, visits to hair stylists and couturiers, and, of course, intimate instruction on sexual activity. Elize was regarded by Gulbenkian as an invaluable aide. He saw her only occasionally, when he would summon her to his Paris residence. Few people were ever allowed to visit him in this ostentatious, gloomy mansion—a treasure house proclaiming his enormous wealth. Sir Kenneth (later Lord) Clark had been engaged as art adviser, and the collection of pictures, sculptures, ceramics, manuscripts, and tapestries were in superb taste. But to Gulbenkian it was their value that was the attraction; almost every acquisition displayed in that silent, lonely residence represented a clever deal, in which rival collectors were outwitted and sellers driven to a hard bargain.

Nor did the sense of family—usually so strong among Armenians —ever greatly occupy Gulbenkian's mind after his children were born. His daughter, Rita, lived in Paris but rarely saw her father; she preferred to provide some comfort for her virtually deserted mother. His only son, Nubar, who in 1896 made his first trip on the Orient Express rolled inside a carpet, was a bitter disappointment to his father. Given the privileged education that only social status or great wealth can offer, the boy was sent to Harrow in 1910, then to Bonn University, and on to Trinity College, Cambridge. He emerged from this meticulous training a cultured playboy, the darling of prewar and between-the-wars society. At a victory ball held at the Albert Hall he met Hermina

Rodriguez Feijo, daughter of a wealthy owner of Cuban estates. They were married secretly in 1922 and parted after three years.

It was then that Nubar, thirty years old, finally broke with his father. He was in love with Doré Plowden, a twice-married music-hall entertainer and minor Hollywood film actress. They married in 1928, but this union was also a failure. For years Nubar's name was linked with that of Mrs. Marie Samuelson, wife of a banker whom Nubar had known since their school days at Harrow. Marie did not obtain a divorce until after the Second World War, and they were married in 1948. Nubar's much publicized private life infuriated his father. The rift between father and son became permanent when they clashed over the only subject they both regarded as vital: money.

The bone of contention was the income derived from an obscure company registered in Canada: Participation and Investments Co. (Pandi). Gulbenkian had set up this company for the purpose of tax avoidance, and a major part of his routine investment income was channeled through it. No doubt to his subsequent regret, he had made Nubar a director.

In 1940 Nubar instituted a high-court action to determine his legal share of the Pandi profits. This action, in the darkest days of the war, seemed like a lawyers' field day when it was known that Gulbenkian, at his Vichy hideaway in France, had issued instructions that steps be taken with the utmost vigor to deprive his son of the claim he was making.

The documents brought into court numbered 987,000. It was expected that this family row would drag on for weeks and possibly months. But abruptly, after only three days of evidence, the parties agreed to withdraw the action, reportedly because of strong pressure from the British and Canadian governments, which were alarmed that the murky details of international intrigue and financial jugglery would inevitably come to light at a critical period of the war.

The outbreak of the Second World War had at first enhanced Gulbenkian's political influence. Although he was dubious about the Anglo-French ability to resist Nazi Germany—as early as 1936 he had moved many of his most valuable works of art from Paris to London —he knew that, short of the Allies' utter defeat, Middle East oil would be a greater source of revenue than ever before. The British and French governments wooed him with hints of honors as well as agreements about money. Britain was reminded by Gulbenkian that in the past his advice had sometimes been ignored to the disadvantage of the country. In 1931, he pointed out, he had told the Treasury that with some minor concessions of the 1927 Treaty of Jedda plus £20,000 in gold, he could have bought Saudi Arabia's oil concession from Ibn Saud, to the great benefit of Britain—less, naturally, his own 5 percent. The British Treasury, then in the throes of Britain's greatest economic crisis, had declared it could not afford the price. So Gulbenkian had turned to the United States, and American oil companies got the Saudi concession.

In the Second World War Gulbenkian's attitude was no more than that of a friendly neutral. When the Nazis overran France, the Low Countries, Denmark, and Norway, he hedged his bets. It became apparent that Hitler could become the ruler of Europe, so after the French surrender Gulbenkian went to live in Vichy, where he established friendly contact with the French collaborators around Marshal Pétain, thus building a bridge to the Nazis. As another cautious move, he had acquired Persian nationality. But then Persia became involved in the war and parts of it were occupied by the Red Army. Gulbenkian's good friend Reza Shah Pahlavi, who had plotted with Nazi agents, was forced to abdicate by the British and Soviet commanders. Gulbenkian remembered him when he was still an army sergeant, who led three hundred cavalrymen in 1925 in a successful attempt to overthrow the Kajar dynasty, which had ruled Persia since the eighteenth century.

With the Persian debacle in 1941, Gulbenkian thought it wise to remove himself to neutral Portugal. There, at the Grand Hotel Avis, among affluent exiles from many warring countries, the oil magnate still tried to retain his power over the oil trade, implicitly believing that he would live for another quarter of a century.

After the defeat of the Axis powers, Gulbenkian returned to liberated Paris. But he now loathed the French capital and complained that brash American officers had the run of the best hotels. He quickly left for his vast mansion and park near Deauville, which he had bought in 1930 and on which he had spent a fortune in creating a park where sixty gardeners tended trees and exotic plants imported from all over the world. While much of northern France lay in ruins, his estate at Deauville had remained unscathed by the Normandy landings. But he preferred the placidity of Portugal and he returned to the Avis Hotel. If his vigor and skill at intrigue were declining, the power of his enormous and carefully invested fortune remained as great as ever. Between 1945 and 1948 he obstinately demanded redress for the income he claimed was due him from the Iraq Petroleum Company, the assets of which had been confiscated during hostilities. His persistence, supported by a retinue of lawyers, paid off. He was given back payments from 1941 onwards—at his usual 5 percent of the total revenue from an annual average of two million tons of oil pumped to the terminals at Tripoli and Haifa.

The unfamiliar experience of failure in his negotiations for future fortune-making spurred the old man's determination to get his own way even if it meant reversing earlier policies. According to an ingenious scheme proposed by a Soviet emissary, Gulbenkian was to get his usual 5 percent on a deal permitting the Soviet Union to share in the oil from the Middle East in return for compensation for oil revenues withheld from stockholders in Russian oil firms since the Revolution. To Gulbenkian's consternation and fury, the proposal was turned down with contempt by President Harry Truman and the U.S. Secretary of the Interior, Harold L. Ickes.

Then came the greatest blow to his self-esteem—and a considerable erosion of his income. As a greatly venerated commercial counselor to Iran for thirty years, he told the Iranian government in the spring of 1951 not to nationalize the Anglo-Iranian Oil Company. But Iran was in the clutch of the National Front, with the eccentric prime minister Mossadegh, to all intents and purposes, the country's dictator. Gulbenkian's advice was rejected and his warning ignored. The latter was a statement that if the oil wells at Abadan were confiscated, the British would send an expeditionary force to retrieve them. Gulbenkian felt certain that he could virtually force Britain into adopting this policy, and he telephoned the newly appointed Foreign Secretary, Herbert Morrison, to tell him that Mossadegh was merely bluffing. But the British were timid. The British cabinet and the army and navy chiefs doubted that any effective force could be mounted in time.

Gulbenkian, by then over eighty years old, was not a man to give in lightly. Despite the previous rebuff by Washington to the strange Soviet scheme, he once more turned to the Americans. By sending cables and making interminable telephone calls he convinced the President, Secretary of State Dean Acheson, and the heads of American oil companies that an intervention by the CIA in Iran could yet be fruitful. Thus it came about that the U.S. government approved Operation Ajax. Kermit "Kim" Roosevelt—the CIA's most experienced senior agent on Middle East affairs, who had already scored success with Colonel Gamal Nasser in Egypt—was rushed with a small team to Teheran. The situation there was explosive. Prime Minister Mossadegh was secretly negotiating with Moscow and had allied himself with the Communist Tudeh Party. The Shah had left the country ostensibly for a holiday in Switzerland but in fact had gone into voluntary exile. Kim Roosevelt first offered Mossadegh a bribe of $8 million, but the old man refused.

Following Gulbenkian's advice, Kim Roosevelt and his assistant, Colonel Norman Schwarzkopf, a former New Jersey police chief who had served in the OSS in Iran during the war, staged almost overnight a clever coup. Schwarzkopf recruited a handful of Teheran's tramps and beggars, paying each fifty dollars. They, in turn, were ordered to distribute ten-dollar bills to a ragged crowd that began to roam the streets shouting "Death to Mossadegh! Long live the Shah!" Before the wily Mossadegh recovered from his surprise and could mobilize his supporters, Roosevelt arranged with General Zahedi, the chief of staff, that a regiment of the Imperial Guards—probably the only unit of the Persian army remaining loyal to the Shah—would "restore order." Mossadegh was clapped in jail and the bloodless coup ended with Zahedi as head of a new government, ready to undo all the harm Mossadegh was alleged to have done to Anglo-American oil interests. Thus the combined plot by Gulbenkian and the CIA prevented the danger of a Soviet intervention and, possibly, a Communist regime in Iran. Washington hurried to buttress Zahedi's government with economic aid and grants for mutual security to the tune of $200 million a year, and thus laid the foundation for the present-day industrialization and prosperity of Iran—and also for the brutally oppressive regime of Mohammed Reza Pahlavi. Neither Kim Roosevelt nor Gulbenkian lost out on the deal. Roosevelt later became vice president of Gulf Oil Co.; Gulbenkian was rewarded by the Shah with a handsome commission.

In Lisbon the frail old man was eagerly following the events. After the coup succeeded, he wanted to travel to Iran on his proven talisman —the Orient Express—at least between Paris and Istanbul. But the Iron Curtain and the cold war had firmly closed the connection. The Orient Express coaches from Paris were running no farther than Nuremberg.

The era that had made Gulbenkian a modern Croesus was over. He remained in Lisbon.

He died there on July 20, 1955, aged eighty-six. A few days before his death he reminded his doctors that he was destined to live longer than his father by at least twenty years—which meant a life span of a hundred and six. But his often repeated boast that "there was nothing that money could not buy" was disproved. Twenty years more were beyond his ability to purchase, with or without a discount of 5 percent. With the death of Calouste Gulbenkian disappeared the most notorious and eccentric passenger the famous train ever carried.

Chapter Eleven

THE TRAIN
LOST IN THE SNOW

THE GROUP OF PEOPLE ON PLATFORM 2 AT THE PARIS NORD STATION surged toward the lighted cars of the Simplon Orient Express No. 3 as the section of the train from London and Calais backed into the station and was coupled to the Wagons-Lits cars already standing there. The staff gave the welcome call *"En voiture, messieurs et 'dames."* Inside there was warmth and shelter from the freezing wind that howled through the vaulted roof of the station, bringing eddies of snow and sleet.

It was Sunday, January 29, 1929, and the time was a little before 11 P.M. The London section of the train had been delayed by gale-force blizzards on the English Channel ferry crossing, but the engineer had made up time on the Calais-Paris run despite being twice held up by frozen signaling. Now in barely ten minutes the train wound its way on the link route to Paris-Lyons station and thus to the main track and onward to the Simplon tunnel on the frontier between Switzerland and Italy, and then to Milan and Venice.

Only a few British travelers had braved the rigors of the sea crossing and the ominous weather reports on that winter's evening. One of them, peering through the misted window at the people entraining at Paris Nord, was in a locked compartment. On the seat beside him, linked to his wrist by a chain, was a heavy leather bag bearing on its clasp the crown flanked by the lion and unicorn of England. Major Alfred Francis Custance, the King's Messenger, was on one of the innumerable journeys he made aboard the Orient Express since joining twenty years earlier the select corps of special diplomatic couriers of the British Foreign Office.

The dispatches he carried were for delivery to the British ambassador in Turkey's capital. Even though Major Custance did not know the contents of the top-secret instructions the Foreign Secretary, Sir Austen Chamberlain, was sending to his ambassador, he was aware that the diplomatic bag he was carrying was of vital importance and its delivery of greatest urgency.

A King's Messenger always traveled alone in a reserved compartment and was not supposed to converse with any of his fellow passengers. But Custance knew the identity of one of them, a tall, distinguished-looking gentleman in his early fifties whom he had seen entering the Wagon-Lit car at London's Victoria Station. He was Sir Gilbert Clayton, a soldier, a diplomat, and an authority on the Middle East. After fighting as a young officer against the "Mad Mahdi" in the Sudan, he served in the Egyptian army under British control, became director of military intelligence in Egypt during the First World War and given the title of Clayton Pasha by the Khedive. Sir Gilbert became a key figure in Britain's activities to create some order out of the chaos following the end of the Ottoman Empire. From 1922 to 1925 he had been chief secretary of the government of Palestine, negotiated the Treaty of Jedda, which led to the creation of the kingdoms of Hejaz (now Saudi Arabia) and Transjordan. As one of the most respected experts on Arab politics he was appointed high commissioner and commander in chief of the British forces in Iraq, and on that fateful February day was on his way to take up residence in Baghdad.

Clayton suffered from no restrictions on alleviating a long and tedious journey by chatting to some fellow passenger. Consequently he was happy enough to have a few words with a young woman who had also joined the train in London. She was Anne Poole, the private secretary to the British ambassador in Turkey, returning from vacation leave in England.

During the brief stop at Paris Nord the Gallic fuss and arguments over luggage, reserved compartments, and last-minute farewells to friends and relatives were missing. The *chef de train* had a list of some eighty passengers all told with tickets for travel to Milan, Venice, Trieste, Zagreb, Vienna, Belgrade, and other intermediate stops, with only a handful going straight through to Constantinople. Normally this large number would have necessitated all that combination of courtesy and firmness which every member of the Compagnie's staff had been trained to display in order to have the well-heeled and critical passengers settled in the cars. But tonight the bitter cold erased protests and complaining inquiries. All that the passengers wanted was to move into the comforting warmth of the train.

First aboard were a couple of Jesuit priests bound for a missionary station in Arabia. They had little baggage and politely refused any help with it. Behind them came a bearded and gowned imam, Hadji Jacuof Fuad, who, either through language difficulty or hostility to the infidels around him, gave no information about his ultimate destination beyond Constantinople. Most of the other men were more forthcoming. They included Captain G.T. Ward, a grizzled, gray-haired giant of a man who had been enjoying the fleshpots and other attractions of Paris before taking over the mastership of an oil tanker lying in an eastern Mediterranean port; a voluble Austrian banker, Arthur Vetter; the counselor of the French embassy in Turkey, Jeloure; a fellow countryman of his, Castlenau, general manager of the French-owned Constantinople Water Company; and an Italian businessman, Guido Famadotta.

One more passenger arrived at the last moment. He was a swarthy individual, dressed in an overcoat that reached almost to the ground and had a huge astrakhan collar. His black homburg was curled at the brim and worn at a rakish angle. He demanded two porters to carry his four cases. At last, inside the train and having approved his sleeping compartment after demanding a vase for the red carnation he wore in the buttonhole of his coat, he strolled along the corridor to introduce himself to his fellow passengers, who were congregating in the restaurant car. He said his name was Alphonse Souf, a Turkish subject though proud of the distinguished Armenian family of whom he was a member. He implied that his was a business trip concerned with an important but unspecified enterprise in Turkey. His captive audience, according to their experience or their gullibility, reacted individually to his remarks that this was just another routine trip for him. He had traveled on the Orient Express on dozens of occasions, the train being almost his mobile home and office as he kept his finger on the pulse of his continent-wide business interests. But his claim of being a VIP was marred in the eyes of the more discerning, who noted that the *conducteurs*—trained to treat every passenger, young or old, known or unknown, with deference and near obsequiousness—barely concealed their amused contempt for Souf's condescending manner. He was, had he but known it, on the semiofficial list of "passengers to be watched."

Souf quickly found that his loquacity was defeated by the main topic of interest among the passengers. As the train gathered speed the cars periodically shuddered as they were bothered by tremendous gusts of wind. On the left side all the windows were rapidly becoming framed in a thick rim of frozen snow. Icy cold penetrated every crevice, and even with the heating at maximum, the floor became uncomfortably cold to the feet. Despite the insulation constructed to ward off every discomfort of the exterior world, the fact that this was the most vicious winter known in Europe for more than a century became an awesome reality.

Since long before Christmas the newspapers had told the shivering people of Europe how the phenomenon of the Arctic Circle shifting nearly a thousand miles south was affecting normal life on the Continent. Apart from the British Isles, protected by the warmth of the Gulf Stream from the paralyzing cold and enduring only periods of heavy snow, virtually all Europe was facing economic and social chaos.

Holland's canals and the Zuider Zee were frozen solid, as were the lower reaches of the Rhine; all German ports were icebound, with floating ice paralyzing Hamburg, Bremen, and Wilhelmshaven, and closing the Kiel Canal. Many smaller ships were badly damaged and stranded, with huge blocks of ice partially thawed by day and then congealing at night. The situation in the Baltic was even worse, with every port from Lübeck to Danzig blocked. The German cruiser *Schleswig-Holstein*, fitted with icebreaking equipment on her prow, made vain attempts to keep a shipping lane open and to rescue hundreds of vessels locked in the ice.

West of Berlin and Vienna the first three weeks of intense cold had brought comparatively little snow, the high-pressure area creating winds predominantly north-northeast passing over the land mass of northern Russia. Consequently, though temperatures regularly dropped to minus 5 degrees Fahrenheit, freezing land and water solid, transport services could be maintained, though with great difficulty on icy highways and on railroads with switchgear thawed by burning thousands of fires in braziers. The determination of the Compagnie to maintain the Orient Express services in such conditions was understandable if risky. What was perhaps less easy to condone was its failure to investigate more thoroughly the strange and ominous absence of news from the Balkans.

News-agency messages from towns in East Prussia and Poland reported climatic conditions threatening to ruin the already depressed state of the economy on the threshold of the worldwide depression that was marked by the collapse of the American stock exchanges eight months later. Polish factories had been closed, and a hundred and forty thousand workers drafted to help the army clear roads and railroads. From Vienna came accounts of people walking and skating on the Danube, the first time the river had been frozen over since 1889, and less happy reports of the emergency hospitals set up in the Austrian capital and in Budapest to deal with the thousands of cases of frostbite, cardiac collapse, and respiratory sickness.

At first, reports and photographs reached the newspaper offices of Central and Western Europe because telegraph, mail, and train services were still being maintained. The trickle of news about conditions in the Balkans and Turkey was almost entirely secondhand or by brief radio announcements. Stories were filed "from Belgrade via Vienna," "from Bucharest via Athens," or reported by agencies in the towns still in communication as travelers' tales.

These stories told of the Danube frozen solid from Budapest to Belgrade, of temperatures in Yugoslavia dropping to 30 degrees below freezing night and day. Official sources were quoted on hundreds of deaths through exposure and of complete paralysis of communications. Weather experts interviewed about the phenomenal drop in temperature stated that in the Arctic and sub-Arctic regions, where such conditions were the regular seasonal occurrence, they were the harbingers of another change for the worse: prolonged and heavy snowstorms. Amazing reports came from as far south as Sicily; in Palermo temperatures of 9 degrees below freezing were reported, the Dalmatian coast was snowed under; snow was falling in Syria, and frost and storms had interrupted road, telegraph and telephone communications between Beirut, Damascus, and Haifa.

The outriders of the blizzards that swept into Central and even Southern Europe during the last week of January were in evidence as Orient Express No. 3 pulled out of Paris Nord that Sunday night. The farther south the train traveled the heavier became the fall, though boisterous wind kept the railroad track fairly clear right through France. In Switzerland the railroad authorities, accustomed to tackling snow, had plows out round the clock, and again there was no severe delay. As the train labored on across the northern plain of Italy those who were not asleep could glimpse the sight of a countryside blanketed in white, and in the Venice station they saw men working to clear the platforms of several inches of hard snow.

The Compagnie representative in Venice gave the locomotive engineer and the *chef de train* the latest reports on the situation as far as Vienna. This was a routine practice, with information on track repairs and so on, together with what were usually reliable weather reports. The Paris headquarters normally maintained a reporting service through the telegraph and telephone links from station to station. It was well aware of the abnormal conditions that had steadily developed over the previous weeks. Just before the departure of the train a telegram from Timişoara on the Hungarian-Rumanian border, delayed for some hours, had been received reporting a temperature of minus 35 degrees Fahrenheit and heavy snowstorms. The figure seemed so abnormally low that it was queried as a transmission error. In any event, severe winter conditions had existed for three weeks and the trains had got through, the incidents being minor delays and a few mishaps to the train employees, including cases of frostbite when, for one reason or another, they had had to lean out of windows. Two conductors had slipped and injured themselves on the ice-covered steps of the cars. But no passenger had been involved in any trouble beyond that of some delay in reaching a destination.

Consequently, the train was authorized by the Compagnie agent in Venice to proceed. It was now heading northeast directly into the wind which was settling down from its earlier periodic gusts to a steady gale. When dawn came, visibility was hardly more than that of twilight with low clouds scudding across the sky. But in the warm and cozy conditions of the cars, with breakfast served just as usual, the scenery, if awesome, was magnificent. The steep folds of the mountains had disappeared under packed snow. The villages of the Tyrol were little more than white silhouettes of buildings almost completely buried. A myriad of fir trees stood like intricately carved white statues, every branch and twig glittering with snow congealed into ice. But it was a dead world: not a sign of animal or human being, and no contrast to the all-pervading whiteness except for the thin double black lines of the railroad behind the train where the wheels had temporarily crushed and removed the layer of packed snow.

After a brief period of merely heavy cloud at dawn the snowfall began in earnest, at first whirling in wisps and then into a steady slanting blizzard of whiteness. The fireman, piling on fuel to keep up the boiler pressure of the laboring locomotive, created a pall of smoke that was immediately caught by the snowflakes and plastered all over the train, covering the windows with a gray mass. But inside the cars the unremitting attention of the staff continued as usual. The luncheon precisely as offered on the menu was served on time while the train approached Linz. Vienna was reached with a delay of less than an hour. The only slight inconvenience to the passengers had been the freezing of part of the steam-heating pipe, turning some compartments into refrigerators. Their occupants had been moved to vacant compartments.

The Austrian capital was the destination of the majority of the eighty passengers who had boarded the train in Paris. A few more, with a caution that proved lucky for them, decided that they would go no farther. Only a few newcomers took their places, either because they dismissed the possibility that any act of God or man could interfere with the reliability of the Orient Express or because they needed to get to their eastern destinations as quickly as possible. Among the new passengers was a fragile-looking blonde, her face almost hidden in the collar of her fur coat. "I am Paula von Werner," she said to the *conducteur*. "I have a reservation to Constantinople. Please show me my compartment. She stressed the "von" of her name, implying her aristocratic status. She gave him a battered little suitcase and was obviously glad to settle down in the snugness of her second-class *couchette*. Normally, she would have had to share the compartment with three others, but as there were only twenty passengers left—and only one other lady, Miss Poole—the *contrôleur* made the compartment all her own. She was a Viennese cabaret singer down on her luck. Because of the weather conditions Vienna's vaudeville houses were almost empty. Having lost her engagement, she had eagerly accepted an agent's offer to go to Constantinople to appear in a rather sleazy night club. As mentioned before, the Balkans, Turkey, and the Near East usually provided a refuge for "resting" show girls in the West.

The train remained in the Vienna East station for some forty-five minutes. The Est 2–2–0 locomotive of the French railroad company had hauled the train from Paris. Efficient as this engine was, it had clearly been inadequate in such weather conditions. It was an indication of how little the railroad authorities knew of the real situation ahead that the train had not been allocated one of the 2–4–1 *La Montagne* locomotives that the Est Railroad had developed a few years earlier—the largest and most powerful express locomotives running in France. Nor was this type available in Vienna. Instead, the train was now hauled by one of the Austrian State Railways' locomotives, a Series II "ten-wheeler" 2–3–0. Though the line surveyors knew that heavy snow was still falling, they were satisfied that the plows that had been working since midnight were keeping the tracks reasonably clear. They hoped that the "ten-wheeler," with the strong adhesion of its six driving wheels and overall weight, would encounter no difficulties.

When the train pulled out and rapidly gathered speed, the passengers could note the excellent work that had been done with well-cleared snow piled on either side of the track. During the five-hour journey to Budapest there was no difficulty beyond a decrease in speed once darkness had fallen because some signals were out of action and the engineer had "to feel his way." But in the Hungarian capital, except for the station staff, there was hardly a sign of life. The Danube, completely frozen, was an expanse of white with the snow overlaying the ice. Few streetlights were burning because some gas mains and electric cables had been damaged.

After a conference between the locomotive crew and the Budapest railroad officials it was agreed that the Compagnie's headquarters in Paris should be asked if the journey should continue. After long delays the *chef de train* managed to get through on the telephone. He reported that the Budapest superintendent suspected that the route was partially blocked in Rumania, and that Bulgarian lines were virtually impassable; he admitted that he had been unable to obtain confirmation because telephone communication had been interrupted. Partly because of the mail the train was carrying, but largely because of the reputation the Orient Express had earned during forty years of service, Paris gave the terse instruction: "Proceed."

Dinner was served as the train crossed the Rumanian-Hungarian border. During the usual long and leisurely meal the winds reached almost hurricane force, with two mainstreams of air battling for supremacy: one from the north, where temperature in the Carpathian Mountains had dropped to minus 40 degrees Fahrenheit, sweeping downwards over the Transylvanian Alps; and the other, predominantly easterly, storming across the Danube basin. The train rocked under the impact of wind, and the engineer reduced speed to a crawl to minimize the risk of derailment. The double gale winds had the effect of decreasing the snowfall, but the rattle of stone-hard crystals periodically hitting the sides of the cars was a bad omen.

After a stop at the Rumanian border town of Turnu-Severin, where a dozen railroad workers struggled to load frozen lumps of coal into the tender and managed to thaw the water cistern long enough to replenish the locomotive's tank, the train faced the long stretch across Bulgaria. The Rhodope Mountains to the south were forcing the winds upwards, bringing calmness as compared with the earlier conditions. Relieved passengers prepared for bed. Few were aware that beyond the windows, rendered opaque with ice on one side and moisture on the other, heavy snow was falling—feathery, cloying flakes that impacted wherever they lay. The snow adhered to the left-hand side of the train, a foot thick in some places. In the locomotive cab the fireman had to shovel away huge lumps of half-frozen slush to get at the fuel, itself frozen into massive blocks that had to be broken with a crowbar before they could be dispatched, hissing, into the fire.

At Svilengrad, the last stop before the Turkish border, the stationmaster warned that the track inside Turkey had not been cleared for two days and was now impassable. But the *chef de train,* obedient to the orders from Paris, decided that the journey should continue. Scheduled timing was now forgotten. The train moved at hardly above walking pace. Two or three times the engineer had to reverse in order to force a way through small drifts that had covered the line. Finally, a few miles west of Çorlu, near the flag stop at Cherkes Keui, the train shuddered to a stop, the front of the locomotive half buried in an enormous drift that rose far above the smokestack. The area was an ominous one to the employees of the Compagnie—they had all heard or read about the notorious and historic holdup of the Orient Express by bandits thirty-eight years earlier.

There was no chance of reversing the train. The drifts that had been effectively tackled by the heavy locomotive would inevitably derail the light truck at the rear of the train if it was pushed into even a small accumulation of snow. In any event, snow was still falling so heavily that within minutes the sides of the entire train were concealed under a white blanket reaching almost to the roofs of the cars.

For the locomotive crew the immediate problem was to maintain the fire and steam pressure to heat the cars. There was, in addition, a serious risk of an explosion because, in the absence of motion, the cylinder valves had frozen and it was problematical that the boiler's safety valve was still operative. An attempt to move the train a few feet backwards so as to clear the smokestack and cylinders from the impacted snow proved that the brake valves had frozen, the reversing gear did not operate, and the bogies of the cars had automatically locked in the braked position and could not be released. Even if by some Herculean effort the train crew shoveled away the drift, the train could not have been moved: it was mechanically immobilized.

The absence of motion wakened the passengers, though most remained in their berths, for by then they were accustomed to periodic halts and the staff's frantic activity in the corridors. The first to emerge were the King's Messenger, Major Custance, immaculately dressed and well-groomed as usual, with his chained document case securely held in his arms, and the high commissioner, Sir Gilbert Clayton. After a few quiet words together they went to the dining car, where the *chef de train*, some of his aplomb decidedly weakened, was removing the snow in which he had been enveloped after crawling alongside the train to confer with the locomotive crew. Clayton displayed restrained indignation about the delay and trusted that it would not continue, as he was due to have an audience with King Faisal of Iraq in two days' time. Custance was more constructive: he proposed that the train be reversed to the last station they had passed, where contact with the railroad executives could doubtless be made.

The *chef de train* pointed expressively at the walls of snow by now towering higher than the car roof and added tersely that the locomotive was useless except, just possibly, to maintain some heating in the train. Whereupon Custance stated the obvious: "Something must be done. This situation cannot be tolerated a moment longer than is necessary." To which the distraught official made the equally obvious comment: "M'sieu, I am afraid there is no way we can send a message. All the telegraph wires have been blown down by the storm or broken by the weight of snow. Of that I was informed when we stopped at Cherkes Keui. I am sorry. We are marooned."

By this time most of the passengers had emerged from their compartments. In varying stages of undress and swathed in blankets and coats, they crowded around the *chef de train* and the two Englishmen, expressing indignation and plying them with questions. At this point a waiter announced that coffee was awaiting them in the restaurant car. With commendable foresight the chef had laced it with brandy. This restored some degree of calmness and gave the *chef de train* the opportunity to announce that the locomotive fire was still being fueled to supply steam heat to the car, and there was two days' supply of food in the kitchen—"by which time of course the emergency will be over," he ended, smiling. After a pause he added, as a rather ominous contradiction of his optimism about the duration of the delay, "I would request that you all be economical in the use of water for your washing and personal routines."

Although it was long past daybreak the heavy cloud and curtain of continual snowfall put the restaurant car in semigloom. With the train at a standstill the car dynamos were not generating current and the batteries would run down after an hour's use. In the hope that the acid would not freeze and render them useless, lighting was kept only for nighttime. At first there was no panic—quite the reverse. After taking coffee the passengers returned to their sleeping compartments and dressed. In ones and twos they began chatting in the still quite warm restaurant car, making friendships where previously there had been no more than a dignified nod of recognition. The two Jesuit priests started a philosophic discussion with the imam and the Italian industrialist. The ebullient Souf produced a pack of cards and persuaded the Viennese banker and the French director of the water company to join him in a game of bezique. The two Englishmen attached themselves to the *chef de train* and advised changes in his plans for the passengers' comfort. They agreed to the official's decision to continue to serve complete meals "to keep up morale"—a proposal that was to leave the passengers cold and half starved later on.

Only the cabaret singer Paula von Werner showed signs of unease during that first morning. The French diplomat and the English girl secretary tried to be friendly to her, but she answered only in monosyllables, just sitting in a window seat and staring at the wall of snow that steadily rose thicker along the whole length of the train.

Luncheon, perfectly cooked and with the usual variety of dishes, was served in time. Boredom seemed to improve appetite. By tacit agreement almost all the passengers then returned to their sleeping berths and sought warmth while fully clothed under the blankets. That night dinner was not quite so lavish as the printed menu promised. It was eaten with only a few lights switched on; most of the bulbs had been removed. In an endeavor to keep up spirits the *chef de train* brought a portable gramophone. Unfortunately, he had only two records. When *The Blue Danube* jingled out for the third time there were groans of annoyance; the gramophone was switched off. Some of the men spanned out the time by drinking heavily. Most, except for the imam and the King's Messenger, were soon in a state of somnolence and there was nothing to do but turn in for the night. The Frenchman and the ship captain had lost heavily in their card game with Souf, who seemed to find the situation amusing. By then the wind had dropped and the snowfall was only spasmodic. But the cold had become more intense, and there were sounds like pistol shots as ice cracked under the pressure of the weight of snow above it.

The next morning, with a breakfast of laced coffee again, stale rolls and a little butter, was uncannily quiet. The invisible world beyond the damp and dripping interior of the restaurant car seemed to be dead. All that could be heard was the occasional rasp of a shovel and the crunch of a pickax as the engineer and fireman, enduring appalling conditions in the locomotive cab, eked out the rapidly disappearing load of fuel. No one seemed to visualize the superhuman effort made by these two men hour after hour in their open cab—blazing heat before them and paralyzing cold to the side and rear—to maintain some heating in the cars.

Sheer animal instinct for survival now began to manifest itself among the marooned passengers. There were accusations about taking a second cup of coffee, complaints that the staff were favoring one passenger more than another in the distribution of blankets, tale-telling about someone allegedly wasting water for washing, and pointless demands to any and every member of the train staff to "do something." A valid reproach, though there was nothing to be done about it, was the state of the toilets. With snow building up underneath the cars the outfall had frozen solid and the bowls were overflowing. The same conditions affected the washbowls, and after the first eight hours no one could wash in clean water.

No positive move was made to seek outside aid because of the general conviction of the train staff and the passengers that rescue was on the way and in fact was expected hourly. That an entire train had virtually disappeared off the face of the earth must, of course, have been known in both Bulgaria and Turkey, let alone the Compagnie office in

Paris. It is a measure of the total paralysis of communications, services, and even military logistics that nothing could be done about it. The bitter truth that survival had become a matter of self-help came on the third day. By then the locomotive's fuel was down to debris. It was decided that train heating would have to be abandoned and the little remaining fuel kept for the cooker in the kitchen, where there was also a small stove burning kerosene, which was kept for emergency. Food was cut to one hot meal a day, though coffee, made with melted snow, was served at intervals. It was weak and without milk. Worse, the warming brandy was no longer added, resulting in someone attempting to raid the liquor store at night. The chef thereupon concealed the last two bottles, to be used only in case of illness.

On this third morning of isolation the *chef de train* asked everyone to assemble in the restaurant car. He asked for volunteers to form a party to tunnel through the snow and try to find help. He explained that there was a village about three miles to the south easily seen in normal conditions over the flat country.

All the men, except for Souf who mumbled something about a heart condition that prevented him undertaking any physical work, volunteered. The party, as could be expected, was led by Sir Gilbert Clayton, who was in fact in poor health, and the King's Messenger, who broke every tradition and solemn rule by removing his chained bag and placing it in the train's safe. By general agreement three elderly men—the Jesuits and the imam—were thanked for their offer but told they would be used only if extra hands were vitally needed.

The plan was to work away from the locomotive, where the heat of the dying fire had created a narrow band clear of snow, and then tunnel through the drift on a steady slope upwards until they could move on the surface. The train's emergency equipment provided some shovels and iron bars, and from the locomotive there were the stoker's tools. The *chef de train* divided his workers into parties of two or three, each working for fifteen minutes, by which time they were exhausted from the cold and effort, and returned for rest and to thaw out. Those not actually working on cutting the frozen snow into lumps and carrying them back from the tunnel to force into the drifts along the side of the train constructed makeshift sledges from compartment doors and table legs, which would serve for runners.

At the entrance the tunnel was some fifteen feet below the snow surface. After one squad of three, including the *chef de train*, had penetrated ten feet the entrance collapsed. Frantic digging from outside quickly rescued those trapped inside. Those who had worked for longer than the stipulated fifteen minutes to rescue them had the telltale marks of frostbite on their hands and faces. Although the wooden steps at the car doors were ripped off to help prop up the roof of the tunnel, there were further collapses before—after nearly forty-eight hours of unremitting effort—the tunnelers broke through to the surface.

The chef and two of his kitchen staff were chosen to barter for food in the village that was said to lie three miles to the south. Not only did an increasing blizzard periodically blot out visibility beyond a couple of yards, there was no evidence of any path, field wall, or animal track. After nearly two hours of floundering waist-deep in pockets of piled-up snow, dragging the sledge behind them, the scouts saw no human habitation. Then, in a brief cessation of the snowfall, the men saw a series of undulations, with a wisp of smoke emerging from small hillocks. Breasting a small hill, they got a better view and saw that there was a tiny clearing almost free from snow in which a handful of men were standing. Each of them was pointing a gun menacingly at the strangers.

One of the kitchen hands, an Armenian who spoke Turkish, shouted that they were only seeking help. He caught the word "brigands" in the shouted reply. Whereupon he advanced with his hands above his head and explained that they had come from a train marooned in the snow and sought help and food. Although the villagers lowered their guns, they made no gesture of friendliness when the three cautiously approached until they were in the clearing. The kitchen hand said they wished to buy food. One of the villagers stretched out his hand, pointed with the other at the strangers and then to his outstretched palm, indicating he wanted money. Unwisely, the foraging party had not faced the truth about the likely greed of poverty-stricken peasants. The chef had only his personal money with him. He displayed the coins and notes he had, and the village leader grunted something about preferring real money—gold or silver.

Barter thereupon began with exasperating slowness. The villagers almost gloatingly described that there was no way of reaching Cherkes Keui railroad station, and that they had not seen any official or policemen for more than two weeks. Eventually the rescue party was led into a mud hovel with two rooms. An open fireplace smoldered in one corner. An old woman with plaited hair was crouched over a black cooking pot full of white beans simmering in some strong-smelling liquid. A few scrawny chickens were pecking at the mud floor. A gesture of hospitality came when the man poured a small quantity of slivovitz into a chipped mug. Each of the three men gratefully drank the burning liquid.

The village leader lunged at one of the chickens, wrung its neck and offered the still-convulsive bird. Satisfied with the money given him, he then killed a second bird. After some more argument the deal ended with a few eggs taken from a pile on a shelf and some slabs of stale bread. After nearly two hours the foraging party were back at the train, having to dig away new snow that had blocked the tunnel exit. The chef dressed the chickens, cut them into pieces and made a stew given a little zest with paprika. The eggs and bread were meticulously sliced so that everyone—passengers and train crew alike—had a minute portion. One wonders how Georges Nagelmackers would have felt had he lived to see a menu such as this served by a Cordon Bleu–trained chef aboard the Orient Express. If nothing else, this meal—and a few more that followed—made the catastrophe that befell the Orient Express train No. 3 in February of 1929 into the most memorable event in the entire history of the Wagons-Lits Compagnie over half a century. Only after the meal was served—on gold-embossed bone-china plates and with heavy silver cutlery properly laid—did the chef and the two kitchen hands who had accompanied him remove their boots. Both had severely frostbitten toes.

No one was talking much any more. The general mood was one of fatalistic resignation. Sheer physical exhaustion, plus mental dullness as the result of the cold and lack of food, meant that on that third night everyone slept soundly—all except Paula von Werner. Although by general agreement two or three people now occupied each compartment in order to conserve the heating while it existed and then to gain a little warmth from body heat, the Viennese singer had refused to share a compartment with Miss Poole. Nor had she helped in any chores, lying for hours in her bunk and refusing even the little food and coffee that were available.

A conductor passing her compartment during the night heard low moans. Trying the door, he found it was locked. With the help of other staff he broke down the door. One of the girl's arms was hanging at the side of the berth, blood dripping from the wrist. Her face was white and she was unconscious. On the floor was a broken hand mirror. A tourniquet was applied to her arm and the slash she had attempted on the artery bandaged. Some of the chef's precious brandy was forced between her lips. She gradually came around and began to moan that she wanted to die. Given a sedative, she fell asleep; Miss Poole became her nurse and guardian.

The next day was as cold as ever, but it was clear that the worst of the snowstorm was over. A general collection of money had been made the previous evening, and there was an impressive sum in silver coins of half a dozen currencies, plus a few gold coins from the Jesuit priests, who had brought them for barter in the desert areas where they were to work. Four volunteers, including the chef, who insisted on going again despite his frostbitten feet, set out with two sledges. The villagers were more friendly once they saw the silver, and though they insisted that they were themselves on the brink of starvation they managed to provide two sheep, two goats, cheese, eggs, unleavened bread, and some *su-boregi*, a cheese-flavored pastry. They were also persuaded to sell some logs, which were lashed to the second sledge. When the chef and his companions made off, they saw the villagers, holding their shotguns, following them out of the village. The chef feared that they would be tempted to take the foodstuffs they had sold and silence the four men in the bargain. His alarm increased when, stumbling ahead with the heavily loaded sleds, they heard shouts behind them. Several of the peasants came hurrying toward them, waving some objects in their hands. But the gestures were friendly, and the objects were thin pieces of wood to tie on the feet and operate as snowshoes.

After these useful accessories had been fixed as tightly as possible with bits of cord, the peasants' leader said they would accompany the party for a short distance, excitedly pointing in a westerly direction. The atmosphere had cleared considerably, and a few moments later the party saw in the distance four or five black dots moving fast and haphazardly. The meaning of the peasants' shouts now became clear: wolves. If they scented the carcasses of the sheep and goats they would undoubtedly attack. Two of the peasants fired a couple of shots into the air. The small wolf pack stood motionless and then ran off into the distance. With friendly grins and words of farewell the peasants then turned back. The return journey was made without mishap. The sight of so much food restored the morale of everyone on the train. Staff and passengers alike set to in helping to break up the logs to feed the kitchen fire, cut up the meat, and collect clean snow to melt over the fire, which was soon blazing. Cleaning jobs were allocated to make the restaurant car and the sleeping berths more hygienic and a rotation system was drawn up to maintain a permanent lookout from the roof of the engine cab. The *chef de train* and the *chef de cuisine* estimated the minimum food necessary for a maximum of a further forty-eight hours, and the food was strictly rationed.

It was in the middle of the afternoon on the sixth day that the lookout yelled like a man possessed. Half a mile ahead of the train, moving over the level band of snow, was a motorized sledge; close behind it were five more, manned by Turkish troops and railroad workers, carrying supplies of food and drums of kerosene.

The frantic welcome over, the rescuers described how they had been working their way from Constantinople without respite, except when a bout of snow made movement impossible, for four days and nights. They also reported that a snow plow pushed by two of the heaviest locomotives available had been due to start out within an hour or so of their own departure. But they had to admit that they had not had a glimpse of it. The immediate reaction of the passengers, reveling in the warmth from the section of the restaurant car nearest the kitchen, and greedily eating the scratch meal of bread, olives, and cheese which were distributed by the soldiers, was that the snow plow hardly mattered. The great thing was that their predicament was known to the outside world, and that they had already been rescued.

Before another night's darkness set in, everyone could see the two great plumes of black smoke rising into the now calm atmosphere, creeping steadily nearer. Soon, the plow locomotives came into sight, leaving a black swath behind them, with the metal of the rails gleaming in the last vestiges of a pale and setting sun. More troops and railroad workers were on the rescue train. Though darkness brought a return of paralyzing cold, all the men of the rescue party worked to clear the snow from the train's wheels and to thaw the frozen brake cylinders with kerosene-soaked rags set on fire. They even managed to thaw the steam pipes and connect them to the leading plow locomotive, thus restoring heat to the train.

In a commendably short time the coupling at the front of the Orient Express locomotive was linked to the plow and with much whistling from both of the hauling locomotives the journey to safety began. The Turkish authorities had fixed a second snow plow at the rear of the rescue train, and this was now used to clear away the snowdrifts that had blown across the cleared track.

At last the Turkish authorities restored rudimentary communications, using wireless transmitters. The officers of the army detachment were visibly embarrassed and most apologetic. When Sir Gilbert Clayton told them about his predicament—the possibility of missing the audience with King Faisal of Iraq, the Turkish commander ordered by radio a tank to the scene of the holdup. Clayton was taken in the tank to Rodosto (Tetirdag), on the shore of the Sea of Marmara, only fifteen miles south of the marooned train. There a naval launch was put at his disposal; he reached Constantinople ahead of the train and continued his journey to Baghdad, the weather having greatly improved.

The return to Constantinople, a distance of some eighty miles, was uneventful and made at a snail's pace. None of the passengers who were subsequently interviewed by pressmen complained. But one incident indicated that the complete isolation of the train for so long a period was at least in part due to the inefficiency of the authorities. Even the approximate place of the train's freeze-up had evidently remained unknown to the Turkish railroad officials and the military and police commanders. The Orient Express had, for seven days and nights, simply disappeared into thin air. It was an occurrence worthy of a horror movie, and it did not happen a century or two ago, or in some far-flung desert or jungle, but in 1929, in an area only a short distance between two large and bustling modern cities.

Sir Gilbert Clayton occupied his office as high commissioner to Iraq for only a few months. He became the only victim fatally affected by the Orient Express disaster. He died, on September 11, 1929, six months later at the age of fifty-four, having never recovered from the exposure to intense cold and his strenuous exertions.

Confirmation of the complete breakdown in railroad organization came when it became known that the west-bound Orient Express which left Constantinople at the height of the snowstorm was also held up by drifts in the same area as train No. 3. At what place and time this train must have passed her sister express is not clear, but in normal weather and daylight each train would have been visible to the other. This second train was stopped for ninety-six hours west of Çorlu. It was carrying two hundred and fifty passengers, but being in the first stage of its journey, it carried plenty of food and fuel. Its nonarrival at Edirne alerted the station staff, who dispatched two locomotives to help drag it out of the drift, along with a car carrying a work gang. The train was quickly freed from the drift that had brought it to a stop, but on the route to Edirne another immense drift had meantime blown over the line. It was not particularly deep but stretched for more than half a mile. After the worst of the snow was dug away, the train, now with three locomotives, forced a way through.

The "disappearance" of the Orient Express became a worldwide sensation even among all the other stories of death and disaster in Europe under Arctic conditions. For many days newspapers published largely imaginative stories. Among the latter were the inevitable reports that all the passengers and staff were dead from exposure and frostbite. The Compagnie, naturally reticent about this reflection on their famed care of their passengers, had been as bereft of reliable information as anyone else. The French and British governments had exerted pressure on the Turkish authorities to do something, but once again the problem was communication, cable and telegraph links being interrupted and the radio services almost useless for days because of the phenomenal incidence of static caused by the electrical storms accompanying the blizzards.

All was soon forgotten except, of course, by those who had experienced the freeze-up. The Compagnie provided free accommodation at their Grand Hotel Pera in Constantinople for those who wanted to rest and recuperate, and the frostbitten victims were treated in the German Brandfeld Hospital, to which Paula von Werner was also taken. Doctors decided that the slash she had attempted on her wrist was only superficial. She was diagnosed as a harmless hysteric and discharged after a few days' rest. Within a week she was appearing to full houses in the Constantinople cabaret, billed as "The Singing Heroine of the Orient Express," and with her pay doubled.

The whole incident was something of a reflection on the Compagnie's insistence that, come what may, its famous train had to run, as well as on the incompetence of the Turkish railroad officials. In contrast, the train personnel had acted courageously throughout, and the passengers composed an address of gratitude to them which all signed. They made a collection; the sum of money presented to the heroes of the incident was not revealed, but was said to be generous, as indeed it should have been.

Thus ended one of the most unusual disasters in railroad history. No official inquiry was ever publicly made to apportion blame, possibly because both the Christian and Muslim countries involved were content to ascribe the whole sorry business to an act of God. Better to forgive and forget.

Even before the damaged cars of the stricken train had been shunted out of the platform at the Constantinople terminus another —and immaculate—Orient Express stood alongside, ready for its run across a continent rapidly recovering from the chaos of the century's worst winter.

Chapter Twelve

THE TRAIN IN FICTION
AND ON THE
SCREEN

No FORM OF PUBLIC TRANSPORT HAS ATTRACTED WRITERS IN the unique way that the Orient Express did. Comparatively few people could afford to travel on it, but millions of newspaper readers knew about it. Apart from the appeal it had for authors, who would describe —or criticize—the luxury and glamour of the world's most costly train, there was the fascinating potential inherent in the oft-exploited formula of bringing a group of strangers into a place from which, temporarily, they cannot escape. The haunted country house, the desert island, the lifeboat, the prison, and, more recently, the hijacked aircraft have regularly provided ready-made drama for any writer with the ability to describe human characters and contrive a series of emotional clashes and alliances among them.

The spate of novels with plots involving the passengers on the Orient Express achieved massive popularity coincidentally with the train's best-known period—the time between the two world wars.

In D. H. Lawrence's *Lady Chatterley's Lover*—first published in 1928 and banned in Britain for more than thirty years—Connie (Lady Chatterley) goes to Venice with her sister after the wife of her lover Mellors, her husband's gamekeeper, returns to him. Connie's father, the veteran artist Sir Malcolm Reid, arranges to take his daughter back to England to her impotent husband. "The old artist always did himself well," Lawrence wrote. "He took berths on the Orient Express, in spite of Connie's dislike of *trains de luxe,* the atmosphere of vulgar depravity there is aboard them nowadays." On the train, as it approaches Paris, Connie tells her father that she is pregnant, greatly to the old man's delight. She does not tell him that the father of the child is her husband's gamekeeper.

Lady Chatterley's Lover, Lawrence's last novel, was written after he had searched in Asia, Australia, and New Mexico for a more acceptable society than that offered by the money-grubbing, luxury-loving industrialized society of Western Europe. Ill and poor, he returned to Europe in 1925 to live in the South of France and Italy. To him the Orient Express, carrying the rich, the vicious, and the decadent, seemed the appropriate place for contrasting the honesty of his heroine with the hypocrisy of her father.

Probably the only people who were able to purchase the French-printed edition of the book were precisely those Lawrence meant to attack. It was the reading matter of many Orient Express travelers looking for sexual stimulation as they embarked on an illicit adventure. And the well-thumbed copy, handed from one friend to another on their European travels, was eventually destroyed because of the risk of discovery by customs at the British port of entry.

If *Lady Chatterley's Lover* was for years known to most people only by rumor and hearsay, there was another work that rapidly achieved enormous popularity. It was written by Maurice Dekobra, whose books are now little read, but before, during, and for some years after the Second World War it had huge sales.

Dekobra was a Parisian, born in 1888. Before he turned to novel writing he was a well-known journalist, ranging the world as a foreign correspondent. As a fiction writer, his output was prodigious. Forty of his novels became best sellers and were translated into twenty-nine languages.

His Orient Express story, *La Madone des Sleepings (The Madonna of the Sleeping Cars*)* was the best known. It first appeared in 1927 and ran through edition after edition for the next thirty years. It

*Bestseller Library, Paul Elek, London, 1959.

used the well-tried formula of romance, intrigue, and terror among characters living and loving against a background which was that of the Orient Express route, plus several scenes in Russia.

The book's appeal to the reading public, in the throes of a world depression and facing the ominous inevitability of war, was the fascination of seeing the last survivors of European aristocracy clash with the sinister secret agents of the Soviet Union, fortuitously brought face-to-face by the Orient Express. The cast of characters included princes of nonexistent European principalities, amorous politicians, and an extravagant but almost penniless society woman offering her charms, not necessarily to the highest bidder but to the most virile and satisfying client.

The heroine, Lady Diana Wynham, "descendant daughter of Scottish kings," entrances the reader with her amorous adventures. Without her love of travel and the convenience of the regular schedules of the Orient Express, the story might well have been set entirely in London, where Lady Diana appears naked on the stage at a charity show to the great benefit of an institution for tubercular patients and also the packed audience of "the cream of society." She evades the resultant scandal in Mayfair thanks to the facilities of the Compagnie, whose Express wafts her eastward to Germany and Russia, where she is soon deep in the throes of love and espionage.

Dekobra's characters were tailored to create melodrama. Very few of his readers could ever have met such people in real life. The creation of men and women anyone might meet and know, and to put them in the exciting situation of traveling together on the Orient Express, was left to Graham Greene in *Stamboul Train,** published in 1932.

Previously Graham Greene had done well enough with *The Man Within* and not quite so well with *The Man of Action.* But *Stamboul Train* was to establish him as one of the most fascinating novelists of the twentieth century. At the time writing the book was something of a gamble for him. He left his job on *The Times,* calculating that he had enough money for his wife and himself to live very modestly for three years while he devoted all his days to authorship. They were fortunate enough to find a cottage for a rental of one pound a week

*William Heinemann; London, 1932.

at Chipping Camden in the Cotswold country. Even on the comparatively inexpensive standards of domestic economy before the Second
World War, times were hard for Greene and his wife. He earned a little
money by book reviewing, but was in debt to his publishers, Heinemann, with whom he had an agreement to write three novels in return
for £600 a year for three years (the payment shared with the American
publishing firm of Doubleday).

Greene thereupon took stock of his ideas about writing and decided to adopt a completely new style. *Stamboul Train* was the result,
based on the now famous Greene formula of high adventure and
psychological insight, combined with superb storytelling. The book
transformed Greene's situation. Good reviews ensured large sales.

The train in his story ran for only part of the journey as the Orient
Express. Its route was Ostend-Cologne, Vienna-Belgrade-Istanbul. It
may well be that the author, in his insistence on the veracity of every
detail, felt he was able to portray the western section of the journey
with greater realism than by describing the Calais-Paris-Trieste route,
with which he was not so familiar.

It is testimony to the author's superb ability to create realism in
his stories that *Stamboul Train* fully conveys the excitement and the
sense of glamour experienced by travelers on the Orient Express as well
as the feelings of those viewing the cars' luxurious interior as they stood
beside the tracks. No one, not even an Orient Express *chef de train*,
could fault Greene's description of the train, its personnel, its passengers, and the stations at which the train stopped.

Stamboul Train is not a cliff-hanger in the conventional sense of
the term. Rather, it is a fascinating examination of the clash of people
of widely different background and character thrown together by circumstance, and of the secrets seemingly ordinary people try to conceal
behind a façade of conventional behavior. The book has has gone on
selling, year after year, since 1932.

Two years after the publication of *Stamboul Train* came one of
the most famous detective stories of all time—*Murder on the Orient
Express.** Its author, Agatha Christie, later a Dame of the British
Empire, was a regular traveler on the Orient Express accompanying her

*Collins, London, 1934.

husband, Colonel Archibald Christie, to and from the Middle East. The colonel, after distinguished service in the Royal Flying Corps during the First World War, spent most of his later life as a senior officer in British intelligence. His wife thus gleaned many real-life secret service plots, which she used as backgrounds for some of her thrillers. She retained the colonel's name as her pen name after her first marriage ended in divorce in 1928; afterwards she married Sir Max Mallowan, a renowned archaeologist.

As a result of her trips she was able to write a story in which the background of train and railroad cannot be faulted for any inaccuracy. Her own feelings about the inherent drama of the train are reflected in an early sequence of dialogue between her famous detective, Hercule Poirot, and a director of the Compagnie, M. Bouc:

"Ah," M. Bouc sighed. "If I had but the pen of a Balzac! I would depict this scene [on the departure platform at Istanbul]."

"It is an idea, that," said Poirot.

"Ah, you agree? It has not been done, I think? And yet—it lends itself to romance, my friend. All around us are people, of all classes, of all nationalities, of all ages. For three days these people, these strangers to one another, are brought together. They sleep and eat under one roof, they cannot get away from each other. At the end of three days they part, they go their several ways, never, perhaps, to see each other again."

Devotees of Christie's detective stories know immediately from this airy supposition that the seeds of mystery and mayhem have been planted. Wherever Poirot went mysteries had to be solved.

The gentle, tiny Belgian detective made his debut in Christie's best seller, *The Mysterious Affair at Styles*, published in 1920. He was clearly the *alter ego* of the author, who, through him, could conceal her lack of knowledge of police routine in countries outside Belgium where the action of her stories takes place, and also avoid any discussion of masculine strength by making Poirot reticent and quite old, relying entirely on his famous "little grey cells" to outwit the criminal.

The author's ability to create an array of believable characters who all seem potentially innocent but possibly guilty makes any Christie novel a classic of its genre. *Murder on the Orient Express* is probably the best she wrote based on this formula. At first the grouping of ill-assorted strangers seems to stretch the long arm of coincidence beyond credibility, but gradually and believably Agatha Christie—or, rather, Hercule Poirot—forges link after link to bind them together and extract the damning evidence.

The sleeping car on the Istanbul-Calais section of the Orient Express presented a perfect background for the story. Agatha Christie knew what traveling in the carriage was like from her many experiences on it after a wearisome journey from Syria on the Taurus Express, which ran from Baghdad via Ankara and Adana, arriving in Istanbul a couple of hours before the Orient Express's departure.

In the story, there are fifteen passengers: one detective, one future murder victim, and the significantly ominous total of thirteen suspects.

With the author's meticulous study of the makeup of the Orient Express on its first stage of the east-west route, and of the actual layout and interior fitting of the cars, down to the position of the toilet and the conductor's seat at the end of the corridor, the reader is given a picture of almost photographic precision. Behind the locomotive was the restaurant car, the door to which was locked except at mealtimes. Then came the sleeping car occupied by the story's characters, watched over by the conductor from his seat at the far end of the corridor, thus effectively excluding the possibility of a total stranger entering from the cars making up the remainder of the train—unless the conductor himself was an accomplice.

Not the least fascinating feature of the story is the typical mixture of passengers who traveled on the Orient Express in the 1930s. From the writer's own experience during that decade the Christie assembly could have been seen on the train at almost any time during the busy season. The only anomaly is that the train was so full in midwinter, a situation that becomes a key factor in Poirot's unraveling of the mystery.

As the passengers are having luncheon Poirot's "little grey cells" begin examining them. At the table across the aisle sit three men—a big, swarthy Italian, a spare Englishman "with the expressionless, disapproving face of the well-trained servant," an American "in a loud suit" with an equally loud voice. Beyond them, sitting by herself, is one of the ugliest old ladies Poirot has ever seen, but dressed and bejeweled as only someone very rich can afford to do: a Russian princess whose husband, long since dead, had had the perspicacity to take himself, his wife, and his wealth out of Russia before the Revolution. At a large table are three women—a pretty English girl, an elderly American lady boring her companions and everyone within earshot with interminable stories about her daughter, and an apparently harmless middle-aged woman "with an amiable face rather like a sheep." Immediately behind the English girl is the stiff, straight back of someone obviously military —a colonel in the Indian army. He sits alone, and Poirot wonders why, as he had overheard him talking intimately to the English girl before the train started.

Poirot's little eyes begin their survey of the passengers at the tables on his side of the dining car. At the far end is a woman who looks like a lady's maid from some North European country—she is probably Scandinavian, possibly German. Then, at a table for two, an animated couple—the man in his thirties, the girl at a guess no more than twenty. Newlyweds? Finally there are two men, the young McQueen with whom Poirot had shared a sleeping berth on the previous night and who had explained that he was secretary to an American tycoon named Ratchett, with whom he is now sitting. Superficially Ratchett appears to be a bland old man perpetually smiling on a kindly world. Only his eyes belie that assumption. They are "small, deep-set and crafty." The devotee of whodunits will be left in no doubt as to the identity of the victim: Ratchett is typical of the characters in the reasoned mystery story who display more than the normal proportion of evil to tempt hitherto law-abiding citizens to rid the world of them. In fact Ratchett is to die that night, unpleasantly and in silence, of multiple stab wounds.

Of course, the simple and obvious solution of the murder of a man safely ensconced in a first-class sleeping berth on the world's most carefully controlled and lavishly staffed train would be an athletic miscreant who boarded the train somewhere, hid himself in an improbable niche, and leaped without injuring himself onto a soft embankment, disappearing into some obscure Balkan town till the hunt was given up and the Express roared on.

But Agatha Christie was well aware of climatic conditions in the Balkans in midwinter. Her journeys on the Orient Express were usually in the colder months, because her husband organized his excavation work in the desert terrain to avoid the hot season. She therefore used a situation that she knew quite frequently occurred—a complete stoppage when the train ran into a snowdrift and the delay until snowplows could clear the track. All she had to do for her story was to make the snowstorm exceptionally severe, preventing plows from getting through for many hours. She also used a familiar source of argument among the passengers—the correct time. There was irrefutable evidence from witnesses of the murder that the crime must have taken place at two different times a full hour apart. This ostensibly impossible situation was created by having the murder committed as the train crossed the Yugoslav border and moved from Eastern European time to Central European time.

For the reader interested in railroad timetables Agatha Christie presents plenty of facts. The train leaves Istanbul at 9:00 P.M. On the uneventful stage of its run it takes twenty-three and three-quarter hours to reach Belgrade. It leaves Belgrade at 9:15 P.M., with an additional coach from Athens at the rear. The weather is deteriorating and the train takes nearly three hours to cover the 100 miles to Vinkovci, arriving there twenty minutes behind schedule. By then it is snowing hard. In spite of the appalling weather the *chef de train* and the locomotive driver decide to risk going ahead on the stretch across flat, almost uninhabited country to the next stop at Brod. The decision is a wrong one. On the 35-mile run between the two towns the train plowed into an impassable drift. Most of the passengers insisted that they were unaware of the hold-up until they awoke at dawn—to find a wall of snow on either side of the train. But at least one passenger had been awake that night: to leave a fellow traveler mutilated and dead.

It would be unfair to the few who have not read the Christie book or seen the movie based on it to elaborate on the extraordinary background of the thirteen passengers which Poirot uncovers and thus finds a solution to the murder.

Agatha Christie provided a fine description of the Orient Express during the 1930s; for the period following the Second World War one of the most accurate records of the postwar train is in the final chapters of Ian Fleming's *From Russia, with Love,** his best James Bond thriller. Not everybody is an admirer of Fleming's literary genre, but Fleming's books remain favorites with the mass readership. Fleming wrote *From Russia, With Love* in 1956, four years after the first James Bond adventure brought him international fame and resulted in phenomenal sales all over the world. In one year, in 1965—though not since—twenty-nine million copies were sold. And millions of people have seen the James Bond films, which were better than the books they were based on.

"Not that it matters, but a great deal of the background to this story is accurate," the author writes in a preface to the book. The knowledgeable traveler with experience on the Orient Express would agree with this statement. Here is a passage that evokes nostalgia for the romance of the railroad age:

The great trains are going out all over Europe, one by one, but still, three times a week, the Orient Express thunders superbly over 1400 miles of glittering steel track between Istanbul and Paris. Under the arc lights, the long-chassied German locomotive panted quietly with the laboured breath of a dragon dying of asthma. Each heavy breath seemed certain to be the last. Then came another. Wisps of steam rose from the couplings between the carriages and died quickly in the warm August air. The Orient Express was the only live train in the ugly cheaply architectured burrow that is Istanbul's main station. The trains on the other lines were engineless and unattended —waiting for to-morrow. Only Track No. 3, and its platform, throbbed with the tragic poetry of departure.

Agent 007 is about to board the train with an attractive Russian girl. He is unaware that she is working for SMERSH, the most secret of all Soviet espionage organizations. So the journey is fraught with the possibility of murder, treachery, and mystery.

*Jonathan Cape, London, 1957.

. . . the train screeched slowly round Seraglio Point. The lighthouse lit
up the roofs of the dreary shacks along the railway line . . . With a jolt and
a screech of couplings, the Orient Express took the points and swerved away
from the through line. Four sets of rails with grass growing between them
showed outside the window, and the empty length of the down platform
. . . It was a typical Balkan wayside station—a façade of dour buildings in
over-pointed stone, a dusty expanse of platform, not raised, but level with the
ground so that there was a long step down from the train, some chickens
pecking about and a few drab officials standing idly, unshaven, not even trying
to look important . . . The engine whistled, a new kind of whistle, the brave
shrill blast of a Greek engine driver . . . The front section of the Orient Express
began to move. The section that would be taking the northern route through
the Iron Curtain—through Dragoman on the Bulgarian frontier, only fifty
miles away—was left beside the dusty platform, waiting.

The train is scheduled to reach the Greek-Yugoslavia frontier at
1:00 A.M. after the train has "laboured up the moonlit valley of the
Vardar towards the instep of Yugoslavia." After the Greek frontier
station at Idomeni, hours pass before the Orient Express steams slowly
into Belgrade. But punctually at nine the new engine takes the long
train out on its all-night run down the valley of the Sava. "Vinkovci
came and Brod, and then, against a flaming dawn, the ugly sprawl of
Zagreb. The train came to a stop between lines of rusting locomotives
captured from the Germans and still standing forlornly amongst the
grass and weeds on the sidings."

Zagreb left behind, the train "hammered into the mountains of
Slovenia where the apple trees and the chalets were almost Austrian."
After Ljubljana the train stops at Sezana. When the train pulls into
Maestre "there was the beginning of canals. A cargo gondola full of
vegetables was moving slowly along a straight sheet of water into the
town" . . . Venice a minute or so later. "Padua came, and Vicenza, and
a fabulous sunset over Verona flickered gold and red through the cracks
of the [compartment's] blind."

Now Bond's journey approaches its climax as it roars into the
Simplon tunnel. Then Domodossola and soon the Italian frontier
. . . the lights of Switzerland. "Soon the train would be slaloming fast
down through the foothills of the Alps into the Canton Valais . . .

Lausanne came, and, an hour later, the French frontier at Vallorbe."
It is 4:30 in the morning, and another hour to Dijon. Why, for Bond,
the journey of the Orient Express ended there rather than at the Paris
terminal is the climax, or near climax, of the story.

Cecil Roberts, who at the age of twenty-three became the literary
editor of the *Liverpool Post* and during the First World War was a
British war correspondent with the Grand Fleet and thereafter a high-
ranking public servant with the Ministry of Munitions, had become
well known in the United States through his books, his six American
lecture tours, and between 1940 and 1946 as a member of the British
government mission in Washington. A prolific author—he wrote more
than fifty books of poems, biographies, travelogues and romantic novels
—was in 1937 tempted by the glamour of the Orient Express and its
cargo of bizarre and mysterious passengers to combine a sort of guide
to the places on the train's route with a fictional adventure. *Victoria
Four-Thirty,** the title embodying the departure time from the London
terminal of the boat-train connection with the Orient Express in Paris,
has the almost standard basis of these travel stories of thrusting a group
of strangers into the confinement of a train for days and nights on end.
To emphasize the luxury surrounding them, Roberts launches his story
through the eyes of a poverty-stricken porter on the London station
platform.

The passengers are a varied lot. There is Gollwitzer, the noted
musical maestro, who is en route to the Mozart festival at Salzburg, and
Nikolas Metaxa, surely the only Greek to fail to make a success of
running a restaurant in London's Soho, who has rescued sufficient
money from the debacle to buy a second-class ticket back to his home
in Athens. Inevitably, as in all such between-the-wars novels, there is
a Balkan crown prince, orphaned since his father lost his throne and
his life in a bomb explosion. He is only thirteen and evidently too young
to realize that this may well be a journey to a similar bloody end, for
he is solely preoccupied with the loss of a pet rabbit he reared with
loving care at his English boarding school. Then there is the newlywed
couple en route to Kitzbühel, Austria, for their honeymoon; their
dialogue is characteristic of the sexual mores of the period.

*Hodder & Stoughton, London, 1937.

Leads to potential heroes, heroines, and villains are generously supplied before the train leaves London. Is Sister Teresa just a nun returning to her vocational duties in her native Transylvania or someone very different from a virginal religious? How long will General Zoronoff, once of the imperial Russian army and now a chauffeur-guide to American ladies doing Europe in search of culture, be content to do nothing about the menace of Russian communism? Will Percy Bowler manage to elude the irate management of a Midlands engineering works and his relatives, and get away with the money he has apparently embezzled from both firm and family? And who is the Turk Alexander Bekir?

If the lack of real drama in the ensuing sequences as the Orient Express rumbles across Europe is a valid criticism of Roberts's skill as a novelist, he can at least be commended for his ability as a travel writer —which was, of course, his chief métier.

At about the same time that Roberts's book was published, a Dutch author, A. Den Doolard, had considerable success in his country with *Orient Express.** It was a historical romance based on careful research and dealt largely with the Macedonian Question—the problems of the territory lying between the southern frontier of Bulgaria and the Gulf of Salonika. At the time Doolard was writing his book the hopes of Macedonian autonomy had collapsed with the establishment of a military dictatorship in Bulgaria in 1934 and the suppression of the Macedonian revolutionary organization, the Komitadshi, and expulsion of its leader Mihailov.

Since the turn of the century Macedonia had been in a state of almost perpetual anarchy, with the Orient Express maintaining its route through the turbulent area with varying degrees of success. These conditions the author saw at firsthand, looking out of the train window while "drinking iced plum brandy in the luxurious Wagon-Restaurant of the Orient Express."

The book is a mixture of fact and fiction. There are factual references to at least seven attempts by the Macedonians to blow up the train. "If they pick the right day," Milja, the heroine, is told by her

*English translation by David de Jong, published under the title *Express to the East,* Arthur Barker, London, 1936.

uncle, a Komitadshi leader, "many a high-stationed gentleman will go up in the air with it, and when that happens they imagine that all of Europe will be concerned about Macedonia once more, and make it at last independent . . ."

Milja is in fact a key operator with the freedom fighters. She marries their chief and works as a courier, constantly traveling on the Orient Express in the guise of a wealthy woman with a cosmopolitan background. These journeys revive her memory of the first time her uncle had taken her as a young girl to see the train. He had said: "It's an important line, Milja. Once a day a train passes which comes from Athens by way of Solun and goes to Belgrade, and then way off to the capital of France. The Orient Express, it is called. It's a train for rich people, you see. Everyone of any importance rides in it—ministers of state, wealthy merchants and the like, all high Europeans, as I call them. Often I stand here watching it pass. We'll see it pretty soon, for it comes by in the late afternoon. The cars are painted blue with yellow stripes, and when they go by I say 'There rides money, Kosta, and power; but there does not ride happiness.' "

In the conventional manner of espionage couriers, Milja never really knows what she is doing or what she is carrying. There are the usual instructions, to be obeyed unquestioningly, of sitting in cafés at specified times waiting for contact with mystery men, and receiving sealed envelopes to be taken to some town on the Orient Express route. Unlike the stereotypical beautiful spy, Milja never enjoys her luxurious all-expenses-paid existence. The contrast between the comfort of the train and the wretchedness of a peasant woman in the fields alongside the track is too great for her. She is ashamed of the luxury in which she is cosseted:

Here she sat, doing nothing but lean on soft pillows and stare outside, spending enough money to support this woman and her husband and her children for a whole week . . . In the dining-car she had been scrutinised as if she were some odd animal just escaped from its cage. All that polite bowing and whispering, only because she had put money on the table—money for the polished and warmed monogrammed plate with its austere W.L., money for the silverware, for the polished windows which seemed too intricately fastened for any common mortal to raise, money for the electric fan, money for the rosewood woodwork . . .

Dedicated communist that she is, Milja leaves her luxury first-class sleeping berth and goes to the third-class coach to sit with some peasants—Serbs whom she had been brought up to hate.

Respecting the factual basis of the story, the author eschews a happy ending. Milja's husband is killed in a skirmish with government forces, and she dies when the train is wrecked, possibly by accident but probably by sabotage, to be buried secretly in one of her uncle's fields, the corpse safe from the marauding Turks who made a practice of mutilating the dead bodies of their Macedonian enemies. The thunder of the Orient Express passing close to her unmarked grave was her daily requiem.

No one knew where Milja's grave was. But whenever Kosta [her uncle] ploughed in the spring, plodding patiently behind his two buffaloes, he thought of her. Twice daily the Orient Express thundered by. It appeared and vanished again, all in the space of ten seconds, and a moment later the smoke from its engine had drifted away over the barren hills. That train came from a strange world in which Milja had lived, a world of which he understood little more than did his black buffaloes, who snorted as they dragged the wooden plough through the crumbling earth.

Lawrence Durrell, author of the *Alexandria Quartet* and superb descriptive works on the Mediterranean islands of Corfu and Cyprus, wrote a memoir* of the time he was connected in 1951 with the British embassy in Belgrade, in the decade after the end of the Second World War. It was a time when Iron Curtain restrictions, lack of passable roads, and shortage of gasoline made the Orient Express, however dilatory and irregular its service, the only artery through which contact with the West was maintained. Durrell provides a delightful account of the varied passengers who arrived and left on the Express, always to the fascination of the ordinary people of Belgrade. The picture of the scene is put into words by the author's colleague, Antrobus, a British

Esprit de Corps, Faber, London, 1957.

diplomat, "portentous, always dropping into a whisper, clicking his tongue, making a po-face, pursing his lips . . ."

Another author attracted by the glamour of the Orient Express was Eric Ambler, described by his contemporary Graham Greene as "unquestionably our best thriller writer." Ambler's *The Mask of Dimitrios** is the story of a master criminal. After a body identified as that of Dimitrios is pulled out of the Bosporus, by chance a British writer of detective stories, Charles Latimer, learns of the dead man's fantastic career of crime and begins his own investigation, which involves him in dangerous adventures and surprising discoveries.

The route of the Orient Express across Europe provides the locale of the plot—or series of plots. The train had been the main source of Dimitrios's criminal activities: murder in Turkey, involvement in political assassination in Bulgaria, robbery in Yugoslavia, espionage throughout the Balkans, Greece, and Turkey, white-slaving and drug trafficking in Paris. Latimer, in tracing this master criminal of Europe between the wars, goes from town to town served by the famous train—Istanbul, Athens, Sofia, Belgrade, Geneva, Paris.

The Mask of Dimitrios is the only major story of its genre which involves the meticulously screened personnel of the Orient Express in criminal activities. One of Dimitrios's most profitable activities was the manufacture, supply, and distribution of cocaine, heroin, and morphine in France and Western Europe. The main processing factories were in Bulgaria and Turkey, and more than a hundred pounds of drugs were shipped every month to France—via the Orient Express. On one occasion the drugs came in a coffin escorted by one of the gang, but the usual way was to put them in packages to be loaded in the Orient Express baggage cars. Still more was brought by a sleeping-car attendant who brought heroin and morphine with him when he went on duty at Sofia and handed it over when the Express was shunted through the track sidings into the Paris terminal. This last method was discovered by the police, and the sleeping-car attendant and six of the Paris gang were arrested.

The book begins with the detective traveling to Istanbul. It ends

*Hodder & Stoughton, London, 1939.

as he catches the Orient Express in Paris and returns to Sofia, his adventures over and the mask that had for so long concealed the true features of Europe's most ruthless criminal finally torn away.

One novel with an Orient Express theme, even though it did not achieve best-seller status, was to become the basis of the first—and still the best—movie featuring the train. Its author was Ethel Lina White and its title *The Wheel Spins.* * The Balkans—the rich mine for writers of whodunits—once again provided the background, and there was the standard mixture of travelers who, for one reason or another, had selected that turbulent area as their destination.

Iris Carr is attractive, rich, independent, and an orphan. She rather inadvisedly has opted for some obscure Ruritarian resort for a vacation. She suffers sunstroke while waiting at the station to catch her train back to England and is thereby in a daze for the entire journey. Her headache is not alleviated by one of her companions on the train, an English governess of indeterminate age but forceful personality, who loses no time in telling Iris that she can speak ten languages—an accomplishment she believes may be useful before the train journey is over.

Settling down for the journey are such unusual passengers as a doctor whose sinister appearance might well intimidate any patient; he is accompanying a person with face and body completely swathed in bandages. No experienced reader of thrillers would take the bland clergyman and his wife at their face value; nor the honeymooners who the governess, if no one else, is positive have never participated in the marriage service. And there is a baroness—who, in Orient Express fiction, is always a phony or, worse, a conspirator in some political plot. Add to this motley band a train crew with a menacing air, and we may be sure that this is one journey of the Orient Express bound to unnerve the directors of the Compagnie.

Alfred Hitchcock, already a master at keeping moviegoers on the edge of their seats, bought the film rights of the book and put two British writers, Frank Launder and Sidney Gilliat, on the job of writing the screenplay for a film called *The Lady Vanishes.* They injected

*Collins, London, 1936.

humor, drama, and mayhem into the story with all the ingredients that have made every Hitchcock movie a masterpiece of its kind.

Margaret Lockwood played the heroine. Two aging English men about town, whose lives never moved very far from cricket pitches and golf courses, replaced the elderly spinsters in the novel. The only passenger who is above suspicion was played by Michael Redgrave, since then an honored Shakespearean actor and a Knight of the British Empire. The governess in the novel became a British secret service agent in the movie, and was played by Dame May Whitty. She is en route to Whitehall with a code book on which world peace depends. Her baffling disappearance while the train is in motion is the film's high point, which Hitchcock handles in his inimitable way.

Although the movie managed to re-create the excitement of traveling on the Orient Express and the atmosphere of Eastern Europe, many of the sets were studio mock-ups, partly for reasons of economy and also because the political situation in Europe made filming on the Orient Express route difficult and risky. But the film was one of the first major productions to exploit the fascination of transcontinental rail travel. It was so successful that Hitchcock decided to pursue the genre in *Night Train to Munich* and *Crook's Tour*.

With *The Lady Vanishes* the train-drama movie came of age, after passing through a long period of development. One of the first films of this genre was *Arrival of a Train at a Country Station*, made by Louis Lumière in 1895. It was shown in London, at the Polytechnic in Regent Street, and sound effects were provided by apparatus behind the screen. The sight of a locomotive steaming head-on toward the audience was too much for some people, who rushed for the exits.

Show business saw that the "living pictures" could well be a gold mine, even at the price of a penny or two for admission. With France then leading in movie technology, the train theme naturally attracted producers to the idea of a film about the world's most famous train, the Orient Express. However, the design of the coaches inhibited the photography of the passing scenery. The idea was taken up in America, where a camera was set up on the observation platform on a train running through the Rocky Mountains. The film was first shown at the St. Louis Exhibition of 1903 and was advertised as Hale's Tours. The floor of the narrow auditorium was made to thump up and down while the film was screened. The film became a fairground attraction all over Europe. Showmen were not averse to misrepresentation then as now, and in France, Germany, and Italy, the film of the trip through the American Rockies was advertised as a journey on the Orient Express through the Austrian Alps.

These films were merely novelties portraying allegedly real events. The first story picture, *The Great Train Robbery*, made by Edwin S. Porter, became a worldwide success, and is still shown periodically by film clubs and societies. It was in fact made on a train running on the Lackawanna Railroad near Patterson, New Jersey. Once again some exhibitors in Europe enhanced the appeal of the film by alleging that the holdup occurred on the Orient Express in a lonely area of the Balkans, in spite of the fact that the film showed an obviously American sheriff and his posse in hot pursuit of the thieves.

The long saga of filmed train dramas ended—at least temporarily —with *The Lady Vanishes*. The outbreak of the Second World War brought more exciting plots for movies and, in any event, trans-European trains no longer ran except in an ersatz version under the swastika. After the war there was a spate of war movies featuring air force and naval exploits, commando raids, and life in Nazi-occupied countries.

The two movies to commemorate the life and death of the Orient Express, which had made its reappearance by 1945, were the James Bond box-office winner *From Russia, with Love* and *Murder on the Orient Express*. In 1974 another *Murder on the Orient Express* movie, based on Agatha Christie's book and by far the most expensive picture involving the famous train, became a worldwide box-office success. Its director, Sidney Lumet, capitalized on the public's nostalgia for a glamorous period. Records and photographs from the Compagnie's files were used for the mock-ups of the sleeping-car interiors and the sumptuousness of the restaurant car. The movie was a period piece, in terms of both the plot and the atmosphere.

It was a disappointing movie despite its box-office success resulting from a massive publicity campaign and a line-up of stars unequaled in the ailing film industry: Sean Connery, Vanessa Redgrave, Wendy

Hiller, Sir John Gielgud, Richard Widmark, Ingrid Bergman, Lauren Bacall, Anthony Perkins, Michael York, and Albert Finney, who was miscast as the diminutive Belgian detective Poirot.

All in all, however, *Murder on the Orient Express* was not a bad curtain for a train that by the time it was seen by millions of movie fans—most of whom had never seen the train or even heard of it—was no more.

Chapter Thirteen

THROUGH THE WAR
AND THE IRON CURTAIN

Between march 1938 and march 1939—that is, between Hitler's proclamation of Greater Germany, when his troops crossed the Austrian frontiers, and the annihilation of Czechoslovakia—Britain and France wavered between the alternatives of appeasement and resistance to Hitler's ever-increasing threats. The Führer had torn up all treaties he had signed, which included those governing the control of international railroad communications.

When the *Anschluss* of Austria was completed, the Reichsbahn took over the Austrian State Railways and broke all the contracts that existed with the Compagnie. The control of all international railroad services, running from the German frontiers in the West to those of Austria in the East, were handed to Mitropa, the German counterpart of the Compagnie. The same occurred in 1939 in Czechoslovakia, and after 1940—when France, the Netherlands, and Belgium were occupied by the Nazis—with Mitropa control stretching from Hendaye on the Spanish frontier to Hungary.

During the winter of 1939, the Simplon Orient Express continued to run from Paris to Athens and Istanbul avoiding Germany, of course, but incongruously accepting at Belgrade the Berlin sleepers sent to the then neutral Yugoslavia. This lasted until the end of the "phony war," when Hitler attacked the Low Countries and brought France to her knees.

When the war reached its initial climax, with the Dunkirk evacuation of British troops, the French armistice, and the Battle of Britain in the air, the Nazis did their utmost to prove their control of Western Europe by maintaining an ersatz version of the Orient Express. Hitler's Reich Ministry of Transportation and the Reichsbahn made a great fuss about their "luxury train" running to the gates of Asia. Only the Nazi elite could travel on the new German Orient Express, and soon such journeys became extremely dangerous. French Resistance fighters were quick to sabotage the tracks and to place explosives on the trains, as did, later, those in Yugoslavia.

The Compagnie's offices had been transferred from Brussels to Paris and their directors put up a stubborn resistance to German pressure. Obviously, they could achieve little. The Compagnie's staff remained loyal and never abandoned the carriages, although the engine drivers and *conducteurs* were often cut off from their homes for weeks, stranded in some far-away places, subjected to bombing by the Royal Air Force, to sabotage actions by the French Maquis, and to continuous derailments caused by blown-up tracks. Some of the Compagnie's employees were, in fact, members of anti-Nazi Resistance and often carried secret messages and conveyed information to Allied agents. A number of them were arrested by the Gestapo, deported to German concentration and labor camps, and seven were executed as "spies" and "terrorists."

In 1941 the Mitropa managers ordered that many of the sleeping cars be used as "hotels" in various French towns, because they were considered safer for housing Nazi officials and SS officers than accommodations in the urban areas, which were often subjected to Resistance sabotage. In Italy—particularly after Mussolini's fall—Greece, and the Balkans, the ersatz Orient Express was the target for similar actions of guerrillas. For some months after the successful German invasion of the Caucasus the train maintained some semblance of a reliable service between Berlin, Vienna, and the Balkans.

Many of the notorious Nazi bosses traveled on the train between

Berlin and the Balkan capitals on their diplomatic missions, which, in fact, meant carrying Hitler's orders to his puppets, such as Marshal Antonescu of Rumania, Admiral Horthy of Hungary, or the Croatian *Poglavnik* Ante Pavelić. Among frequent travelers were Admiral Canaris (chief of the German secret service), Franz von Papen (who presided over the Nazi espionage network in Ankara), and an SS general with the ominous name of Killinger who was the Nazi overlord of Rumania.

Occasionally diplomats of the few remaining European countries were given facilities by the Reich Foreign Ministry to use the ersatz Orient Express in order to reach their embassies in the Balkans or to return home. One of these privileged neutral passengers on the Nazi-run Orient Express in early July 1944 was Raoul Wallenberg, who belonged to the wealthiest banking family in Sweden. His tragic story could have provided the basis for any of the thrillers that fiction writers have woven around the famous train.

In June 1944, a few days after the Allied invasion of Normandy, Wallenberg was invited to a meeting at a quiet house on the outskirts of Stockholm. His hosts were the U.S. minister Herschel V. Johnson —after the war the U.S. representative on the Security Council of the United Nations—and President Roosevelt's special representative on the U.S. War Refugees Board in Sweden. The proposition they put to Wallenberg was brief and to the point: Would he go to Hungary to try to save the surviving Jews in Budapest's ghetto from the Nazi gas chambers and slave labor camps?

"As regards money," Johnson said, "my government will provide virtually unlimited funds in any currency you wish. The amount is really dependent on what you can take with you. I must stress that officially the Swedish consul general in Budapest will know nothing about your mission on behalf of the United States. Even wholly humanitarian activities by a neutral could seriously compromise your country. You will be appointed third secretary, a minor post which is hardly likely to cause undue interest either in Germany or Hungary."

Wallenberg's reply was immediate: "If I can save a single person I will go."

He left Stockholm a week later with only the luggage he could keep by him as personal cases and bags. He carried some packets of

German and Hungarian banknotes quite openly among his clothes and official papers. In the unlikely possibility of a check of his luggage at the German port of entry little suspicion would be aroused in view of the weakness of exchange rates in Hungary. But much more money had been concealed in the lining of two cases. The really sensitive material —lists of Hungarian anti-Nazis and dossiers on members of the Horthy administration known to be secretly pro-Allied and preparing to negotiate with the Russians—he kept in an official briefcase.

Wallenberg's journey through occupied Denmark and as far as Berlin was without incident, his ultimate destination at that stage not being revealed, and the Nazi security services were effectively misled into believing that he was taking up an appointment in the Swedish embassy in the German capital. He did in fact stay there for three days. The embassy was able to get him a reservation on the Nazi Orient Express due to leave Berlin the following night. He was the only foreign civilian among the Wehrmacht and SS officers en route to the Balkans; there were also some Germans, businessmen or officials of some ministry.

The train consisted of three coaches, one a sleeper with blinds already drawn and carrying a "reserved" notice with the SS death's-head insignia. The communicating doors to the other coaches were locked. Followed by a woman porter wrestling with his bags and cases, Wallenberg walked to the train and found his compartment. Three Wehrmacht officers and a civilian were already seated in it. The latter immediately made sarcastic remarks about the inconvenience of having a large amount of luggage in the compartment on a hot night, and insisted that the luggage be placed in the covered wagon-car attached to the third coach. Wallenberg looked suitably contrite and apologetically showed his diplomatic identity card. The civilian grunted in annoyance and then lapsed into silence.

On the interminable journey, as time after time the train was shunted onto sidings to allow troop and armaments trains to pass in one direction and an ominous number of hospital trains in the other, Wallenberg left the train for more than a few yards only once—when an air-raid warning in the Dresden area brought the train to a halt and the guard ordered everyone out to take cover in a culvert just ahead of the train.

He arrived in Budapest exhausted after a trip that took a little over thirty hours of actual running. He had not dared to do more than doze, and his only meals were snacks of black bread and ersatz sausage sold at the main stations. On the final stage of the journey, after the train had crossed the Hungarian border, the loquacious civilian ceased his questioning and began talking about himself. He claimed that he was personal assistant to Riecke, the state secretary for the Reich Ministry of Food, and was on the way to supervise the collection and transport of grain and fruit pulp about to be harvested in Hungary. He put Wallenberg on the alert for a trap by making snide remarks about German bureaucratic inefficiency and also by repeating rumors he had heard of Allied successes in France. Later Wallenberg described the man and repeated the gist of his conversation to Hungarian anti-Nazis, who ascertained that he was no purchaser of bulk food supplies, but an SS colonel of the Gestapo.

Once established at the Swedish legation in Budapest, Wallenberg began his rescue campaign. Jews were told how to insist that they had never taken up Hungarian citizenship, or if the evidence was to the contrary, how to forge papers to indicate they were subjects of Turkey, Lebanon, or any other country still beyond the grasp of the Reich. Hungarian police were being more cautious in riding roughshod over legal niceties as the Soviet forces drew nearer, and the Jews with the claims to neutrality could with some certainty rely on a long legal inquiry to confirm or deny their statements. Some twenty thousand Jews who had put in such claims received a sign from Wallenberg to stick on the door of their homes: "Under the protection of the Swedish Legation." Jews who had already lost their homes were put in thirty houses Wallenberg rented, which were crammed from cellar to attic.

In October, when Russian and Rumanian troops were within sixty miles of Budapest, Wallenberg believed his work was over. Horthy asked for an armistice, but he was abruptly deposed by Hungarian Nazi extremists led by Szalasy, and the hunt for Wallenberg was on. He fled to the Russians in January 1945.

If he was dubious about the welcome he would receive from the

Soviet army as the man who had saved thousands of Jews from extermination, he did believe that he would be treated with the consideration due a diplomatic emissary of a neutral country. Marshal Rodion Yakovlevich Malinovsky, the commander in chief of the Soviet forces in Hungary, indeed behaved with propriety toward him. But Beria's NKVD had other ideas. Wallenberg was arrested as a spy, taken to Moscow, and imprisoned in the Lubyanka. For more than ten years the Soviet government refused to reply to innumerable inquiries, notes, and appeals from the Swedish and American governments. Wallenberg had become a nonperson. Only after the death of Stalin, the execution of the notorious Lavrenti Beria, and the ascent of Khrushchev did the Soviet Foreign Minister, Andrei Gromyko, send a terse note, in 1956, to the Swedish ambassador, informing him that it had only recently been established that Wallenberg "had died of a heart attack on July 17, 1947." The note gave no further information, and it must be assumed that he died, whether from natural causes or by "liquidation," in a KGB prison. He was then thirty-four years old.

The only record of that errand of mercy, which began with a journey on the ersatz Orient Express and ended in the Lubyanka, was pieced together from recollections of some of the grateful Jews whom Wallenberg had befriended and saved.

AS EUROPE SLOWLY AND PAINFULLY RESTORED THE LINES OF COMMUNIcation after 1945 the Compagnie was ready to introduce, albeit gradually, a semblance of luxury into postwar trans-European railroad travel. Apart from providing personal trains for General Eisenhower and Field Marshal Lord Alexander during the final months of the war, the Compagnie's first public service was its run from Paris to Innsbruck on September 27, 1945. It was called the Arlberg Express, a name taken from the area of mountains between the Tyrol and the Austrian province of Vorarlberg, with the famous tunnel more than six miles long under the Arlberg Pass. A few weeks later the route was extended to Vienna, after the Allies negotiated train-transit facilities through the Russian zone of Austria.

From the first day of operation of this austere version of the original Orient Express the train became a focal point for spies, smugglers, black marketeers, fleeing Nazis and their ex-collaborators—hopefully disguised—and those of the rootless people of half of Europe who were able to pay for the tickets. The almost daily dramas of pursuit and escape increased both in number and bizarre intrigue after November 13, 1945, when the Simplon Orient Express began running once more —daily from Paris to Trieste and Belgrade, and three times a week to Istanbul via Sofia.

The Iron Curtain was not yet as rigid as it was to become later, and the Western Allies and the Soviets concentrated chiefly on screening passengers to ferret out Nazi criminals, who traveled in either direction. Former members of the Gestapo, SS men and quislings from Western Europe, Norway, and Denmark tried to reach Italy or Turkey in order to obtain passage to South America. Those Nazis fleeing from formerly German-occupied Balkan countries tried—often successfully —to go underground in Austria, Switzerland, and Italy.

After the fleeing Nazis came many thousands of people who "voted with their feet": people who wanted to leave countries where, by 1948, Communist regimes had been established. Soviet soldiers boarded the Orient Express and searched it for escapees. Watches, radios, tobacco, and spirits would buy their compliance in overlooking hiding places on the train.

Excesses of looting and assaults were reported by the trains' staff to the Allied Control Commissions, but complaints rarely produced anything but facile excuses from the Soviet members. Tension between Russia and the Allies grew after the breakdown of the Four Powers Conference in December 1947, and within six months the Iron Curtain became almost impenetrable.

Two American reporters, Roy Rowan and cameraman Jack Birns, were sent in 1949 by *Life* magazine to make a trip across the Iron Curtain—to cover the entire route from Paris to Istanbul. The cold war was becoming colder and the controls at every frontier were increasingly severe. Even the French and Swiss examined the passports and baggage thoroughly.

On reaching the Iron Curtain at the Hungarian frontier station of Hegyeshalom, the travelers experienced their first real adventure: the Orient Express was stopped for more than two hours. Gendarmes and

Soviet MGB agents collected all passports and took them to a guard's hut, where they were carefully scrutinized. Then they searched every compartment. Seats were turned up, toilet cisterns examined, and mirrors, picture frames, and electric bulbs unscrewed to look for hidden papers and money. Many passengers were searched and some taken to the station building, where they had to strip. All this was repeated on the Hungarian-Rumanian frontier at Lokoshaz and Curtici. The two American journalists meticulously noted in their report: 300 bulbs unscrewed, 20 toilets examined, including the backs of lavatory lids, 50 passengers frisked. At Lohozada the searchers took two and a half hours; 3 miles farther, at the Rumanian post of Curtici, they lasted from 1:30 in the afternoon to 6:20 in the evening, and the passengers arrived in Bucharest, totally exhausted, at 8:41 the next morning. The journey from Vienna to Bucharest—a distance of about 730 miles— took thirty-five hours, which meant an average speed of about 20 miles per hour. "The Bulgarians flagged the train at every mudhole," noted Rowan.

Few people, other than diplomats and Communist officials and officers of the armed forces of Russia and her Balkan satellites, traveled on the eastern sections of the route. The attempt to maintain a regular schedule was partly for the sake of prestige but also in the optimistic belief that normal conditions—that is, those pertaining up to 1939— would eventually be restored. The Simplon Orient Express became extremely popular among the privileged who could obtain permits to travel. Its cuisine provided the Communist hierarchy with a taste of the luxurious living that even an austerity-controlled Western Europe could manage as part of the normal service to travelers on its express trains.

The Arlberg Orient Express was invariably fully booked on its run through Austria. The Americans, British, and French tenaciously in- sisted on their rights to issue travel permits to their nationals, and in the Viennese headquarters of the Control Commission relationships on a personal level among the four powers were reasonably good. Protests or refusals of permits from the Soviet members were comparatively rare. The secret instructions sent down the line to guards at the checkpoints were another matter. The express left Vienna for western Austria, Switzerland, and Paris at midnight. Apart from those on official business, the train was used by the families of British and American army personnel and civilian officials for skiing holidays in the Tyrol and Switzerland. Every passenger had to have a gray pass in addition to his travel permit and passport. The gray pass was the target for Soviet guards when they had instructions to harass passengers; something could always be found to be wrong with it.

Typical of what occurred was the experience of two American women, Mrs. Lucile Vogeler and her sister, Wilhelmine Eykens. As a celebration of Wilhelmine's twenty-fourth birthday the two women planned a few days' skiing in the Tyrolean Alps. It was a cold March night in 1948 when, armed with the vital gray passes, they boarded their sleeper at Vienna's Westbahnhof. The train left on time at midnight.

Three hours later, the train stopped, as usual, before the bridge over the river Enns (a tributary of the Danube), which marked the division between the American and Russian zones.

Russian soldiers climbed aboard and, shouting, roused the sleeping passengers. A corporal took the American women's passports and gray passes. After a quick glance at the name on each passport he growled in bad German, "Your papers are not in order." He had barely troubled to glance at the passes. Clearly, he had been ordered to identify Mrs. Vogeler and her sister and take them off the train.

He betrayed the real motive for his attitude by shouting at Mrs. Vogeler: "We know you hate us. Hurry up and get dressed!"

The two women dressed as slowly as they dared, hiding their few valuables in their clothing. Mrs. Vogeler did her best to contrive the appearance of early pregnancy and her sister, who was by nature frail, heightened the pallor of her face to suggest illness. These subterfuges, they hoped, would minimize the usual risk of such Soviet checkpoint investigations—rape.

When they opened the compartment door the Russian corporal jerked a hand at the four suitcases, indicating that the women should pick them up and move toward the door at the end of the coach, where two soldiers waited with automatic rifles in the firing position.

Outside, under the floodlights, stood a Soviet army officer and a sergeant. As soon as the women were clear of the train the officer gave a wave with a sweep of his arm to order the locomotive driver to take the train across the bridge. It was all too clear that the two passengers he had been ordered to remove from the train were the only persons who interested him.

When the rumble of the train died away as it pulled up at the U.S. checkpoint on the far side of the bridge, the Russians shut off their floodlights. The officer, after a few words to the corporal guarding the two women, strolled off into the darkness. Half a dozen of the soldiers who had boarded the train or mounted guard on each side of the track disappeared into the gloom to a small wooden hut which was the only shelter at the checkpoint. By then sleet was falling steadily. Two soldiers and the corporal remained outside to guard the women, who had to stand beside the track until the corporal eventually ordered them to follow him to the shed.

Inside there was a stove burning lumber, surrounded by soldiers drinking some kind of alcohol from a large jar. There was a sergeant there, and after a time he told two of his men to let the women sit on their boxes near the fire. Some of the soldiers had a smattering of English and German, and they began asking questions about life in the United States in a friendly and clearly envious, if only half-believing, fashion. To enhance this amicable atmosphere Mrs. Vogeler did her best to answer brightly and amusingly, and the situation became easier until the sergeant tried to make the women drink some of their liquor. Both women politely refused. This infuriated the sergeant, who drank the lot and then hurled the jar at the wall of the hut.

He was quickly maudlin drunk and began fondling Wilhelmine, an action that encouraged the corporal to sidle up to Mrs. Vogeler. When both women repulsed them the sergeant took his pistol from his belt, released the safety catch and threatened to shoot either or both of them if his sexual proposition was refused. He next ordered his men out of the hut and began to undress. His eyes never left Mrs. Vogeler, her sister's frailty and paleness suggesting to him that she was hardly a desirable sex object. Then Wilhelmine began to vomit. Her sister went over to her to hold her head. She told the sergeant that her sister was very ill and beseeched him to permit her to take the sick girl into the nearby town of Sankt Valentin, which Mrs. Vogeler knew was only about a mile away and where there were one or two hotels and inns.

Nearly four hours had passed since the women had been taken off the train. With dawn the sleet had ceased. The lustful sergeant had by then disappeared, but his men, accepting that he had authorized their prisoners to walk to Sankt Valentin, did nothing to stop them.

In the village the women sought out the post office and asked to make a phone call to the U.S. High Commission in Vienna. They were told by a sympathetic but frightened woman assistant that no calls were allowed without written permission from the Soviet commander of the district. Infringement of the order meant imprisonment and probable execution. After some argument and pleading the woman agreed to transmit a telegram, addressed personally to General Keyes, the U.S. high commissioner, asking for urgent help. They then returned to the checkpoint on the railway, hoping that another train for Vienna would come along and they would have more success in boarding it. But there no train was due till midday. Meanwhile the corporal who had taken them off the train arrived with two MGB officers. One of the officers spoke fluent English and asked Mrs. Vogeler to recount what had happened. This she did in detail. Soon the corporal was cringing under a stream of Russian invective from one MGB man, while the other cursed the two women for causing so much trouble. "Get the next train to Vienna and never let yourselves be seen traveling in the Soviet zone again," he said.

There had in fact been a technical victory in that Mrs. Vogeler's telegram resulted in the Russian High Command in Vienna sending the MGB officers to the checkpoint and Sankt Valentin. A terse announcement was later issued by the Russians that "the guilty persons had been punished." The motive of the Russians in their badly organized plot to kidnap the two young women was that Mrs. Vogeler was the wife of a man whose name was prominent on the MGB list of suspected spies.

Robert A. Vogeler was the thirty-six-year-old assistant vice president of the International Telephone and Telegraph Corporation and its representative in Eastern Europe. A New Yorker, the son of naturalized French and German parents, Vogeler spent some time at the U.S. Naval Academy at Annapolis and subsequently was a student at the Massachusetts Institute of Technology—both activities duly recorded by Soviet intelligence as evidence of espionage training after Vogeler's name went on the list of potential spies and saboteurs during the war.

Vogeler was manager of the special products division of the Kellogg Switchboard and Supply Company in Chicago when Germany invaded Russia in 1941. He was in charge of producing equipment for the U.S. forces and, also, fifty thousand field telephone sets for the Soviet forces. Russian inspectors at the factory accused Vogeler of supplying them with inferior products, a groundless charge but, of course, duly noted in Moscow. In addition, he was denounced to the FBI by someone in the factory for making anti-Russian statements. The FBI took no notice of the report, but inevitably the same informant gave a more elaborate account to the Russians.

Before the end of the war Vogeler moved to a subsidiary of ITT and was sent to Vienna soon after VE day in 1945. In June 1946 Vogeler was able to obtain a house in the American sector of Vienna, where his wife and children joined him. It was a base from which he regularly visited Budapest and Prague, with periodic trips to Zurich and Rome to confer with ITT executives. These journeys to and from Soviet zones of influence served to confirm the suspicions of the Soviet counterespionage and security departments that Vogeler was a major spy.

His dossier grew, with voluminous reports of his journeys both by train and car, and in the space of two years—up to August 1949—there were records of twenty-three trips between Vienna and Czechoslovakia, more often than not by the Orient Express, a safer means of travel than a car, because driving always involved the risk of being stopped on some flimsy pretext by Soviet troops bent on looting or merely intimidating an American civilian. Vogeler also traveled by train for nine visits to Budapest in the spring of 1949, journeys that aroused the interest of the Hungarian State Defense Authority, Állam-védelmi Hatóság (AVH), the political police. Encouraged by their Russian MGB masters, the AVH eventually brought Vogeler in for questioning at its dreaded headquarters at Stalin Avenue, No. 60, in Budapest, where files on nearly every Hungarian adult, as well as hun-

dreds of other nationals, were kept. The interrogation, followed by
degrading treatment, threats of torture, and steady building up of
"evidence" of a major conspiracy against the state, fell into the familiar
pattern. Along with six others (including a Briton, Edgar Sanders),
Vogeler was put on trial. He was charged with espionage and sabotage,
and every effort was made to show that he had been the leader of a
major spy ring.*

The trial—with carefully rehearsed evidence and the promise that
if he made a full confession the sentence would be lenient—began at
the Criminal Court on Marko Street on February 17, 1950. Vogeler
admitted having "illegal contacts," was found guilty, and was sentenced to fifteen years' imprisonment. He remained in prison for only
one year. Efforts by the American authorities, plus a statement that he
had been well treated and had had "a fair and just trial," resulted in
his release in April 1951. He was handed over to a U.S. consular official.

It is doubtful whether the Hungarian and Soviet counterespionage
chiefs genuinely believed that Vogeler was a professional CIA agent.
More likely the charges were used as an excuse to arrest Hungarian
political malcontents by saying they were members of an American spy
ring headed by Vogeler. It would have been all too easy for the Hungarian political police to dispose of a secret agent by making him
"disappear," since such disappearances were a stock-in-trade of Communist political police.

Sometimes intended disappearances were crudely handled and
arranged "accidents" became simple murders. Such a case occurred five
days after Vogeler was taken in for questioning. The victim was one
of his friends, Captain Eugene S. ("Fish") Karpe, a wartime naval
intelligence officer. Karpe, from Delhi, Louisiana, had been appointed
naval attaché to the U.S. legation in Bucharest. This perhaps reasonably intrigued the Rumanians and Russians, for no one could pretend
that the maritime activities of Rumania in its coastal waters of the
Black Sea could really justify such an appointment. If Karpe had
confined his activities to those implied by his official position he might
have been tolerated. Military, naval, and air force attachés are tacitly
accepted by all nations, whether communist or capitalist, as genteel

*Robert A. Vogeler, *I was Stalin's Prisoner,* W. H. Allen, London, 1952.

spies, by custom and tradition strictly confining themselves to an intelligent assessment of the resources and policies in the host country of the parallel branch of its armed services.

Karpe would have been the first to admit that his activities far exceeded conventional duties. He was away from Bucharest as often as he was in his office, traveling like a long-distance commuter on the Orient Express to Hungary, Czechoslovakia, and Yugoslavia, and remaining for many days in Vienna. There is little doubt that he was engaged in intelligence work.

It was on one of these Orient Express trips that Karpe and Vogeler met. They became friendly, and when it was feasible they arranged to travel at the same time. This regular travel in company with each other, usually in the same two-bunk sleeping compartment, was, of course, noted by the MGB and AVH. Indeed, at Vogeler's trial it was alleged that he was one of Karpe's agents. But the allegation was not pursued.

The two men apparently did work together for their mutual benefit. Karpe, who had reliable or well-bribed friends among the station staff in Bucharest and other towns, as well as among the crews of the Orient Express, was highly successful in smuggling Rumanians and Hungarians to safety; some were helped by him because their names had been given to him by Vogeler as prewar employees of ITT in local factories and offices. Their continued loyalty to the company brought them the risk of arrest.

By early 1950 either Washington or CIA agents in Vienna came to the conclusion that Karpe's activities were putting him in extreme danger. He himself had reported that he was getting special attention. On three occasions, while traveling on the Orient section of the Arlberg Express from Bucharest to Vienna, he had as a fellow traveler a pretty blonde, a Hungarian who got on the train at Budapest. Karpe was a bachelor. On the first occasion he was happy enough to say yes when the girl asked if he would mind if she sat at his luncheon table. Conversation was inconsequential. The girl noted Karpe's rank by his uniform, asked how far he was traveling, and explained that she herself was going right through to Paris. She gave no explanation as to why she was traveling from one end of Europe to the other. When she joined the train on a second occasion, Karpe's suspicions were aroused.

When it happened a third time his forebodings were confirmed. Karpe reported his meetings with the girl after the second incident, and CIA agents checked up on her. To their amazement they discovered that she was the mistress of Matyas Rakosi, head of state of the Hungarian People's Republic. That Rakosi's currently favorite girlfriend had been employed to entice Karpe was evidence enough of the extreme danger he was in. The State Department ordered his immediate transfer. The order came on the same day as news of the opening of Vogeler's trial. Captain Karpe rejected the plan to get him out in an automobile under full diplomatic privilege and opted to travel by his familiar method on the Orient Express. He stopped off in Budapest and subsequently in Vienna, getting in touch with agents he had previously employed to smuggle out refugees from Hungary and the Russian zone of Austria.

This time, mainly on the grounds of friendship but also because of his strong streak of an almost schoolboyish sense of adventure, he hoped to get Vogeler out of prison and then onto the train. Vogeler was confined, with other top-security prisoners, in the old Maria Theresa barracks. The vast complex of buildings was surrounded by a high stone wall. A watchtower was manned day and night by guards with submachine guns at the ready. Nothing short of a wartime-style air attack, followed by a commando assault, could possibly have freed Vogeler.

Nevertheless Karpe was determined to make the attempt. He contacted men he optimistically believed were a hundred percent reliable, checked the duty roster of the train personnel to identify his helpers on the run between Budapest and Vienna, and tried to ascertain from an ex-prisoner the routine of exercise times, guard changeovers, and so forth. But he got little support for either his bizarre idea of an open assault on the prison or a scheme for kidnapping off-duty guards and penetrating the prison disguised in their uniforms.

Moving on to Vienna, he spent nine frantic days meeting CIA agents and Hungarian double agents. Karpe himself was determined to lead the rescue foray. He had an unusually designed cigarette lighter of Vogeler's that was to be used as a recognition item when the prisoner was contacted. Whether Karpe eventually abandoned the harebrained idea as impossible or whether he proposed to mount a more resourceful plan worked out with CIA agents in the West remains unknown. What is known is that he left Vienna on the night Arlberg Express bound for Paris.

Karpe was last seen by passengers and train staff in the dining car late on the evening of February 23. This was two days after Vogeler had been sentenced. The waiter subsequently said that the American had asked for a soft drink, explaining that he had tenderness in his foot which he suspected was gout. This contradicted rumors that Karpe had been drunk when he went to his sleeping compartment. The sleeping-car attendant knocked on Karpe's door when the train reached the Swiss border and passengers had to be awakened for passport and customs control. There was no reply. The door was unlocked and the compartment empty. The bedclothes were unruffled.

After the train had been searched, the U.S. authorities in Vienna were contacted by telephone. A search over hundreds of miles of track began. Karpe's mangled body was found in the Pass Lüg tunnel south of Salzburg. The face was unrecognizable, and the condition of the body suggested that he had been hit by more than one train after death. Among the papers and personal items in his pockets was Vogeler's cigarette lighter.

Rumors circulated in Vienna that Karpe was a notorious alcoholic and must have been so drunk that he opened the door of the sleeping car believing that it was the door to the other coach. But the U.S. authorities suspected that Karpe had been murdered.

Agents of the U.S. Counter Intelligence Corps in Vienna boarded the Arlberg Express on the same schedule as that taken by Karpe. They took with them a sandbag of the same height and weight as Karpe. When the train reached the Pass Lüg tunnel they opened the sleeping car door and let the sandbag drop out. It fell intact in the gap between the train and the tunnel wall—a space generously wide to allow men working on the line to stand in safety when a train passed.

Repeating the experiment, they found that two hefty CIC men had to grab the sandbag, lift it up, and hurl it with all their strength to overcome the wind pressure and to make the sandbag crash against the tunnel wall. It was quite clear that Karpe had been thrown out, with more than one man involved in the effort. Examination of the tunnel showed traces of blood and hair on the wall more than a yard above ground, with shreds of clothing and flesh where the body had then bounced under the wheels of the coaches.

Long before these experiments had been carried out or the findings issued—in fact, within a few hours of Karpe's death—Mrs. Vogeler in her Vienna apartment received a telephone call from a woman.

"Have you heard what happened to your friend and his fatal accident on the Arlberg Express?" the woman asked.

Mrs. Vogeler said that she had.

"Well, you'd better keep his fate in mind if you want to see your husband again." Then the phone went dead.

Many months later the Swiss police questioned a Rumanian, Rian Tarescu, who claimed that he and two students, on orders given them by a "foreign organization," had attacked Karpe and pushed him out of the train. How they managed to board the train, presumably in Vienna, elude the checks of the American guards at the checkpoint beyond the Russian zone, and conceal themselves in Karpe's sleeping compartment while he was having dinner has never been satisfactorily explained. It must be assumed that not all the traveling staff members of the Orient Express were anti-Communist.

Chapter Fourteen

JOURNEY'S END

THE DEATH OF THE ORIENT EXPRESS WAS PERIODICALLY ANNOUNCED over a period of several years ever since French railroad officials announced in the spring of 1961 that its final run would take place on May 27. But the demise, in the immortal words of Mark Twain, was on this and many later occasions "greatly exaggerated."

In 1961 the train was not running beyond Bucharest, and its restaurant cars went only as far as Vienna, where the majority of passengers alighted. But improvements in the track in Rumania and Bulgaria and the desire of the Balkan countries to have the benefits of this easily controlled means of communication with the West resulted in the train not only surviving that "final run" in 1961 but in slowly resuming its earlier routing as far as Istanbul, with a line to Athens. For almost ten years the Orient Express, though greatly reduced in size, luxury, and reliability, ran to and fro between Paris and Istanbul, poorly patronized by passengers traveling the whole distance but valuable for intermediate journeys; more and more stops were scheduled, so that the train became a series of "local" expresses linking the capitals and major towns of Austria, Hungary, and the Balkan countries.

Only exceptionally did a complete train cover the entire distance of 1,880 miles on the best route between Paris and Istanbul. Normally only one or two cars were retained during the many changes in direction, separation of cars and reassembly of different rolling stock. As many as twenty different locomotives might be used according to the varied resources of the companies involved. Cars for local passengers were attached and detached; not unusually a few cattle trucks would be added. Restaurant cars were frequently unavailable, necessitating longer stops so that meals could be obtained at some stations.

It is, however, pleasant to report that with all the restrictions imposed and nervous passengers sometimes being ordered to alight at some temporary stop to undergo yet another inspection, there were also occasions that did not lack humor. Gordon Brook-Shepherd, the distinguished biographer and historiographer of the Hapsburg monarchy, recounted how an Austrian businessman traveling eastward in midwinter of 1960 was pulled off the train at one checkpoint after a careful scrutiny of his passport and marched off to a military barracks nearby. His agitation deepened to terror when he found himself led before a Soviet captain. The salt mines of Siberia seemed to lie straight ahead. To his bewilderment, however, he was merely treated to several strong drinks and much back-slapping and finally led back through the snow unmolested to the waiting train. It happened to be the Russian captain's birthday, and he had ordered his minions to search the train for any passenger born on the same day to come and share his lonely celebration with him.

That the Wagons-Lits trains continued to run virtually without final cancellation of any service was a measure of the diplomacy and resourcefulness of the Compagnie in dealing with the railroads and governments of eight nations, some of whom for all practical purposes had severed normal relations with their neighbors. The Simplon Orient Express, in particular, was still leaving dead on time and arriving with only occasional delays. Nor was the train's slowness through some of the Balkan countries too exasperating for the passengers. High speeds remained routine from Paris to Budapest thanks to electrification. In addition to the French section with speeds unbeaten anywhere else in Europe, the 580 miles between Basle in Switzerland and Vienna had been electrified, and most of the lines east of the Austrian capital were also electric, although diesel-electric locomotives, with their capacity for rapid acceleration with heavy loads, were increasingly used.

By 1972 the death warrant of the Orient Express had been signed. By then it existed in name only, being in fact a succession of separate trains to which Wagons-Lits sleeping cars were coupled on and off. The state-owned railroad companies through whose countries the trains ran had taken over from the Compagnie the ownership of the sleeping cars. In 1974 the Thomas Cook Group ceased to represent the sleeping services on the Continent. Nagelmackers' Compagnie dropped from its title the proud "Grands Express Européens" and ominously added "du Tourisme."

SADLY RESEMBLING AN OVERAGED AND SLIGHTLY RADDLED PRIMA donna, the Direct-Orient Express, in "positively last and final appearance," sang its swan song along the tracks across Europe in May 1977. It was to have been a grand event as a mournful but fitting end to a spectacular performance that had lasted, with periodic interruptions as wars raged through Europe, for ninety-four years.

Only the twin ribbons of steel spanning Western Europe to the gate of Asia remained much the same. Since the Orient Express first laboriously rumbled on its historic route the Austro-Hungarian, German, French, and Italian empires had faded away. Emperors and princelings, sultans and caliphs, fascist and communist dictators, had risen and fallen. National boundaries had been redrawn, overrun, and drawn again. Nations had been broken up and new ones created. Difficult gradients on the track had been leveled, tunnels to shorten the distance blasted from rock, bridges built to span rivers and swamps, stations that tried to symbolize national wealth and prestige had risen in place of the whistle-stops of the nineteenth century. The greatest change of all was the sometimes invisible but all too frequently tangible and menacing testimony to the disunity of a continent—the Iron Curtain. The Orient Express had eventually managed to penetrate it, after the usual arguments, bickerings, and intrigues. But it was defenseless against its real enemy: the aircraft that telescoped the train's most usual schedule of sixty-seven hours for the whole journey to less than three hours.

The last run was timed to leave the Gare de Lyon in Paris at seven minutes before midnight on May 19, 1977, to commemorate the Orient Express's traditional reputation by departing precisely on time. It did not. There was a delay in shunting and coupling the locomotive, and the train did not leave until 12:13 A.M. on May 20. This was a technical calamity for the enterprising London firm that had sold thirty thousand commemorative envelopes bearing a French 80-centime stamp and franked Paris Gare P.L.M. 19–5–77; the envelopes were taken aboard in sacks and were given an additional Turkish stamp of 125 kurus and franked at Istanbul on May 22.

Nor was there much evidence of the old glories. No opulent sleeping and restaurant cars; merely one rather shabby sleeping car and three ordinary day coaches. French railroad officials had been understandably unenthusiastic about supplying the additional sleeping cars that could easily have been filled: they had the bitter experience of mysteriously losing some of their air-conditioned, luxury coaches for weeks on end in the Balkans and eventually finding them doing service on local expresses to furnish a touch of Western decadent luxury for Communist government officials.

Only eighteen passengers on this last Orient Express managed to get sleeping berths. Most were press reporters or TV men. The genuine enthusiasts had to settle for seats in the three-day coaches, taking with them food and drink to last for the journey; no meals were provided on the train, though facilities for buying it at stations en route were vaguely and cautiously promised. But in addition to the roast chickens, French bread, and vacuum flasks of soup and coffee, most of the passengers had managed to bring along bottles of champagne. Some of it was shared with a small crowd of shivering onlookers on the Paris platform as the barrier was shut and the guard blew his whistle. The night had little of the poetic springtime in Paris about it; there was a cold wind and the sky was overcast. As the train of four coaches and a locomotive rumbled slowly past the long and modernistic crack French expresses standing at the adjacent platforms the occasion inevitably became more of a funeral wake than an impressive, if nostalgic, commemoration of a milestone in the history of transport.

But for some hours, for those enjoying a degree of comfort in the sleeping car, nothing could erase the glamour of this final journey into the past. By daybreak the train was running along the shores of Lake Geneva, with the snow-capped peaks of the Alps on the eastern horizon. After the stop at the Swiss border the train passed through the 12-mile Simplon tunnel to emerge into the brilliant sunshine of Italy, and, after numerous and inexplicable stops, across the flat countryside to Milan. Mussolini's palatial station provided the now hungry and grimy passengers with the opportunity to wash and snatch a quick meal. Then on to Venice. The train was by now running late and no one was quite certain how long the stop would be; in any event it was midafternoon and the station seemed to be sharing the siesta of the Venetians.

Then came Trieste, with another long wait while passports and identity papers were examined. The border between Italy and Yugoslavia was jealously guarded by officials of both nations, none of whom seemed to be impressed—or even aware—that this was a historic train. But the station café was well stocked with food and Western drinks—inexpensive for those who could pay in U.S. dollars. More delays, with Italian and Yugoslav customs officials examining the baggage. Before the train started at twilight, a crowd of swarthy men, festooned with shabby valises and parcels, maneuvered for the best remaining seats in the day cars. At almost every stop ahead more people were due to board the train. For years the Orient Express had been the homeward-bound train for Turkish migrant workers, such as waiters, laborers, and workers in the engineering plants of Switzerland and western Germany, returning with their savings—souvenirs of high wages and good jobs—a thousand miles to their native villages.

The train traveled slowly across the Yugoslav plains, frequently halting at wayside flag stops, where in the darkness there were shouts and altercations as more people, with or without tickets, tried to scramble aboard. A good many were unlucky, though not every seat was by then occupied. The earlier arrivals simply barred entrance to their compartments. None of the distraught would-be passengers dared to shoulder past the train officials guarding the doors to the sleeping cars; these at least were kept inviolate for the "real" passengers.

At Belgrade more day cars were coupled to the front of the train, and there was a long wait while the hungry passengers besieged the mobile stalls selling food and cold drinks. There was even coffee in plastic beakers brought to the train by one of the staff. With still more time lost, the train eventually jerked into motion and crept along a single track through lush farmlands. The train slowed still more as the locomotive labored onto the limestone foothills to the west of the Balkan Mountains. Then came a halt for Yugoslav police and border officials to check papers. The VIP passengers were given only a routine check. But it was different in the crowded day coaches. Indignant men and women protested in vain in half a dozen languages and dialects as the security men methodically read every page of their passports, entry visas, exit visas, and work permits, and then probed into packages and baggage. But the inspectors remained polite and even-tempered even in the face of angry protests.

The officials eventually left, and the train moved slowly over a network of lines to the outskirts of Dimitrovgrad, the frontier town of Bulgaria, a large and modern industrial complex created after the war. It marked a change in atmosphere. The Yugoslav brand of communism had been tolerant toward the Westerners making this final journey. But Bulgarian border security guards and customs men were officious, and some were armed with submachine guns. Unsmiling, they snapped orders to everyone to open their baggage and hand over papers. Transit visas were read, taken away, and finally brought back with a stamp of approval. The train staff and railroad personnel had made themselves scarce and there were few onlookers.

Almost as soon as the train resumed its journey a Bulgarian inspector moved through the train checking the tickets that had been scrutinized a few minutes earlier. There proved to be no people bumming a ride, and the train moved fast—for a time at least—through heavily wooded country and then across intensely cultivated farmland. Men and women working alongside the track in the fields seemed to be gangs of some kind of labor force. A few paused long enough to wave to the crowded day cars. Sofia presented a large and immaculate station. The restaurant was spacious, the tables were set with gleaming cutlery on white cloths, but there was no evidence of anyone enjoying a meal there. In any event the officials waved the would-be customers back to the train, pointing to the station clock and shrugging their shoulders. Evidently an attempt was being made to make up time, and the only source of food was a quick-service café that sold a great variety of sandwiches, cakes, sausages, candies, and soft drinks. The obstacle to buying these goodies was that the only money acceptable was Bulgarian stotinki and levas. Only a few of the experienced travelers in the day cars had any, and there was apparently no money-exchange bureau.

The mysterious stops at wayside depots or in desolate country continued through the night as the train rattled to the Turkish frontier. Border guards checked the right of passengers to leave Bulgaria and then to enter Turkey, and the train rumbled slowly on a deteriorating track past villages with mosques crowned with minarets to prove that the world of Islam had at last been reached. From the day cars the wailing sound of singing rose as the glittering blue of the Sea of Marmara came into view.

Five hours thirty-eight minutes behind schedule the train came to a stop in Serketchi station in Istanbul. The two dozen passengers who had made the historic journey as a gesture to nostalgia rather self-consciously gathered outside their sleeping car and opened a few bottles of champagne while the Englishmen sang "Auld Lang Syne"—to the utter bewilderment of the railroad staff and the crowd of small boys hoping to earn tips for carrying their baggage. There was no more to be done. If the ghosts of nearly a century of the Orient Express operation hovered over them, they did not materialize.

It was all over.

But was it?

On that May day in 1977 the Orient Express may have been relegated to history, but the rails on which it ran still snaked their way across Europe, and if one was willing to change trains and sample the Soviet version of railroad travel, it was still possible to follow in considerable luxury that memorable route from Paris to Istanbul.

It was left to private enterprise to make at least a symbolic gesture to the past. The Zurich travel agency Intraflug began organizing package tours in October 1976, with clients traveling one way by air and the other by train. The flight between Zurich and Istanbul was scheduled for four and three-quarter hours; the train journey, rather optimistically, at about fifty-six hours. A second package tour, organized between Lausanne and Athens, was named the Simplon Orient Express.

Again the trip was one way by air and the other by train. The cars, hired or purchased, were all originally used on the "real" Orient Express. To them were added new dining cars and a shower car.

The Swiss enterprise of a package Orient Express tour was something as unique in its way as the original concept of a luxury transcontinental train—a privately run project making use of state-owned track facilities. A train staff of twenty handled deliveries of the finest foods Europe could provide—salmon flown in from Scotland, pheasant from an English farm in Norfolk, fresh fruit from Provence and Italy, a hundred bottles of champagne from the Rheims cellars, and caviar from the Soviet Union. The menus were to be up to the highest standard ever attained in the heyday of the train's career.

Eighty passengers booked on what they believed was indeed the Orient Express's last journey. On the return journey by train most of them changed into evening dress for dinner—to the bewilderment or amusement of the inhabitants of Belgrade and other towns who glimpsed this evidence of the decadent luxury of the West when the splendidly illuminated train made late-evening stops to pick up local wines, clean bed linen, and fresh food. After a brief stay to see the sights of Istanbul the passengers returned to Zurich, none of them having booked on the trip for any reason other than to revive past memories.

So successful was this first unofficial Orient Express trip that the Intraflug agency decided to repeat it in the spring of 1977, and this time the journey was made by rail in both directions by two trains, one named the Arlberg Orient Express, running from Basle and Zurich via Innsbruck, Vienna, Belgrade, and Sofia to Istanbul (still described as Constantinople in the firm's prospectus), and the other as the Simplon Orient Express starting in Lausanne and running via Milan, Venice, Ljubljana, Belgrade, and Salonika to Athens. Thus the entire family of the old Wagons-Lits system was resuscitated; there was, of course, no question of a regular service, and the journeys were made—and continue to be made in 1978 and 1979—a few times each year as holiday package tours for people who could afford to pay for the luxury offered. On the first few trips the price of a tour was about 3,000 Swiss francs (at the exchange rate then prevailing, $1,300 or £900). With the depreciation of the dollar and pound value, present-day tours became less affordable by the Anglo-Saxon tourists, although the fares were still not unreasonable, considering that the journey to Istanbul and back included a sojourn at the Hilton Hotel on the Bosporus, and that to Athens a stay at the Hotel Grand Bretagne, with "gala dinners" and a number of organized excursions and sightseeing tours, as well as short stays in Salzburg, Belgrade, and Sofia. At first seven sleeping cars, with single or double beds, two Pullman parlor cars, and a restaurant-and-bar car were used. The whole tour to Istanbul and back was scheduled for five days; that to Athens and back, for seven.

Because the names of the Orient Express and the Simplon Express continued to be used in official timetables, the agency appropriately named their special trains "The Nostalgic Orient Express" and "The Nostalgic Simplon Orient Express." For tens of thousands of now aging people who had worked on the railroads or lived near them, only their memories can conjure up the sights and sounds of the magnificent trains that embellished the Golden Age of rail travel. But for the select few there will still be tangible evidence of the trains' existence and even the chance to sample the kind of luxury travel unattainable today in aircraft or automobiles.

The idea of reviving the famous trains as tourist and vacation attractions was emulated by an American tycoon, James Sherwood, president of the Sea Containers, Inc., who owns the Cipriani Hotel in Venice, Italy. Starting in 1979, his company will run once weekly from London's Victoria Station a luxury train via Newhaven and Dieppe to Paris, and than via Lausanne and Montreux to Venice. Both the managing director of the Swiss agency and Sherwood were eager to acquire several Wagons-Lits cars—the first, to add them to his Nostalgic Orient Express; the other, to obtain authentic rolling stock for his Venice train. The opportunity came when the Compagnie put up several of its cars for sale at an auction on October 8, 1977, appropriately enough in Monte Carlo, perhaps the last bastion of Europe's "gracious life." The sleeping cars were built in 1929, each with bathrooms, and with décor by the best-known designers of the period, Prou, Morrison, and Nelson. One of them operated as the mobile headquarters of the German Wehrmacht during the Second World War. The dining car is older, built in 1926, and has two dining rooms seating thirty-two second-class passengers and twenty passengers, respectively. The *salon* contains wing chairs designed by Prou and wall panels by Lalique.

The announcement of the Wagons-Lits sale brought buyers from all over the world. A few of the privileged and wealthy, as well as notables such as Princess Grace of Monaco, aides of the shah of Iran and the king of Morocco, were aboard the train when it made its final run to the sale site from Nice—a trip of only 15 miles along the coast, but taken slowly enough for a champagne breakfast to be served by white-gloved waiters with all the deference of the good old days.

At the sale, which lasted only thirty minutes, the auctioneers—the famous firm of Sotheby Parke Bernet—the five Wagons-Lits cars fetched 1,450,000 francs (about $340,000). Two sleeping cars were bought by Sea Containers, Inc.

The *salon* car, with its two separate drawing rooms, and one sleeping car were bought by André Paccard, a French interior decorator who owns an estate near Annecy, in the foothills of the Alps, which is big enough for a stretch of private track where the cars will stand in nostalgic glory and occasionally move for a short run. The restaurant car, with its two dining rooms, pantry, kitchen, linen cupboard and wine cellar, was the only one destined to return to its original route. It was bought by the Swiss Intraflug.

There were souvenirs galore at the Monte Carlo auction for the enthusiastic but less wealthy admirers of the Orient Express. Linen and blankets from the sleeping berths, fittings and furnishings executed in the Art Nouveau and Art Deco styles of the 1920s, and lamps, chairs, and marquetry panels from the car walls were all snapped up by collectors. New York's Museum of Modern Art bought a water jug with silver mounts, and an anonymous collector in Virginia successfully bid by telephone for several lots, including a 1925 carpet designed by Marie Laurencin. Altogether these items brought in more than 2,300,000 francs (about $550,000).

Some other Orient Express cars are continents distant. Eight first-class cars and a locomotive were bought in June 1977 for exhibition in Otsu, Japan, the country's ancient capital on the shores of Lake Biwa and a popular tourist center. Otsu is also the site of a locomotive manufacturing plant, and the Orient Express rolling stock is shown as an example of Occidental style to be compared with Japan's own products of the past and present.

With the dispersal of its uniquely luxurious cars the Orient Express—at least in its official and historic mold—came at last to its not inglorious end.

Bibliography

Abbott, G.F., *Turkey and the Great Powers*, London, Scott, 1916.

About, E., *De Pontoise à Stamboul*, Paris, Hachette, 1884.

Allen, P., *On the Old Lines*, London, Cleaver-Hume, 1957.

Ambler, E., *The Mask of Dimitrios*, London, Hodder & Stoughton, 1937.

Arthur, G., *Life of Lord Kitchener*, London, Macmillan, 1920.

Auty, P., *Yugoslavia*, New York, Walker, 1965.

Bac, F., *La fin des temps délicieux*, Paris, Hachette, n.d.

Baicoianu, C.I., *Le Danube, Aperçu historique et politique*, Paris, Recueil-Sirey, 1917.

Baker, G.I. *The Passing of the Turkish Empire*, London, Seeley Service, 1913.

Bardens, D., *Zaharoff*, London, Humanity, 1936

Barsley, M., *Orient Express*, London, Macdonald, 1962.

Basch, A., *The Danube Basin*, London, Kegan Paul, 1944.

Behrend, G.H.S., *The History of the Wagons-Lits*, London, Modern Transport Co., 1959.

———, *Grand European Expresses*, London, Allen & Unwin, 1962.

———, *Pullman in Europe*, London, Ian Allan, 1962.

Benson, E.F., *King Edward VII*, London, Longmans, 1933.

Berghaus, E., *History of Railways*, London, Barrie & Rockliff, 1964.

Bird, M., and G. Kino, *Foreign Office Confidential*, London, Souvenir Press, 1961.

Blowitz, H. Opper de, *Une Course à Constantinople*, Paris, Plon, 1884.

———, *My Memoirs*, London, Arnold, 1903.

Buchanan, M., *Queen Victoria's Relations*, London, Cassell, 1954.

Busch, M., *Bismarck, Some Secret Pages of His History*, London, Macmillan, 1898.

Carmen Sylva (Queen Elisabeth of Rumania), *Mein Penatenwinkel*, Munich 1908.

Cars, J.des, *Sleeping Story*, Paris, Juillard, 1976.

Christie, A., *Murder on the Orient Express*, London, Collins, 1934.

Clough, S.B., and P. Gay (eds.), *The European Past*, New York, Macmillan, 1964.

Clissold, S. (ed.), *Yugoslav Handbook*, Cambridge University Press, 1965.

Colquoun, A.R., *Whirlpool of Europe, Austria and the Hapsburgs*, New York, Harper, 1907.

Commault, R., *Georges Nagelmackers*, Paris, La Capitelle, 1966.

———, *Le Wagon de l'Armistice*, Paris, La Capitelle, 1969.

———, *Bibliographie des écrits de Richard Wagner* (in *Revue Palladienne*, Paris).

Cookridge, E.H., *From Battenberg to Mountbatten*, New York, Day, 1968.

Corbin, T.W., *Romance of Modern Railways*, London, Seeley Service, 1922.

Corti, E.C., *Das Haus Rothschild*, Graz, 1945.

———, *Unter Zaren und gekrönten Frauen*, Graz, 1949.

———, *Leben und Liebe Alexanders von Battenberg*, Graz, 1950.

———, *The Downfall of Three Dynasties*, London, Methuen, 1934.

Cotterel, S. *Railway Handbook*.

Cougham, R., *Gulbenkian, Life and Times*, New York, 1960.

Courcy, J. de, *Searchlight on Europe*, London, Eyre & Spottiswood, 1940.

Cowes, V. *Edward VII and His Circle*, London, Hamish Hamilton, 1936.

Crompton, R.E., *Reminiscences*, London, Constable, 1928.

Cuddon, J.A., *The Owl's Watchsong*, London, Barry & Rockliff, 1960.

Davey, R., *The Sultan and His Subjects*, London, Chatto & Windus, 1908.

Daye, P., *Leopold II*, Paris, Fayard, 1934.

Dekobra, M., *La Madone des Sleepings*, Paris, Baudinière, 1925.

———, *The Madonna of the Sleeping Cars*, London, Paul Elek, 1959.

Demachy, L., *Les Rothschilds, Une famille des financiers juifs*, Paris, 1925.

Doolard, D.A., *Express to the East*, London, Barker, 1936.

Dorys, G., *Abdoul Hamide—intime*, Paris, 1902.

Drage, G., *Austria-Hungary*, London, Murray, 1909.

Durand, P.M.F., *La SNFC pendant la guerre*, Paris, Hachette, 1968.

Durrell, L., *Ésprit de Corps*, London, Faber, 1957.

Ellis, C.H., *Railway History*, London, Studio Vista, 1966.

———, *Rapidly Round the Bend*, London, Parrish, 1961.

———, *The Royal Trains*, London, Routledge, 1975.

———, *Steam Railways*, London, Eyre & Methuen, 1975.

Encyclopedia of Railways, London, Octopus, 1971.

Fenino, F., and Y. Broncard, *The Last Steam Locomotives of France*, London, Ian Allan, 1977.

Fichtenau, H. (ed.), *Beiträge zur neueren Geschichte Österreichs*, Vienna, Böhlaus, 1974.

Fleming, I., *From Russia with Love*, London, Cape, 1957.

Foxwell, E., and T.C. Farrer, *Express Trains*, London, Smith Elder, 1889; reprinted London, Ian Allan, 1965.

Giles, F., *A Prince of Journalists*, London, Faber, 1962.

Glaser, R., *Fürst Alexander von Bulgarien*, Bensheim, 1901.

The Golden Age of Trains, 1830–1920, London, Hamlyn, 1977.

Grant-Carteret, J., *Popold II, Roi des Belges et des Belles*, Paris, Michaud, 1908.

Greene, G., *Stamboul Train*, London, Heinemann, 1932.

Hantsch, H., *Geschichte Osterreichs*, Vienna, Styria Verlag, 1962.

Hecquard, A., *La Turquie sous Abdul Hamid*, Paris, 1901.

Hermant, A., *Souvenirs de la Vie frivole*, Paris, Hachette, 1933.

_____, *Souvenirs de la Vie Mondaine*, Paris, Plon, 1935.

Hewins, R., *Mister Five-Percent*, London, Hutchinson, 1957.

Hogg, G., *Orient Express*, London, Hutchinson Junior Books, 1968.

Hurmuzaki, I., *Documente privatoare la istoria Romanitor*, Bucharest, 1904.

Husband, J., *The Story of the Pullman Car*, New York, 1917.

Jelavich, C. and B., *The Balkans in Transition*, Berkeley, University of California Press, 1963.

Judd, D., *Eclipse of Kings*, London, Macdonald, 1975.

Kay, F.G., *Steam Locomotives*, London, Hamlyn, 1974.

Kerner, R.J. (ed.), *Yugoslavia*, Berkeley, University of California Press, 1949.

Kitchenside, G. (ed.), *Steam*, London, David & Charles, 1975.

Klaber, H., *Fürst Alexander of Bulgaria*, Dresden, Heinrich & Co., 1904.

Knappich, W., *Die Habsburg Chronik*, Salzburg, Bergland, 1959.

Kreidler, E., *Die Eisenbahnen im Machtbereich der Achsenmächte während des Zweiten Weltkrieges*, Frankfurt, 1959.

Kremnitz, M., *König Karl of Rumänien und Carmen Sylva*, Berlin, 1906.

Lamouche, L., *La Bulgarie*, Paris, Rieder, 1923.

Lawrence, D.H., *Lady Chatterley's Lover*, London, Pan, 1970.

Lengyel, E., *The Danube*, London, Gollancz, 1940.

Lendvai, P., *Eagles in Cobwebs*, London, Macdonald, 1970.

Lhotsky, A., *Österreichische Geschichtsschreibung*, Vienna, Universitätsverlag, 1962.

Lichtervelde, L. de, *Leopold II*, Brussels, Dewit, 1926.

_____, *Leopold of the Belgians*, London, Stanley Paul, 1929.

Lockhart, Sir Robert Bruce, *Retreat from Glory*, London, Putnam, 1934.

_____, *Friends, Foes and Foreigners*, London, Putnam, 1957.

Logno, G.C., *Bulgaria Past and Present*, Manchester, Sherrat & Hughes, 1936.

Marie-José, *Queen of the Belgians, Albert and Elisabeth de Belgique*, Paris, Plon, n.d.

Maurois, A., *King Edward VII and His Times*, London, Cassell, 1933.

Maxwell, H. (ed.), *Railway Magazine Miscellany*, London, Allen & Unwin, 1958.

Miller, W., *The Balkans*, New York, Putnam, 1899.

———, *The Ottoman Empire and Its Successors*, Cambridge University Press, 1934.

Minshall, M., *Guilt Edged*, London, Bachman & Turner, 1975.

Morand, P., *Tendres Stocks*, Paris, Gallimard, 1921.

———, *Ouvert la nuit*, Paris, Gallimard, 1922.

———, *Fermé la nuit*, Paris, Gallimard, 1923.

———, *Journal d'un attaché d'ambassade*, Paris, La Table Ronde, 1949.

Morgan, B.S., *The End of the Line*, London, 1955.

———, *The Great Train*, London, Patrick Stephens, 1973.

Morgenthau, H., *Secrets of the Bosporus*, London, Hutchinson, 1918.

Neave, Lady Dorma, *Romance of the Bosporus*, London, Hutchinson, 1949.

Neumann, R., *Zaharoff, The Armament King*, London, Allen & Unwin, 1935.

Newman, B., *Unknown Yugoslavia*, London, Jenkins, 1960.

Nichols, B., *No Place Like Home*, London, Cape, 1936.

Nock, O.S., *Railways Then and Now*, London, Elek, 1975.

———, *Railways of Western Europe*, London, Black, 1975.

———, *The Golden Age of Steam*, London, Black, 1973.

Page, M., *The Lost Pleasures of the Great Trains*, London, Weidenfeld & Nicolson, 1975.

Pears, Sir Edwain, *Forty Years in Constantinople*, London, Murray, 1920.

———, *The Life of Abdul Hamid*, London, 1917.

Pécheux, J., *L'Age d'or du Rail européen*, Paris, Berger-Levrault, 1975.

Perleman, S.J., *Westward Ha!* New York, Simon & Schuster, 1947.

Poujardhieu, G., *Les Chemins de fer*, Paris, Hetzel, 1883.

Price, M. (ed.), *International Timetable*, London, Thos. Cook.

Pudney, J., *The Thomas Cook Story*, London, Michael Joseph, 1953.

Rae, W.F., *The Business of Travel*, London, Thos. Cook, 1891.

Rappoport, A., *Leopold the Second*, London, Arnold, 1903.

Raschdau, L., *Ein Sinkendes Reich*, Berlin, Mittler, 1934.

Renon, P., *Histoire de La Compagnie Internationale des Wagons-Lits*, Marseilles, Terras, n.d.

Ristelhuber, R., *Histoire des peuples balkaniques*, Paris, Fayard, 1950.

Roberts, C., *Victoria, Four-Thirty*, London, Hodder & Stoughton, 1937.

Roberts, H.L., *Rumania*, New Haven, Yale University Press, 1951.

Seton-Watson, R.W., *Rise of Nationality on the Balkans*, London, Constable, 1917.

————, *History of the Rumanians*, Cambridge University Press, 1934.

Slade, R., *King Leopold's Congo*, London, 1962.

Stackelberg, N.von, *Aus Carmen Sylva's Leben*, Berlin, 1885.

Stadtmuller, G., *Geschichte Südosteuropa's*, Munich, Oldenburg, 1950.

Stinglhammer and Dresser, *Leopold II au travail*, Brussels, 1946.

Stoeckl, F., *Die Zwölf Besten Züge Europa's*, Salzburg, Selbstverlag, 1956.

————, *Europäische Züge mit klangvollen Namen*, Darmstadt, Rohrig, 1958.

————, *Die Eisenbahnen der Erde*, Vienna, Ployer, 1961.

Stojadonovic, M.D., *The Great Powers and the Balkans*, Cambridge University Press, 1939.

Sturdza, D., *Charles I, roi de Roumanie*, Bucharest, 1910.

Tapié, V.L., *Monarchie et peuples du Danube*, Paris, Fayard, 1969.

Temperley, H., *History of Serbia*, London, Longmans, 1919.

————, *England and the Near East*, London, Longmans, 1936.

Theroux, P., *The Great Railway Bazaar*, London, Hamish Hamilton, 1975.

Thomson, D., *The Third Republic*, London, Royal Institute for International Affairs, 1946.

Toynbee, A.J. (ed.), *The Balkans*, Oxford University Press, 1915.

Wechsberg, J., "Take the Orient Express," *The New Yorker*, April 22, 1950.

Westwood, J., *Locomotive Designer in the Age of Steam*, London, Sidgwick & Jackson, 1973.

Wheeler-Holohan, J., *The History of the King's Messengers*, London, Grayson, 1935.

Whitaker, M., and A. Hiss, *All Aboard with E.M. Frimbo*, London, Deutsch, 1975.

White, E.L., *The Wheel Spins*, London, Collins, 1936.

Whitehouse, P.B. (ed.), *Railway Relics and Regalia*, London, Country Life 1975.

Williams, A. (ed.), *Railway World Annual*, London, Ian Allan, 1977.

Vogeler, R.A., *I Was Stalin's Prisoner*, London, W.H. Allen, 1952.

NEWSPAPERS AND MAGAZINES

American Historical Review
Berliner Illustrierte Zeitung
Constellation, Paris
Crapouille, Paris
Cri de Paris
Cri de Peuples, Brussels
Daily News, London
Guides Bleus
Illustrated London News
L'Actualité, Paris
L'Illustration, Paris
L'Independence, Brussels
L'Independant du Rail, Paris
Le Figaro, Paris
Le Matin, Paris
Le Monde, Paris
Le Temps, Paris

Morning Post, London
New York Herald Tribune
New York Times
Neue Freie Presse, Vienna
Neues Wiener Journal, Vienna
Paris Match
Pétit Parisien
Revue des Deux Mondes, Paris
Railway Gazette
Revue des Voyages
Revue des Wagons-Lits
The Daily Telegraph, London
The Times, London
The Tattler, London
Town Topics, New York
Vie de Rail
Vossische Zeitung, Berlin

Index

Abdul Hamid II, 54, 67–68, 75, 78, 191
About, Edmond, 31–32, 34–36, 37, 38, 39, 40, 41, 43, 56, 57, 64, 69
Acheson, Dean, 205
Adana, 235
Adenauer, Konrad, 150
Adrianople (Edirne), 70, 75, 77, 82
Aga Khan, 158
Ahmed Pasha, 67
Albany, Prince Leopold, Duke of, 22
Alexander, king of Serbia, 140
Alexander, king of Yugoslavia, 132
Alexander of Battenberg, prince of Bulgaria, 62
Alexander II, czar of Russia, 24, 141
Alexander, Sir Harold (Lord Alexander), 252
Alexandroúpolis, 96
Alfonso XII, king of Spain, 112
Alfonso XIII, king of Spain, 62
Algeria, 89
Ali Khan, 158
Allamvédelmi Hatóság (AVH), 258
Allcard, William, 33
Ambler, Eric, 242–43
American Edison Company, 40, 43
Anatolian Express, 90
Anasthatos, 72–73, 76, 77
Andrássy, Count Gyula, 164, 170
Anglo-Iranian Oil Company, 198
Ankara, 233
Ansbach, 184
Antonescu, Ion, 249
Arlberg, 91, 94, 96, 252
Arlberg Orient Express, 94, 95, 97, 252, 254, 262
Aslanian, Raoul, 113, 114
Asshwell, Robert, 172
Athens, 89, 93, 94, 96, 242, 264, 270
Augsburg, 40
Augustus, prince of Saxe-Coburg, 135
Aure, J.C., 178
Auriol, Vincent, 150
Austria, 4, 17, 93, 94, 95, 247, 253

Austrian State Railways, 27, 30, 42, 247
Austro-Hungarian Empire, 7, 25, 41, 45, 49, 93

Bacall, Lauren, 245
Baden State Railways, 27
Baden-Powell, Robert, 167–68
Baghdad, 235
Bahrein, 200
Baker, Josephine, 183
Baku, 188
Baldwin, Stanley, 133
Baldwin Locomotive Works, 98
Balkan Express, 96
Baltimore & Ohio Railroad, 4
Baring, Thomas, 194
Basle, 94, 265
Battenberg, princes of, 62
Bavaria, 4
Bebra, 26
Bedaux, C.E., 134
Beirut, 212
Bela Palanka, 80, 84
Belgian State Railways, 31, 38
Belgium, 4, 5, 15, 91, 247
Belgrade, 80, 93, 95, 96, 99, 139, 211, 242
Bennett, James Gordon, 32
Bergman, Ingrid, 245
Beria, Lavrenti, 252
Berlin, 15, 26, 248
Bernhardt, Sarah, 159
Bethlen, Count István, 160
Biatorbagy, 182, 183
Bibescu, Prince Georges, 126
Birns, Jack, 253
Bismarck, Prince Otto, 135
Blowitz, Henry Opper de, 31, 32, 35, 39, 47, 50–55, 56–58, 60–61, 63, 68
Blowitz, Anne Amélie Opper de, 52
Boris III, king of Bulgaria, 136–39
Boulogne, 91, 94
Bowen, James H., 13
Boyer, Georges, 57
Brackenbury, Sir Henry, 53

Branson, Lionel, 166
Bratislava (Pozsony), 44
Bremen, 90, 210
Brenner Pass, 17
Brook-Shepherd, Gordon, 265
Brouet, 154
Bruce, David K.E., 175
Bruch, Max, 161
Brussels, 87–88, 248
Bucharest, 54, 61, 91, 93, 95, 254, 264
Budapest, 44–45, 80, 91, 97, 139, 211,
    215, 258
Buddicom locomotives, 33
Bulgaria, 28, 61–62, 79, 80–81, 85, 95,
    239, 264
Bülow, Hans von, 161

Cairo, 90, 193
Cairo-Luxor Express, 90
Calais, 89, 94, 131, 207
Callas, Maria, 162
Canadian Loco Co., 98
Canaris, Wilhelm, 249
Carnot, Sadi, 146
Carol II, king of Rumania, 141–46
Caruso, Enrico, 162
Casimir-Périer, Jean, 146
Cassel, Sir Ernest, 156, 198
Castel Peles, 55, 58
Castelnau, 209
Central Pacific Railroad, 9
Chaliapin, Fyodor, 162
Châlons-sur-Marne, 34
Chamberlain, Sir Austen, 208
Changchun, 90
Chantilly, 100
Chaplin, Sir Charles, 134
Charles I (Carol I), king of Rumania, 50,
    54, 55–56, 59–60
Charles I, emperor of Austria, 140–41
Chastel, Comte de, 88
Cherbourg, 90, 146
Cherkes Keui, 70, 74, 216
Chevalier, Maurice, 160
Christie, Agatha, 231–36, 245
Christie, Archibald, 232
CIA (Central Intelligence Agency), 175,
    205, 259–62
Clark, Sir Kenneth (Lord Clark), 201
Clayton, Sir Gilbert, 208, 217, 220,
    225, 226

Clementine, princess of Bourbon-
    Orléans, 135
Codreanu, Cornelius, 144
Cologne, 26
Commault, Roger, 147, 152–53, 162
Compagnie Internationale des Wagons-
    Lits, 17, 26, 27, 85, 87–90, 91, 93,
    94, 95, 102, 139, 153, 178, 211, 222,
    247, 248, 265, 268
Compiègne, 100
Congo, Belgian, 129
Connery, Sean, 245
Constanţa, 87, 89
Constantinople (Istanbul), 28, 66–67, 80,
    85, 86, 93, 94, 95, 96, 105–6, 225,
    264, 270
Cooch Behar, Maharaja of, 157–58
Cooper, Peter, 4
Çorlu, 216, 226
Coty, René, 150
Crampton, Thomas Russell, 33
Crompton, Rookes Evelyn, 139–40
Curtici, 254
Custance, Alfred Francis, 208, 217
Custer, General George A., 20
Cuza, Alexander, 50
Cyril, Archimandrit, 128
Czaribrod, see Dimitrovgrad
Czechoslovakia, 96, 141, 247

Dalziel, Davison (Lord Dalziel of
    Wooler), 88, 89, 90
Dalziel, Elizabeth (Mme. René Nagel-
    mackers), 90
Damascus, 212
Danzig, 211
Daudet, Alphonse, 32
Daudet, Ernest, 32
Daudet, Léon, 32
Darlan, Jean, 150
Dautry, Raoul, 103
Debussy, Claude, 161
De Falla, Manuel, 162
de Gaulle, Charles, 100
Delane, John, 53
De Lara, Isidore, 161
Defterdar Ahmed Bey, 130, 131
Dekobra, Maurice, 229–30
Delloye-Matthieu, 30
Denmark, 4, 108, 203, 253
Deschanel, Paul, 148–50

Deterding, Sir Henry, 156
Diaghilev, Sergei P., 162
Dieppe, 272
Dietrich, Marlene, 160
Dimitrov, Georgi, 84n
Dimitrovgrad (Czaribrod), 84, 269
Direct-Orient Express, 97, 184, 266
Disraeli, Benjamin, Lord Beaconsfield, 53
Doderer, Wilhelm, 58
Domodossola, 237
Doolard, A. Den, 239–41
Drake, Edwin, 20
Dreyfus, Alfred, 51
Dulles, Allen, 175
Duncan, Isadora, 162–63
Durrell, Lawrence, 241
Duse, Eleonora, 159

Eddy, William, 175
Edinburgh, Prince Alfred, Duke of, 24
Edinburgh, Prince Philip, Duke of, 62, 132
Edirne, see Adrianople
Edward VII, king of Great Britain and Ireland, 22, 24, 131, 132, 151–52, 156
Edward VIII, king of the United Kingdom, 132–34, 156
Egypt, 16
Eisenhower, General Dwight D., 150 252
Elizabeth, empress of Austria, 115, 131
Elizabeth, queen of Rumania (Carmen Sylva), 55–56, 59–60
Espero, 64, 66, 69
Essayan, family, 189–90, 191
Eykens, Wilhelmine, 255–57

Faisal I, king of Iraq, 217, 225
Famadotta, Guido, 209
Farnoux, Annette, 179
Faure, Félix, 146
Feleggyhaza, 127
Ferdinand I, czar of Bulgaria, 81, 82, 126, 134–37, 172
Ferdinand, king of Rumania, 141, 143
Field, Benjamin, 11
Field, Norman, 11
Finney, Albert, 245
Fitzgerald, Scott, 159
Flamented, Albert, 90
Flandin, Pierre-Etienne, 149

Fleming, Arthur H., 100
Fleming, Ian, 177, 236–38
Foch, Marshal Ferdinand, 99–100
Fokine, Michel, 162
France, 4, 25, 91, 98, 203, 247, 248
Francisco, duke of Marchena, 111–12, 114, 116, 118, 119
Franz Josef I, emperor of Austria, 41–42, 112
Frankfurt-am-Main, 26, 181
Frère-Orban family, 5
Freundinger, Jean, 71, 72, 73, 76
Fuad, Hadji Jacuof, 209
Fusan, 90

Geneva, 94, 244
George V, king of the United Kingdom, 147
George VI, king of the United Kingdom, 132, 165
Gerlach, Walter, 75
Germany, 91, 93, 94, 95, 98, 135, 197, 247, 258
Gestapo, 139, 248, 251, 253
Gielgud, Sir John, 245
Gilliat, Sidney, 243
Giscard d'Estaing, Valéry, 150
Giurgiu, 30, 61
Gladstone, William Ewart, 53, 68
Gleichen, Lord Edward, 166
Glen, Sir Alexander, 177
Goering, Hermann, 100
Grant, Ulysses S., 13
Great Britain, 4, 16, 17, 91, 203, 247
Great Western Railway, 33
Greece, 95, 108, 248
Greene, Graham, 230–31, 242
Greger, Oskar, 73
Grévy, François Paul Jules, 31
Grimaldi, princes of Monaco, 119
Grace, princess of Monaco, 273
Grock (Andrien Wettach), 160
Gromyko, Andrei, 252
Guimet, 163–64
Guitry, Lucien, 160
Guitry, Sacha, 160
Gulbenkian, Calouste, 120, 186–206
Gulbenkian, Nevarte, 189, 190, 192, 193
Gulbenkian, Nubar, 191, 192, 193, 201–2
Gulbenkian, Rita, 194, 201
Gustav VI, king of Sweden, 62

Haghop Pasha, 195
Haifa, 212
Haile Selassie, emperor of Ethiopia, 158
Hamburg, 90, 210
Hamdi Pasha, 77
Hankey, Sir Maurice, 159
Harand, M., 87
Hauke, Julia Teresa, 62
Hawkins, Rev. John, 167
Haworth-Leslie, Martin, 172
Hegyeshalom, 97, 253
Helen, queen of Rumania, 142, 144
Herkulesbad, 49
Herzl, Theodor, 159
Hiller, Wendy, 245
Hitchcock, Alfred, 243
Hitler, Adolf, 100
Ho Chi Minh, 150
Hohenlohe-Langenburg, Duke of, 166
Hollan, Ritter von, 42
Hoover, Herbert, 159
Horowitz, Vladimir, 162
Horthy, Miklós, 141, 182, 249
Hoskins, Henry, 175
Houdini, Harry, 160
Hungary, 93, 169, 249

Ibn Saud, king of Saudi Arabia, 203
Ickes, Harold L., 204
Imperial Railways of Alsace-Lorraine, 27
India, 16
Innsbruck, 95
International Macedonian Revolutionary
    Organization (IMRO), 135
Intraflug, 270
Iran, 203
Iraq, 190, 198
Iraq Petroleum Company, 197, 198
Irkutsk, 90
Israel, Moritz, 73, 74–76
Istanbul, see Constantinople
Italy, 4, 95, 248, 253
ITT (International Telephone and Tele-
    graph Corporation), 257, 258

Jantzen, Mijnheer, 35
Japan, 90
Jelour, 209
Joachim, Joseph, 161
Johnson, Herschel V., 249
Joseph, archduke of Austria, 7

Juan, prince of Bourbon, Spanish Crown
    pretender, 145

Kahniar, Onody, 46
Kaiser Ferdinand Nordbahn, 42
Karlsruhe, 40
Karpe, Eugene S., 259–63
Kassel, 26
Katowice, 93
Keyes, General, 257
Khrushchev, Nikita, 252
Kiel Canal, 210
Kiliseli, 74, 76
Koelsch, Oskar, 73
Komitadshi (revolutionary organization),
    239
Kreisler, Fritz, 161
Kubelik, Jan, 161
Kuwait, 199, 200
Kviat, Georgius, 74

Lacroix, Caroline (Baroness Vaughan),
    130
Lambrino, Zizi, 141–42, 143
Lane, Frederick, 196–97
Langtry, Lillie, 22–23, 24
Larissa, 93
Launder, Frank, 243
Lausanne, 91, 270, 272
Laval, Pierre, 158
Lawrence, D. H., 228–29
Le Gaulois, 57
Le Figaro, 57
Le Havre, 90
League of Nations, 94
Lechat, Etienne, 30
Lee, Robert E., 13
Lehár, Franz, 161
Leipnik, Janos, 183
Leopold I, king of Belgium, 5
Leopold II, king of Belgium, 7, 14–16, 25,
    26, 128–31
Leria, Carlotta, 60
Lesseps, Ferdinand de, 52, 53
Liège, 16, 89
Lifar, Serge, 162
Liman, Karl, 58
Lincoln, Abraham, 12, 13
Linz, 91, 213
Lisbon, 205
Litvinov, Maxim, 165

Ljubljana, 237
Lloyd-Triestino Shipping Co., 64
Lockhart, Sir Robert Bruce, 168–72
Lockwood, Margaret, 244
Lokoshaz, 254
Lohozada, 254
London, 19, 24, 203, 244, 272
Louis Philippe, king of France, 7
Lübeck, 211
Ludwig II, king of Bavaria, 26
Lumet, Sidney, 245
Lumière, Louis, 244
Lupescu, Elenitza (Magda), 142–46
Lvov, 93

Mafia, 180
Mahler, Gustav, 160
Malinovsky, Rodion Y., 252
Mallowan, Sir Max, 232
Manchurian Express, 90
Mann, William d'Alton, 18, 19–26
Mantachoff, Alexander, 193–94, 196–97
maquis (French Resistance), 248
Maria, duchess of Marchena, 111–19
Maria Christina, queen of Spain, 116
Maria Theresa, 45
Marie, queen of Rumania, 132
Marie Alexandrovna, 24
Marie Valerie, archduchess of Austria,
    155
Markham, Reuben, 175
Marquet, Albert, 73
Mascagni, Pietro, 161
Mason, Michael Henry, 177
Massine, Leonide, 162
Mata Hari (Margaret Gertrud Zelle),
    163–64
Matuska, Sylvester, 183–84
Maurois, André, 162
Maxim, Hiram Stevens, 113
Maxwell, Elsa, 159
Meade, Stephen, 175
Meinertzhagen, Richard, 166
Melba, Nellie, 155–56
Menelik II, emperor of Ethiopia, 158
Menton, 26
Mérode, Cléo de, 25, 130
Metcalf, Major Edward, 133
Mexico, 199
Michael, king of Rumania, 142
Midhat Pasha, 68

Miguero y Azcarate, Count Fermin, 111
Milan, 91, 268
Milan I, king of Serbia, 139
Minshall, Merlin, 176–77
Mishak Effendi, 35, 47
Mistinguett (Jeanne Bourgeois), 160
Mitropa Gesellschaft, 94, 95, 247, 248
Monaco, 119
Mont Cenis, 16, 17
Monte Carlo, 119, 162, 272
Montreal Loco Co., 98
Montreux, 272
Morand, Paul, 125–28
Morrison, Herbert, 204
Moscow, 96
Mossadegh, Mohammed, 204, 205
Mosul, 120, 195, 199
Moszkowski, Moritz, 162
Munich, 26, 40, 41, 93
Murad V, sultan, 68
Murphy, Sara and Gerald, 159
Museum of Modern Art, 273
Mussolini, Benito, 95

Nagelmackers, Edmond, 5, 6, 7, 14
Nagelmackers, Georges, 5–10, 13–18,
    24–28, 41, 44, 80, 81, 87–90
Nagelmackers, René, 90
Namur, 33
Nancy, 34
Napoleon III, emperor of France, 52
Nasser, Gamal, 205
Neef-Orban, Octave, 88
Netherlands (Holland), 4, 203, 247
New York, 23, 89
New York Central Railroad, 32
New York Express, 90
New York Herald, 32
Newhaven, 272
Nice, 118
Nicholas II, Czar, 146–47
Nijinsky, Vaslav, 162
Nish, 80, 81, 82, 135
Nobel, Alfred, 188–89
Nord-Express, 174
Nordenfelt, Torsten Veilhelm, 108
North German Lloyd, 90
Norway, 203, 253
Nuremberg, 93, 96

Offenbach, Jacques, 42

Olanescu, 54, 56
Oliphant, Lawrence, 52–53
Opper de Blowitz, *see* Blowitz
Opper, Marcus, 51
Orban, Neef, 88
Orsova, 30, 49
Ostend, 96
Ostend-Vienna-Orient Express, 95
OSS (Office of Strategic Services), 175
Ostrorog, Count, 116
Ottoman Empire, 31, 95, 191, 199
Ottoman Railway Company, 82, 197, 200
Otsu, 273

Pacelli, Eugenio, Cardinal (Pope Pius XII), 158
Paderewski, Ignace, 162
Paccard, André, 273
Page, Martin, 176
Palermo, 212
Palestine, 208
Palffy, Count Joseph, 182
Papen, Franz von, 249
Paris, 26, 29, 85, 89, 90, 91, 94, 95, 264, 266
Patton, General George, 101
Pavelić, Ante, 249
Pavlova, Anna, 162
Peking, 90
Peninsular & Orient Line, 16
Perkins, Anthony, 245
Pétain, Marshal Henri-Philippe, 149
Peter II, king of Yugoslavia, 132
Pioneer, 12, 13
Pirot, 81, 84
Ploesti, 54, 173
Plovdiv, 80, 82, 135
Plowden, Doré, 202
Pohl, Leonie, 43, 47
Poincaré, Raymond, 147
Poland, 91, 96, 211
Pompidou, Georges, 150
Poole, Anne, 208, 223
Porges, 40
Port Arthur, 89
Port Said, 90, 194
Porta Orientalis, 49
Porter, Edwin S., 245
Portugal, 145, 203
Pozsony, *see* Bratislava
Prague, 91, 93

Prussia, 4, 211
Pullman, George Mortimer, 10–14, 22

Qatar, 200

Rachmaninoff, Sergei, 162
Radowitz, Josef von, 75
Rakosi, Matyas, 261
Ralli, Sir Stephen, 77
Rappoport, Eugène von, 79
Raymond, Eugène de, 78
Redgrave, Sir Michael, 244
Redgrave, Vanessa, 245
Regray, 66
Rénard, Jean, 182
Reza Shah Pahlavi, 203
Ribbentrop, Joachim von, 133
Richemont, Count de, 81–82
Roberts, Cecil, 238–39
Rockefeller, John D., 196
Rodriguez Feijo, Hermina, 202
Rodosto (Tetirdag), 225
Roet, Franz, 73
Rome, 164, 258
Roosevelt, Franklin Delano, 249
Roosevelt, Kermit, 175, 205, 206
Rothschild (family), 53
Rothschild, Baron Alfred, 156
Rothschild, Baron Eugène, 133
Rothschild, Baron Ferdinand, 156
Rothschild, Baron Henri, 164
Rowan, Roy, 253
Royal Dutch Petroleum Company, 195, 198, 199
Rudolf, Archduke, 131
Ruffier, François, 78
Rumania, 28, 48, 49–51, 79, 91, 95, 173, 264
Rumanian State Railways, 27, 54
Rumelia, 30
Ruschuk, 28, 30, 61, 62
Russia, 109, 174, 199, 253, 258

Said Pasha, 67
Said Halim Pasha, 67, 199
St. Germain-des-Fossés, 149
Saint James, Jean, 146
St. Petersburg, 24, 164
Salisbury, Robert Arthur Talbot Gascoyne-Cecil, marquess of, 53
Salonika, 89, 93, 96, 101

Salzburg, 91
Samuel, Herbert (Viscount Samuel), 194
Samuel, Marcus, 195
Samuelson, Marie, 202
Sanders, Edgar, 259
Saudi Arabia, 203, 208
Scala, Karl von, 42
Scala, Madame von, 43, 47
Schleswig-Holstein, 211
Schroeder, Napoleon, 30
Schultz, Johann, 58
Schwarzkopf, Norman, 205
Sea Containers, Inc., 272, 273
Ségur, Marquis de, 88
Serbia 80, 82, 139; *see also* Yugoslavia
Sheker Pasha, 67
Shell Transport and Trading Company, 195
Shepelev, General, 62
Sherwood, James, 272
Sheytandjik, 63
Shibly Jemal Effendi, 159
Siemens (electrical firm), 43
Simplon Orient Express, 91, 93, 94, 95, 96, 97, 101, 120, 159, 178, 207, 247, 253, 254, 265
Simplon Tunnel, 91, 207, 265
Simpson, Bessie Wallis (Duchess of Windsor), 133–34
Sinaia, 55
Skuludis, Stephen, 107
Slivnitza, 85
Smyrna (Izmir), 130
Snyatin, 93
Sofia, 81, 83, 95, 96, 242, 269
Sopron (Odenburg), 141
Sotheby Parke Bernet, 273
Souf, Alphonse ("Slim"), 180, 210, 218, 220
Soulas, Elize, 201
Spain, 4, 112–13
Stalin, Joseph, 174, 252
Standard Oil Company, 196
Starhemberg, Prince Ernest Rüdiger, 154
Stirling, Edward, 159–60
Stockholm, 249
Strasbourg, 40, 93
Strauss, Johann, 42
Strauss, Oscar, 161
Strauss, Richard, 161

Stuttgart, 41
Subotica, 91, 93
Suez Canal, 52, 53
Svilengrad, 96, 216
Sweden, 108
Switzerland, 17, 94, 253
Sylva, Carmen, *see* Elizabeth, queen of Rumania
Syria, 212
Szegedin, 46

Tatar Pazardzhik, 30, 80, 82, 83, 84
Tauern Express, 96
Tchtaldja, 180
Temesvar (Timişoara), 46, 145, 212
Thibaud, Jacques, 161
Tibot, Roger, 133
Time, magazine, 133
Times, The (London), 24, 32, 52–53, 68, 77, 107[n]
Timişoara, *see* Temesvar
Tom Thumb, 4
Toscanini, Arturo, 162
Transjordan, 208
Trans-Siberian Express, 89, 147
Trefeu, Jules, 57
Trieste, 91, 95, 268
Trotsky, Leon, 174
Truman, Harry, 204
Tukhachevski, Marshal Mikhail, 164–65
Turkey, 179–80, 199, 216, 253; *see also* Ottoman Empire
Turnu-Severin, 215

Ulm, 40
Umberto, ex-king of Italy, 145
Union Pacific Railroad, 9
United States, 4, 5, 8, 23, 98, 159, 174, 200, 203
Vansittart, Sir Robert, 158
Varna, 28, 63, 64, 86
Venice, 91, 212, 272
Venezuela, 199
Vetsera, Maria, 131
Vetter, Arthur, 209
Vickers Sons & Company and Vickers-Maxim Co., 117
Victoria, Queen, 5, 7, 131, 135
Vinkovci, 91, 93
Vienna, 40, 41, 43, 91, 93, 95, 96, 211, 213, 254, 264, 265

Vishinsky, Andrei, 96
Vitry-le-François, 181
Vladivostok, 89
Vogeler, Lucile, 255–57, 263
Vogeler, Robert A., 257–59, 259n, 260, 261
Voisseron, 151–52
Vulcan Locomotive Works, 98

Wagram, 42
Waldorf, Leopold, 116
Wallenberg, Raoul, 249–52
Ward, G.T., 209
Warsaw, 91, 93, 96
Wenger, Leon, 173
Werner, Paula von, 214, 218, 222–23, 227
Weissel Pasha, 71, 77
Westinghouse, George, 9–10, 33
Weizmann, Chaim, 159

White, Ethel Lina, 243
Whitty, Dame May, 244
Widmark, Richard, 245
Wilde, Oscar, 22
Wilhelmshaven, 210
William II, emperor of Germany, 75
Wolf-Ferrari, Ermanno, 161
Württemberg State Railways, 27
Wyntner, Philip, 172

York, Michael, 245
Ysaÿe, Eugene, 161
Yugoslavia, 93, 95, 98, 141, 173, 211, 248
    see also Serbia

Zagreb, 91, 99
Zaharoff, Sir Basil, 35, 104–11, 112–13, 156, 187
Zahedi, General, 205
Zurich, 94, 95

E. H. COOKRIDGE was educated in Vienna, London, Paris
and Lausanne and made his acquaintance with the Orient
Express as a cub reporter more than forty years ago. Before
the Second World War he worked for American and British
correspondents who used the famous train to cover Central
Europe and the Balkans. As a wartime intelligence agent he
traveled on some of its last runs through the Balkans before
the Nazis gained control over the area in 1941. After the war
he distinguished himself as a foreign correspondent and once
again became a frequent passenger of the Direct-Orient
Express and the Simplon Orient Express, using them also for
vacation trips when he was a political lobby correspondent in
the House of Commons. He has appeared as a commentator
on British, American, French and Canadian radio and television. Mr. Cookridge has written many important documen-
tary works on espionage and the Second World War, including *The Net That Covers the World, Philby: The Third
Man, Traitor Betrayed, Set Europe Ablaze* and *Gehlen: Spy
of the Century,* as well as several biographies, such as *From
Battenberg to Mountbatten* and *The Baron of Arizona.*